D1254001

Greater Cincinnati
Bicentennial History Series

Board of Editors
Zane L. Miller
Gene D. Lewis

Making Better Citizens

Making Better Citizens

Housing Reform and the Community Development Strategy in Cincinnati, 1890–1960

Robert B. Fairbanks (Robert Bruce)

University of Illinois Press
Urbana and Chicago

To my Mother and Father

Publication of this work was supported in part by grants from the Research Enhancement Program of the University of Texas, Arlington, and the Cincinnati Historical Society.

© 1988 by the Board of Trustees of the University of Illinois
Manufactured in the United States of America
C 5 4 3 2 1

This book is printed on acid-free paper.

Library of Congress Cataloging-in-Publication Data

Fairbanks, Robert B. (Robert Bruce), 1950–
    Making better citizens: housing reform and the community
development strategy in Cincinnati, 1890–1960 / Robert B. Fairbanks.
        p.   cm.—(Greater Cincinnati bicentennial history series)
    Bibliography: p.
    Includes index.   *138247*
    ISBN 0-252-01554-1 (alk. paper)
    1. Public housing—Ohio—Cincinnati—History—20th century.
    2. Housing policy—Ohio—Cincinnati—History—20th century.
    3. Community development—Ohio—Cincinnati—History—20th century.
    I. Title. II. Series.
    HD7288.78.U52C54 1988
    363.5′8—dc19   88-1584
                                                                 CIP

Contents

Editors' Introduction   xi

Acknowledgments   xiii

Introduction   1

I   Tenements, Place, and Urban Social Problems   9

1   Tenements, Congestion, and the Problem of the Poor, 1865–1910   13

2   Redefining the Housing Problem: From Inappropriate Dwellings to Inadequate Community, 1910–19   25

II   Housing, Place, and Urban Cultural Problems   39

3   Housing Reform and Comprehensive Planning in Metropolitan Cincinnati: The 1920s   41

4   Reformers and the Decline of the Filter-Down Theory   58

5   Promoting Good Housing: Large-Scale Slum Clearance and Urban Reconstruction, 1929–33   71

III   Government and the Housing Problem   89

6   Implementing the Plan: Cincinnati, the CMHA, and Laurel Homes   91

7   The Consequences of a Community Strategy: From Housing the Poor to Providing Better Housing   104

8   Cincinnati's Vacant Land Project Controversy   114

9   Addressing the Black Housing Problem: Community and Racial Segregation, 1933–44   124

IV Abandoning the Neighborhood Community Approach   147

10 Clearing the Slums: From Community Services   151
       to Individual Desires, 1945–60

       Notes   179
       Bibliographic Note   227
       Index   231

Editors' Introduction

Robert B. Fairbanks's study of the effort between 1915 and 1954 to create an ideal metropolitan social atmosphere as the seedbed for good citizenship is a significant and innovative contribution to our understanding of American history. He concentrates on the movement for low-cost housing, a movement he defines as an attempt to foster a sense of local and metropolitan community through philanthropic urban housing projects, comprehensive city planning, federal public housing and greenbelt town programs, urban redevelopment and urban renewal. He contends that the movement sought especially to reinforce cultural group pluralism, in part by establishing separate but equal neighborhoods for whites and blacks in the central city and its suburbs. He uses Cincinnati as a vehicle for telling this story because of its reputation as a leader in the movement and as the nation's best governed city, but treats the movement as a national phenomenon that stemmed from similar efforts in other cities. The focus on one metropolis also enables him to lay out in compelling detail the extraordinary diversity of participants in the movement and the critical role of ideas in its rise and decline.

Making Better Citizens is the initial volume in the Greater Cincinnati Bicentennial History Series, a monographic series focusing on a broad range of historical topics relating to the entire Cincinnati region. Additional volumes will be published annually for the next several years. The series is a joint venture of the Cincinnati Historical Society and the Department of History and the Center for Neighborhood and Community Studies at the University of Cincinnati. The Cincinnati Historical Society and the University of Texas at Arlington helped defray the cost of publishing this volume.

Gene D. Lewis
Zane L. Miller

Acknowledgments

Although I simply do not have enough space to acknowledge individually everyone who has contributed to this book, certain people must be singled out for thanks. Professor Zane L. Miller, my mentor at the University of Cincinnati, has not only nourished my interest in housing and planning history, but helped me develop a very useful conceptual approach to urban history. He has read more drafts of this manuscript than either of us cares to admit, each time providing challenging and insightful commentary. The shortcomings of this book undoubtedly will be because of my failure to heed some of his good advice.

Although he frequently gave me headaches, Henry D. Shapiro's hard questions have certainly made this a better manuscript. My close association with Miller and Shapiro, as a student in their seminars and teaching assistant in their Laboratory in American Civilization, was clearly the high point of my graduate career.

Other friends and teachers at the University of Cincinnati read and commented on this work in dissertation form; and Roger Daniels and Alan Tuchfarber made valuable suggestions on how to turn my dissertation into a book.

Fellow graduate students Judy Spraul Schmidt, Ellen Corwin Cangi, and Alan Marcus all read parts of this manuscript and helped me sharpen its conceptual basis. Their friendship and intellectual comaraderie have left me wondering about the supposed cutthroat competition at graduate school. Kathleen Underwood, Stephen Maizlish, John Kushma, and Nora Faires, colleagues at the University of Texas at Arlington, also read and commented on various chapters.

Two other scholars reviewed the book in its latter drafts: Peter Marcuse of Columbia University asked me some useful questions about the early chapters, and an anonymous reader for the University of Illinois Press helped me strengthen and clarify some of the book's main arguments. Richard L. Wentworth and Carol F. Saller, also of the University of Illinois Press, provided the necessary guidance and encouragement so useful to new authors. Ed Koranda helped me enter the final revisions into my computer.

Financial support from the University of Cincinnati's Charles Phelps Taft Graduate Fellowship in 1979–81 and from the University of Texas at Arlington Organized Research Fund's New Faculty Support Program in 1986 facilitated the research and writing of this manuscript.

I not only benefited from scholarly and institutional assistance, but from courteous and helpful librarians and archivists wherever I visited. The staffs of the Cincinnati Historical Society and of the Special Collections Department at the University of Cincinnati must be singled out, however. Edward Rider, Alden Monroe, and Francis Forman of the Historical Society spent hours helping me locate documents and suggesting potential sources. Alice Cornell, head of Special Collections, did likewise even though her department was being moved at the time.

Finally, I'd like to thank several people who played a relatively minor role in the actual research and writing of this book, but who have contributed to it in other important ways. Professor Edward K. Spann of Indiana State University first introduced me to the excitement of doing urban history. Emily, my wife, has not only shared my love of cities, but has shouldered an unfair proportion of household work and child care so I could write. And while my parents probably wondered if I would ever complete this manuscript, they masked their doubts, providing encouragement and support as only parents can.

Introduction

This book is about the formulation in the 1920s and 1930s of a federal public housing policy that is codified in the Housing Act of 1949 as "a decent home and a suitable living environment for every American family."[1] It examines persistent attempts to provide low-cost housing by philanthropists and city governments, efforts which ultimately involved the federal government in the Hoover, Roosevelt, and Truman administrations. The attempt to provide low-cost housing also involved city planners who, like low-cost housing advocates, worried about the threat of civic alienation associated with the spread of anomie and social disorganization from slums into more respectable neighborhoods. Indeed, it was this concern for the problem of community—the need to encourage civic coherence and commitment by developing facilities for inculcating an appropriate urban way of life in neighborhoods across the face of the metropolis—that produced the extraordinary form of the first federally subsidized slum clearance public housing projects, large self-contained compounds that I have called "community development projects," instead of individual dwelling units that produced mere shelter for the homeless.

My work on this book stemmed from a fascination with the form and nature of public housing in the 1930s. As a graduate student living on the West Side of the city, I commuted to the University of Cincinnati, just north of the central business district and the inner-city slums. That trip took me daily past English Woods, a community development project built by the Cincinnati Metropolitan Housing Authority (CMHA). Located in an integrated working-class neighborhood well removed from the central business district, English Woods now houses poor blacks and whites in its still attractive setting. Upon observing this, I started reading the work of public housing advocates of the 1930s, the "housers," in an attempt to understand how the segregation of poor people in large projects came about. From that reading, I became convinced that these early middle and upper-class proponents of large scale, self-contained public housing projects saw their efforts as a critical contribution to the betterment not of "the poor" but of low-income wage earners, both black and white. Indeed, public housing intended to foster a whole new way of life rather than merely provide adequate shelter. English Woods, like other CMHA projects at that time, was constructed as a community development project to foster a sense of community among people who seemed about to lose it (or to have lost it) and who appeared destined to fall prey to the social pathology of the slum. I also discovered that in Cincinnati, housers and planners shared a common vision of the metropolis. Moreover, they cooperated with each other and with other civic activists (women and businessmen) from the 1920s into the 1950s on a variety of programs that took as their central focus of concern the problem of community in the metropolis, not the fate, demise, or decay of the central business district, which became a central issue after the mid-1950s.[2] This coalition of civic activists cooperated in programs aimed at making the metropolitan community one that would provide a decent neighborhood for everyone except "dependents," i.e., the very poor who were unprotected by a functional family, and therefore were cared for by charity and social workers, the police and the courts. Only in the late 1950s did the problem of poverty (and the possibility of eliminating poverty) focus great attention on this group. Prior to then, civic activists pursued a community strategy which sought coherence for a culturally pluralistic metropolis. Toward this end they endorsed the segregation of different races or different classes into "communities," all of them conceived as community development projects, but only some of them executed as public housing community development projects.

Traditionally, historians have underestimated the importance of both the emphasis on metropolitan region and the community orientation of civic improvers. Although planners and housers concentrated on different specifics, by the 1920s they both appeared to have adopted what could be identified as the metropolitan mode of thought which acknowledged the metropolitan region as a discrete entity of differentiated yet interconnected parts. And while it is true that some have accused the planners of the 1920s of lacking social consciousness, a careful look at the movement, which sought to channel public and private development into "community development," suggests otherwise. For instance Roderick D. McKenzie, who in 1933 wrote *The Metropolitan Community* for the President's Research Committee on Social Trends, observed that planning was to provide "convenient, healthful, and attractive places in which people may work, play, learn, and otherwise express themselves in well-rounded living." To achieve this social good, planning focused on "problems relating to the physical aspects of the city or other unit—its streets, railroads, waterways, public services; its public buildings, schools, and other cultural centers; parks, recreation grounds, and other open spaces; and the development of housing, industry and other private property."[3]

Clearly, this emphasis on community suggests an alternative explanation of the low-cost housing and planning experience between 1920 and 1954. The conventional wisdom holds that downtown business interests wanted to save the central business district, that planners shared these same economic goals and fought with social-minded housing reformers, and that all of them were racists who treated blacks with benign neglect at best.[4] On this last issue my study questions the ahistorical use of racism as a timeless prejudice embedded in whites (and therefore ineradicable). Rather, it suggests that racism is a historical/social phenomenon and that our decoding of what it meant in different periods of the past helps us to understand that society can be organized in different ways. Thus prejudice is the expression of historically bounded conceptual apparatuses and the organization of society that flowed from them.

This study also led me to the phenomenon of historical discontinuity. When I turned back to the late nineteenth-century tenement reform movement to find the roots of the community development strategy, I found no such roots but a concern for a totally different problem. Tenement reformers wanted to provide sanitary quarters designed to afford family privacy for low-income people. And for tenement reformers, the dependent was seen as different— someone else's problem, to be segregated from the wage earner and placed in public institutions such as the workhouse, the infirmary, and the city hospital.

This discovery forced me to rethink traditional evolutionary models, for it suggested discontinuity rather than a linear progression of events. That discovery greatly influenced the makeup of this book, which will focus on a discrete chronological period characterized by the way in which people conceptualized the housing problem and the city. Although the first several chapters will survey the earlier era of tenement reform, it is done to show the differences, rather than the similarities, between the two eras.

This study does more than merely identify discrete chronological periods, however. It defines history as the process of people defining and solving problems, and therefore it details the process of problem solving within these discontinuous segments of time, a process that yields ultimately a reconceptualization of the problem and a new process of problem solving. Thus this study concentrates on the consequences of certain conceptual schemes, treating the process of problem solving as both the cause of reconceptualization and the consequence of a particular conceptual scheme.

Cincinnati provides an excellent setting to explore the formulation of public housing policy for several reasons. First, the city's manageable size and well-preserved manuscript collections make a careful analysis of its low-cost housing leadership possible. Second, the city fits the general trends of the twentieth century for cities in the urban-industrial heartland. Demographic trends such as declining immigration, increasing black migration, and slower growth rates all appeared in Cincinnati after 1920 as in the rest of the industrial Northeast. The city also experienced the spatial changes typical of the twentieth century: growing differentiation by function, decentralization, and residential segregation based on economic and racial criteria. Politically, the city also conformed to the tradition of bosses versus reformers characteristic of the first one-third of the twentieth century.

Of course Cincinnati did vary in detail from the norm. By 1920 the city experienced slower growth and attracted fewer immigrants but contained greater housing congestion than most cities of the urban-industrial heartland. Although in 1860, the period of its most rapid expansion, more than 45 percent of Cincinnati's citizens were foreign born, by 1920 the proportion of foreign born had dwindled to 10.7 percent of the population, less than half the percentage found in similarly sized cities such as Milwaukee and Minneapolis. At the same time, the city's black population formed 7.5 percent of the total, giving it one of the higher proportions of blacks in the urban North. While the city's black population experienced increased segregation after 1920, the Queen City's largest immigrant group, the Germans, found ready acceptance and experienced rapid assimilation. Those growth and acceptance patterns, as found in the 1920s, remained consistent over the next thirty years.[5]

Despite the city's leisurely growth in the twentieth century, Cincinnati's age and hilly topography helped make it one of the most congested and poorly housed cities in the nation. Indeed, as early as 1903 New York tenement reformer Lawrence Veiller claimed that outside of New York City and Boston, Cincinnati suffered from the worst tenement housing problem in the nation. Forty years later, the first federal housing census discovered that 14.4 percent of Cincinnati's 114,284 dwellings needed major repairs. Of the twenty-five largest cities, Cincinnati contained the second-highest percentage of deteriorating dwellings.[6]

Despite this apparent lack of progress, Cincinnati ranked as a leading center of low-cost housing and planning activity into the 1950s. Led by the Better Housing League, a citizens group founded in 1916, the city gained a national reputation for housing reform which ultimately helped it secure a number of federal housing projects in the 1930s. Local citizen planning associations, such as the United City Planning Committee (UCPC) and the Citizens' Planning Association (CPA) also addressed low-cost housing problems. The UCPC, founded in 1915, helped Cincinnati become the first large city in the nation to adopt officially a city plan in 1925. The CPA, formed in 1943, fostered the development of the 1948 plan, "one of the most comprehensive and ambitious master plan projects ever undertaken by a major U.S. city," according to *American City.*[7]

Along with these organizations, Greater Cincinnati provided the setting for some of the nation's most widely acknowledged housing ventures. Jacob Schmidlapp's Model Homes Company, founded in 1914, gained nationwide recognition as one of the country's most successful limited dividend housing companies. And during the 1920s, the *New York Times* called Mariemont, a large-scale housing and new town development on the easterly outskirts of Cincinnati, "one of the most important American community developments at the present time."[8] Later, in the 1930s, the federal government's Resettlement Administration chose to build one of its three greenbelt town projects in the Cincinnati metropolitan area.

In addition, many of the city's housers and planners earned both state and national reputations for their expertise. Bleecker Marquette, brought to Cincinnati in 1918 by the Better Housing League (BHL) to serve as its executive secretary, provided the key leadership in housing reform until 1954. Prior to accepting that post, Marquette worked under Lawrence Veiller as the assistant secretary of the New York State Tenement House Committee. Once in Cincinnati, he not only headed the BHL until 1954 but also consulted for the CMHA, helping that organization establish and implement public housing in Cincinnati. Along with Ernest J. Bohn of Cleveland, Marquette pushed through the Ohio Assembly in 1933 the nation's first legislation enabling state housing authorities.[9]

On the national level, Marquette served in 1931 on President Herbert Hoover's Conference on Home Building and Home Ownership. As a member of its Committee on Blighted Areas and Slums he coauthored a part of the committee's report on the definition and causes of blight and slums. Several years later, the National Association of Housing Officials elected him president of their organization. In addition to these honors, Marquette helped Sen. Robert Wagner's assistant, Leon Keyserling, draft the 1937 Housing Act.[10]

Two others committed to resolving Cincinnati's low-cost housing problem through community development were Alfred Bettman and Ladislas Segoe. These close personal friends emerged as key figures in the development of planning both in Cincinnati and in the nation. Indeed, their impressive contributions to the field led one observer to conclude that "there would be no planning today without the technical, legal, and philosophical foundations laid by these two men."[11]

Alfred Bettman, the Harvard-educated corporate lawyer and senior to Segoe by twenty-one years, chaired the meeting which led to the formation of the Cincinnati Better Housing League. He turned to housing and planning while active in reform politics against the notorious Boss George B. Cox machine. After attending a National Conference on City Planning for the first time in 1913, he maintained close ties to the national planning movement and frequently traveled to the United Kingdom to attend summer town planning courses offered by the British Town Planning Institute. And after World War

I, Bettman became a "tangential" member of Lewis Mumford's and Clarence Stein's Regional Planning Association of America.[12] These experiences, stemming from his concern over Cincinnati's haphazard development, help explain why Bettman adopted a planning philosophy which emphasized social as well as physical goals. Because of his strong commitment to comprehensive zoning and planning, Bettman led the movements which resulted in the Cincinnati plans of 1925 and 1948. The corporate lawyer also devoted much of his available time to the City Planning Commission, a body he chaired from 1930 to his unexpected death in 1945.[13]

Bettman's influence went far beyond Cincinnati's city limits. His role in sustaining the constitutionality of zoning through his legal brief for the U.S. Supreme Court in the *Euclid v. Amber* case is probably his most often cited accomplishment, but he helped shape city planning throughout the nation in other ways too. During the 1920s, he served in Secretary of Commerce Herbert Hoover's Division of Housing, where he helped draw up comprehensive model planning legislation needed to permit effective planning for the nation's cities.[14]

During the next decade, Bettman occupied leadership roles in the American Planning Institute, the National Conference of City Planning, and in the newly formed American Society of Planning Officials (as its first president in 1936). In each position, he promoted comprehensive planning for metropolitan regions rather than merely for cities. He also continued to influence planning law through his leadership of the Legislative Committee of the American Institute of Planners and the American Bar Association's Committee on Planning Law Legislature. Finally, his long interest in slum clearance and public housing as part of a comprehensive treatment for cities led him to play a critical role in the early development of the Housing Act of 1949.[15] These activities, as well as his eighty-five published titles in the fields of planning and housing, suggest why one historian of planning has argued that "no single person contributed more to the development of city and regional planning between 1920 and 1945 than Alfred Bettman."[16]

Ladislas Segoe, the city's other prominent planner, also participated in Cincinnati's better housing movements. While earning a Diploma of Engineering at the Technical University of Budapest, Segoe became interested in planning. After graduation, the Hungarian national traveled to the United States in 1922 and joined the Technical Advisory Corporation of New York as a city planner. Sent to Cincinnati to help develop a comprehensive plan, Segoe made the Queen City his home base and played an active role in its planning and housing history. In 1926 he became the city's first planning engineer; several years later, in private practice, he devised site plans for a Cincinnati slum-clearing, limited dividend housing project. Later, he helped draw the metropolitan plan for greater Cincinnati published in 1948.[17]

Segoe and Associates, a firm of city planners and consulting engineers, was used by more than 100 cities and counties including San Francisco, Chicago, New York, Pittsburgh, Philadelphia, and Seattle. In addition, Segoe edited an important and influential text, *Local Planning Administration*, published in 1941 by the International City Managers Association. He also lectured widely at universities between 1930 and 1942, including Harvard, Carnegie Institute of Technology, and Northwestern as well as the University of Cincinnati.[18]

During the New Deal, Segoe helped write the original policies on site planning in public housing for the Housing Division of the Public Works Administration and consulted for the Tennessee River Valley Authority's Planning Department. Even more significant, he directed the National Resources Board's Urbanism Committee. Segoe was largely responsible for its report, *Our Cities: Their Role in the National Economy*, which claimed to be "the first inquiry of national, official, and comprehensive scale into the problems of the American urban community."[19]

Not only did the city possess a number of respected housing and planning leaders, but it had gained national recognition as a model "progressive" city by the late 1920s. Observers cited two factors for its metamorphosis from one of the nation's worst-governed cities to one of its best. First, they credited Cincinnati's newly structured local government. During the mid-1920s, Cincinnatians installed the city manager form of government and reduced the large city council to a body of nine members elected by proportional representation. Moreover, the good-government proponents maintained their reform organization, the City Charter Committee, as an unofficial political party. It not only controlled council from 1924 to 1938, but gave the city capable and nationally respected leaders such as Mayor Murray Seasongood and City Manager Clarence A. Dykstra. Just as bosses George B. Cox and Rudolph K. Hynicka had provided the leadership necessary for effective machine rule, Seasongood's and Dykstra's nationally recognized governing and administrative skills provided Cincinnati with efficient reform government. As a result, the *Survey Graphic* claimed in 1937 that Cincinnatians paid less and got more for their money than residents of "any other city of comparable size in the country."[20]

Although the Charterites pushed both housing and comprehensive planning during their tenure, even when shifting political alignments resulted in the first Republican mayor under the new system in 1938, no major redefinitions of the housing or planning problems occurred until the 1950s. That is, politics affected the specifics of policy implementation, but seemed to have little impact on the perception of the broader problem. Indeed, the movement for the plans of 1925 and 1948 started when Republicans controlled council.

The evidence, then, suggests that Cincinnati is an excellent city in which to explore the low-cost housing movement for two reasons. First, the high level of activity in regard to housing provides an abundant amount of evidence to scrutinize the goals and accomplishments of better housing advocates in one city. Second, Cincinnati's local housing activists participated in the national dialogue over the low-cost housing problem, suggesting they shared the broad assumptions about the housing problem which made communication possible. As a result, after acknowledging that Cincinnati reformers adopted specific solutions to the Queen City's particular problems, it still should be possible to view the Cincinnati experience as symptomatic of the larger low-cost housing movement.

PART I

Tenements, Place, and Urban Social Problems

Americans discovered their neighborhood slums and tenement districts in the late nineteenth century in a way they had not done before. Although the new preoccupation with slums corresponded with the dramatic shifting of populations in the "new city," it should not be dismissed merely as a consequence of this. According to Henry D. Shapiro, by the end of the nineteenth century "place as environment entered social theory as the critical context facilitating or prohibiting the development of particular patterns of relationships between the individuals and the society of that place."[1]

Historian Paul Boyer has observed that by the early twentieth century there occurred "a fundamental shift of interest away from the individual to the group." Furthermore, Boyer has suggested that this shift in social thought "reflected not merely an interest in *studying* social groups, but also in controlling them through the benevolent manipulation of their physical and social environment."[2] The combination of this new focus on place and group, along with the perception that the working-class poor would remain a permanent part of the American urban setting, led to an unprecedented preoccupation with tenement districts and those who lived there.[3]

Indeed, members of the city's middle and upper classes, traumatized by the rapid growth and transformation of their cities, and gravely concerned about the apparent breakdown of order and community in the urban setting, led the assault on tenement districts. Fearful that tenement districts destroyed family life and promoted an assortment of social, political, and medical pathologies, reformers focused on improving the environment of the poor.

This new concern with tenement districts around the turn of the century resulted in a number of investigations of those areas by both federal and state governments.[4] Local surveys which also collected and categorized a variety of social data about such places increased at this time too.[5] Of course, urban reformers were not content merely to collect data on the neighborhoods of the poor, but wanted to develop programs to better the slum environment that they found. Looking back at turn-of-the-century reform, sociologist Ernest Burgess recalled that the city had become the "happy hunting ground of movements." Not only were many of those movements linked to this concern with tenement districts, but they reflected the certain way reformers viewed the city. Commenting more than twenty years later on the variety of those movements (i.e., the public health movement, the social center movement, the social work movement), Burgess concluded that "these movements lack[ed] a basic understanding of the city."[6] What he meant was that while turn-of-the-century reformers could adequately identify separate components of the slum problem, they failed to understand the complex interrelationship of those separate problems in the same way reformers did by the 1920s.

Although turn-of-the-century reformers may not have grasped the complexities of urban problems in a way that pleased Burgess, they clearly identified the evils of environment in the tenement district. When they examined tenement districts they found a heterogeneous, disordered, and artificial setting which seemed to have a disproportionate amount of immorality, criminality, poverty, and ill health. These social problems would remain, according to the middle and upper-class reformers, until the environment of the poor was improved. As a result, much of the era's reform focused on bringing a sense of order and propriety to tenement district dwellers by improving their environment. Nowhere is this better exemplified than in tenement house reform.

Tenements appeared as a microcosm of all that was wrong in slum neighborhoods. Their rental policies indiscriminantly mixed good and bad people together; their cramped and ill-ventilated rooms discouraged family togetherness; their dark halls and shared toilets promoted sexual promiscuity; and their filthiness and physical defects threatened the very lives of their inhabitants. Tenement reformers feared that such a domestic setting threatened family stability. Therefore, they expended almost all of their energies on correcting the worst defects found in the dwellings of the poor.[7] As a result, tenement housing codes became the major legacy of Progressive Era housing reform. The New York Tenement House Law of 1901, passed largely by the efforts of Lawrence Veiller, became the model for tenement house legislation. Veiller, who emerged as the nation's leading tenement house reformer, promoted tenement codes for several reasons. First, he believed they would promote "proper types of new tenement houses" in the future and "forbid the erection of any others." Second, they would help remedy "errors of the past" by altering and improving old tenement houses so as to make them fit for human habitation. Third, the codes would help "maintain present and future tenement houses" in sanitary condition "by promoting adequate supervision." [8]

Although Veiller and other tenement reformers looked forward to the day that they could place the poor in small cottages on the city's outskirts, they also believed that tenement reform would bring about real improvement in the lives of tenement dwellers. Eliminating the worst defects found in tenement district dwellings, then, characterized the housing movement at the turn of the century. Only later would housing reformers promote better housing for the city as a whole. [9]

CHAPTER 1

Tenements, Congestion, and the Problem of the Poor, 1865–1910

Those who have studied the laws of social science know that crowding increases crime. The morals become depraved, intemperance reigns, and men not only often neglect work, but become mentally and morally unfit to faithfully perform it. Nor is that all. Living in such a state of depravity they become the ready tools of unprincipled and avaricious politicians who use their opportunity not only to obtain office where they can rule the public, but to sink their constituents into still a deeper state of degradation; hence our exorbitant taxes, our heavy city debt.
                                                        —Richard Nelson, *Suburban Homes*

Some Cincinnatians identified their city's crowded and unsanitary tenements as a problem long before a distinct organization appeared in 1916 to better them. Although mid-nineteenth-century reformers tended to believe that intemperate behavior caused pauperism, they also recognized clear linkages between poverty and inadequate living space.[1] As early as 1865, the Cincinnati Relief Union, an association founded to aid the needy and worthy poor, complained that unhealthy and unwholesome tenement house conditions contributed to the number of indigent found in Cincinnati. Indeed, one of the union's directors visited the dwellings of between 400 and 500 impoverished families throughout the city and declared that much of the sickness—and hence dependency—could be linked to the deficient living space found within the city's tenement houses. At least one of the tenements so lacked ventilation, air, and sunlight, that the director compared it to the

Portions of chapters 1–3 first appeared in the *Journal of Urban History* 11 (May 1985): 314–34, in an article I wrote entitled "From Better Dwellings to Better Community: Changing Approaches to the Low-Cost Housing Problem, 1890–1925." This material is reproduced with the permission of Sage Publications, Inc.

"black hole of Calcutta."[2] The Relief Union blamed both ignorant tenants and greedy tenement landlords for the "inexpressively filthy and unhealthy abodes" it found, but particularly singled out the landlords for condemnation. According to the union, some of the city's wealthiest citizens derived much of their income from overcrowded, poorly ventilated, and exorbitantly priced tenement houses. Such dwellings, the union's report continued, threatened to contaminate "an otherwise healthy and prosperous city."[3] Nevertheless, it was not only greed, but Cincinnati's unique geography which made it particularly susceptible to the tenement evil.

During the 1860s, Cincinnati occupied nearly seven square miles of low-lying basin on the north bank of the Ohio River. Except for entrances through the Mill Creek Valley on the west, and the Deer Creek Valley on the east, sharply rising hills surrounded the rest of the city and inhibited the outward expansion characteristic of urban America at this time. According to the 1870 census, Cincinnati ranked only behind New York as the most congested large city in the United States.[4] Although the physical boundaries of the city expanded throughout the rest of the nineteenth century, the congestion found in the basin remained.

For instance, in 1879, the Cincinnati Board of Health reported that Cincinnati contained more tenements than Chicago, Philadelphia, Baltimore, and St. Louis combined. From 1869 to 1879, the city's population climbed from 216,239 to 255,139, an 18-percent increase. During the same period, its tenement houses swelled from 1,410 to 5,616, a 298-percent increase.[5]

Cincinnati tenements were generally not as tall as in New York or as "hidden" as in Chicago.[6] The most prominent Queen City tenement contained three stories and was constructed specifically to house the unskilled wage earner. These rectangular buildings usually housed two families per floor, and featured a side entrance and stairways in the middle of the dwelling. Each floor contained two rooms in the front of the house and two in the rear. Water flowed only from a kitchen or hallway faucet. Sometimes toilets were located in the hallway, but many were placed outside in the courtyard. Builders often erected these tenements close together, sometimes two to a lot.[7]

Block tenements also spotted the basin landscape. Some of these units had been constructed for residential use, but others were converted from warehouses or factory buildings. Although not many of these buildings existed in Cincinnati, those few that did ranked among the city's worst residential quarters. In 1879, Rev. Dudley Ward Rhodes referred to the deplorable conditions of these dwellings in his lecture on "The Curse of Tenement Houses." He particularly singled out for condemnation a block tenement called Big Missouri, located on the west side of Sycamore Street between Seventh and Eighth Streets. This five-story brick building, formerly a spice mill, had been converted into a ninety-five-room tenement dwelling. It housed approximately

300 tenants, who were forced to climb rotten wooden stairways and endure foul-smelling hallways and courtyards. Besides living in small, dark, unventilated rooms which rented for between $2 and $4 per month, Big Missouri's 300 tenants shared one water hydrant located outdoors in the courtyard. After inspecting the infamous tenement house, a Cincinnati health officer declared Big Missouri "an outrage against decency and humanity."[8]

Many of the tenements which lined the riverfront and attracted common laborers involved in the river trade had formerly been warehouses or factories. Landlords divided those buildings into tenement quarters by erecting temporary wooden partitions. According to an 1897 Department of Health report, those "grossly unsanitary" quarters housed many of the city's "vicious" poor, and served as the origin for many of Cincinnati's epidemics. After summarizing the deplorable conditions found in the river district, the report concluded that "the slums of Cincinnati, though limited in extent, are equal in squalor and misery to those found in any American city."[9]

A number of single-family houses, now converted into multiunit dwellings, constituted the third type of Cincinnati tenement house. Although such conversions had taken place as early as the 1840s, their numbers proliferated after the 1860s. By then, the recently introduced steam-powered inclined plane allowed horse-drawn streetcars to scale the city's hilltops. The introduction of cables and electric streetcars in the 1880s further encouraged the exodus to the high land. As more of the city's middle and upper-class families exited from the congested basin, speculators bought their old homes, divided them into flats, and rented them to the poor. Usually, these old houses, located on 20' by 90'(or 100') lots, were partitioned into several two-room flats on each floor, resulting in dark halls and stairways, along with inadequate ventilation. Deficient toilet facilities, however, constituted the worst problem. Almost all the converted tenements had outdoor toilets located in the narrow yards between dwellings. Moreover, there was usually only one outhouse per tenement.[10]

Tenements could be found throughout the basin, although those located on the eastern half of the city's core seemed particularly threatening. According to the 1890 census the Twentieth and Twenty-second Wards on the West Side of the basin near the foul-smelling, polluted Mill Creek, contained "thickly settled tenements," while a tenement district "of mixed nationalities" occupied the central basin's Eighteenth Ward (see map 1-A). Prior to 1916, however, most reformers focused on Bucktown, located east of Broadway around Sixth and Seventh Streets (Sixth Ward); or on the lower East End.[11] And when the city finally initiated systematic block inspection of tenements in 1913, the Housing Department chose to inspect an East Side tenement district near the Ohio River first, since it contained "more unsanitary and unsafe conditions . . . than any other [area] in the city."[12]

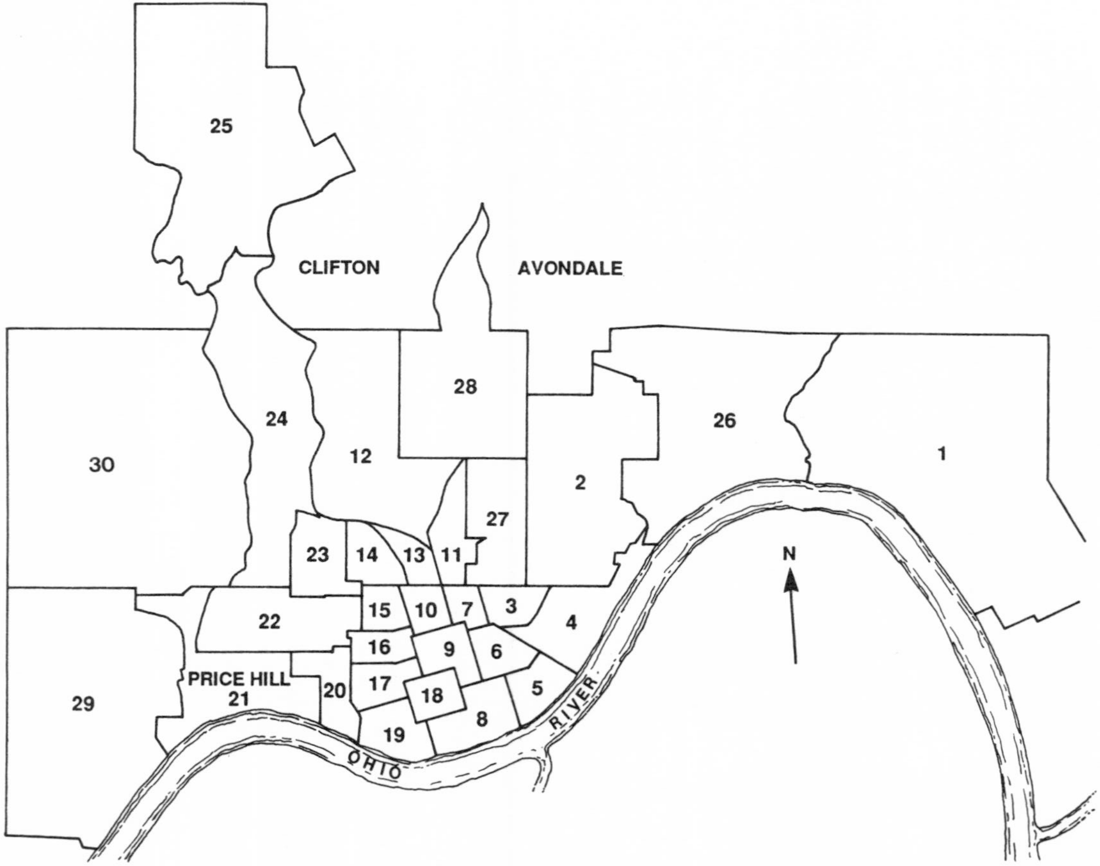

Map 1-A. Cincinnati Wards, 1890

Long before the creation of the city's Housing Department, the Board of Health surveyed the city's tenements and discovered serious problems. Created in 1867 through an act of the state legislature, Cincinnati's first full-time Board of Health investigated the city's tenements two years later. It found that nearly half of the 9,894 families residing in tenement houses occupied but one room. Unhappy with its limited power to order improvements in tenements which lacked adequate sanitary facilities, water, breathing space, or sleeping accommodations, the Board of Health turned to the state legislature for additional powers.[13] Board members proposed legislation modeled after the comprehensive New York State Tenement Law of 1867, which required light and ventilation in each sleeping room, at least one toilet for every twenty occupants, registration and upkeep of all cellars as flats, and specific distances between buildings, heights of ceilings, and dimensions of windows. Many of its requirements applied to existing as well as future tenement dwellings.[14] Although the Ohio State Assembly passed a law in 1875 mandating the improvement of dwellings deemed unsafe for habitation, it failed to approve the type of tenement regulation pushed by the Board of Health until 1888. That year, the state's newly written building code for cities of the first class limited the use of cellars as dwellings, regulated the distances between tenement buildings, and required that each dwelling be properly lighted and ventilated.[15]

Despite this legislative triumph for tenement betterment, there appeared a growing anxiety over basin tenement conditions during the late nineteenth century. This coincided with a new concern over the poor and their environs expressed by many of Cincinnati's middle and upper classes. For as the city continued to extend its boundaries (Cincinnati grew from twenty-two square miles in 1880 to more than fifty square miles in 1910), observers worried about the social implications of the "new city," characterized by much greater segregation than the earlier "walking city." To many it appeared that the new city contained distinguishable social, economic, and geographic parts which performed specific functions within the larger urban system. Most urban reformers adopted this vision of city as social system, composed of discrete yet interconnected parts, and expended their efforts on treating faulty urban components rather than the whole.[16]

Because the new city failed to live up to the expectations of reformers, late nineteenth-century urban America constantly seemed on the brink of disaster. Rather than resemble an orderly and efficient social system, the city appeared to be a jumbled mix of political corruption, physical ill health, and social pathology. Reformers, however, believed they knew the source of much of the urban malaise, and pointed to the neighborhoods of the city's poor working classes. Was it not here that the origins of the ill health and social chaos which threatened the city and taxed its institutions could be found? And had not these neighborhoods furnished the necessary support to maintain the city's corrupt political organizations? Called slums by some, tenement districts by others, the environs of the poor became the target of reformers who wanted to better the city.[17] As a result, kindergartens, settlement houses, social centers, and playgrounds all appeared in the basin at this time. It is within this context, as one of many distinct movements aimed at reconstructing the environment of the urban poor, that tenement house reform emerged as a leading issue during the Progressive Era.[18]

One of the leaders in late nineteenth-century tenement reform, the Associated Charities of Cincinnati, organized in 1879 to institute "intelligent and systematic distribution of the relief given . . . to the poor," founded a Committee on Tenements in 1892 to study "the present conditions of degraded portions of our city." That committee owed its existence to the efforts of the suburban Walnut Hills Congregational Church, made up of people who had fled the chaos of the basin.[19]

Two years later, the Ohio Bureau of Labor, mirroring the government's increased concern with the environs of the poor, investigated Cincinnati's Third Ward (see map 1-A). The investigation, apparently modeled after the federal investigation of the slums of Baltimore, New York, Chicago, and Philadelphia a year earlier, surveyed the ward's demographic and social characteristics as well as the sanitary conditions of its tenement houses. With the exception of the eastern part of the ward which contained railroad switching yards, a dump, and some of the "vilest tenements" in the city, the sanitary conditions in the district, to the surprise of the bureau, were "on the whole, excellent."[20]

The survey, which focused exclusively on the condition of the ward's tenement buildings, investigated both their outside and inside conditions, rating them either good, fair, poor, or bad. According to the inside inspection, which accounted for the cleanliness, the ventilation, and the light of the building, only thirty-one flats out of 513 were judged bad, while another twenty-eight were reported poor. Investigators rated the majority of the inspected tenements good, and noted the excellent condition of some. Outside conditions drew the same type of scrutiny and findings. After examining the general condition of the buildings, the plumbing, the sewage, the water closets, the ventilation, and "all those things over which the individual tenants could have no direct control," inspectors rated only thirty-five bad and another sixty-two poor.[21]

Although the survey discovered that some of the "old rickety weather-worn frame buildings" in the ward lacked adequate plumbing, and that some of the newer tenement houses contained neither sewers nor privies, it nevertheless concluded that there was "no more sickness in the third ward than could be found among an equal number of people in the better residence districts." It also reported few cases of overcrowding among the largely German population, even though most families occupied only two large rooms. Recognizing that such living arrangements could at times create personal inconvenience, investigators concluded that the health of the tenants was in no way endangered.[22]

The report's recognition of the census tract's excellent sanitary conditions, and the praise it lavished on the tenants, did not prevent it from criticizing the "conditions of life" in the "crowded tenement district" as not being "favorable to the development of the highest moral standard." The report particularly worried that "the privacy of the home" and the "dignity of life" could not be preserved in the tenement district. It observed that such a setting seemed inappropriate for children, because "the child is the child of the neighborhood rather than of any one family and while he will profit by the moral precepts that emanate from his own home, . . . he will be quick to imbibe the evil of the whole community."[23]

Despite this recognition of the influence of both the dwelling and the neighborhood on the development of the tenement district's children, late nineteenth-century tenement reformers focused narrowly on improving the dwelling place, either through governmental regulation or through the building of model tenements, and left other aspects of neighborhood improvement to other movements just as narrowly conceived.

For instance, when wealthy German Jews, led by Max Senior, established the United Jewish Charities of Cincinnati (UJC) in 1896 "to relieve the deserving poor, prevent want and distress, and discourage pauperism," they created a three-member tenement committee. That body specifically focused on alleviating the congested conditions of the Jewish poor—largely Russian immigrants—found in the basin. Hoping to improve those "squalid districts," it pushed tenement regulation after another UJC committee complained that its efforts to introduce habits of cleanliness, sanitation, and morality to the newcomers were thwarted by "big, unwholesome and dilapidated buildings."[24]

The Associated Charities, concerned with the non-Jewish poor, pursued the same strategy and campaigned not only for better laws to improve the already built tenement houses, but pushed new regulations to ensure future tenements of a higher minimum standard. As a result of the efforts of the UJC and the Associated Charities, Cincinnati passed its first building code on August 15, 1898, which provided more regulation of tenements than ever before in areas such as lot coverage, water closet accommodations, light shafts, and fire escapes. Despite this success, tenement reformers were still hardly placated. Instead, they complained that the code was too vague and too lenient in regard to tenements.[25]

Not only did reformers want better tenement regulation, they also wanted the existing laws governing them strictly enforced. The tenement committee of the United Jewish Charities was specifically charged with assisting the efforts of the city authorities in their enforcement of the tenement laws.[26] And several years later, the Associated Charities' Central Board passed a resolution instructing its friendly visitors to report any "unwholesome conditions" to the association's central office so that it could report them to the understaffed Board of Health.[27]

In addition to their interest in the passage and enforcement of better tenement regulations, reformers also encouraged the building and establishment of model tenements. Just as tenement regulation was not new to the 1890s, the idea of model tenement building in Cincinnati had been raised earlier. In 1867, the Cincinnati Relief Union reported the formation of a Tenant House Association composed of "thirty-six public spirited men to erect suitable model tenements." Apparently nothing came of this.[28] Nor was the late nineteenth-century effort much more successful. The Associated Charities, probably the strongest proponent of model tenements at this time, leased a tenement from wealthy businessman Thomas Emery, Jr., in 1895 and remodeled it into a model tenement. Rev. and Mrs. F. S. Fairchild managed the Lock Street tenement, and reported their experiences at the local Conference of Charities and Benevolent Organizations four months after they had begun their work. At that meeting, the Fairchilds discussed the importance of sanitation and light in preserving "the respectable character of tenements" and stressed that future tenement houses should "be built in such a manner as to better promote family privacy, without which there is no home."[29] Despite the apparent improvement brought to family life by this experiment, few in attendance chose to follow.

Nor did the Joint Industrial Homes Committee of the Carpenters District and Building Trades Council generate much building activity when it published plans for model tenements in the Central Labor Council's newspaper, the *Chronicle*. Apparently providing "real homes for the workingman" just did not pay a sound enough return on the investment.[30]

Despite the endorsement of unions, the city's prosperous businessmen, professionals, and their wives, working through philanthropic organizations, provided the main initiative for the movement. And as the new century began, they stubbornly continued to adhere to the forty-year-old strategies of regulation and model tenement building.

For example, the Associated Charities launched a major tenement improvement campaign in 1901 which embraced these strategies. In July of 1901, the Associated Charities invited Wallace E. Miller, professor of sociology at Southwestern Kansas University, to survey the city's tenement house conditions. Part of the reason for Miller's survey, reported the Associated Charities, was "to open up the way for model tenement houses in Cincinnati: (1) by ascertaining the real conditions; (2) by locating the needs; (3) by demonstrating to public spirited men of means the practicality of model tenements." The investigation would also discover if model tenements could provide "a reasonable rate of interest." [31]

This latter point proved important since it appeared that Cincinnati tenement reformers subscribed to the "business creed" of housing so appropriately described by Thomas Philpott in his book on Chicago housing reform. The tenets of that creed were simple: "Housing was a commodity for private enterprise to provide at a profit." If model tenements were to succeed, they would have to retain a profit of not less than 5 percent to their investors. A completely philanthropic endeavor never seemed to have been considered by Cincinnati reformers since such housing was seen as detrimental to both the marketplace and the tenant. [32]

Despite these limitations, the attempt to arouse interest in model tenement building seemed to work. The *Charities Bulletin* claimed that "a considerable interest has been shown in the subject of model tenements." It went on to predict that "whenever it can be shown that comfortable, healthful dwellings, providing modern conveniences can be built and rented at a profit it will not be difficult to secure capital for the purpose." That same periodical reported that Dr. S. D. J. Meade's planned tenement house for the East End will "be a model in every respect" and will be "watched with much interest." [33]

Another outsider, E. R. L. Gould, also helped fuel reformer interest in the city's tenement problem. Gould presided over the New York City and Suburban Homes Association, an organization which built model dwellings for the poor. Although he came to Cincinnati in 1903 to lecture on other matters, the leadership of the Associated Charities arranged a meeting with Gould to discuss the local tenement problem. That meeting, held at the YMCA in March, attracted a number of reformers, architects, and realtors. Members of the Associated Charities hoped that the meeting would produce the momentum necessary to establish a model tenement company. [34]

Not only did private citizens push model tenements to combat the tenement problem, but so did government officials. For instance, Clark W. Davis, Cincinnati health officer, observed in his annual report for 1903 that model tenements were desperately needed for the city's poor who were unable to afford new tenement houses built by speculators and were therefore forced to live in congested and unsanitary flats. In his report he asked, "Who is to provide the new tenement [for the poor]? Here," he continued,

> is an opportunity for the real philanthropist—not to give, for alms are not desirable, but to build for investment. This may yield but a small per cent, but it will surely be safe and substantial. This is not giving to the poor; it is simply lending

them money at a low rate of interest. Sanitary tenements are not in the interest of the poor alone; they are in the interest of the well-to-do, as the health of every part of the community is affected by the life and health of every other part.[35]

By building model tenements, then, reformers thought they could combat the immoral and unhealthy conditions which threatened family life and contributed to the social ills of the tenement district. If they built enough model tenements in a district, the theory went, they could eliminate the worst tenements by providing an attractive alternative to them at comparable prices. This procedure would upgrade the entire district and thus help to solve some of the social and health problems caused by congested, ill-designed, and unsanitary tenement houses. Nevertheless, reformers failed to attract the hoped-for capital, so that the most visible legacy of the era was not model tenement building, but stricter and more comprehensive tenement regulation.

Professor Miller journeyed to Cincinnati in 1901 not only to see if conditions warranted model tenements but to "ascertain whether a new State Tenement House Law was desirable for the larger cities of Ohio." Miller found both sanitary and social conditions to be bad in his two-month survey of eight districts selected by the Associated Charities. The results from his survey of the First District, located just to the southeast of the central business district, typified Miller's overall findings. In that district, 25 percent of all families contacted lived in bad or very bad dwellings. Furthermore, Miller discovered that the district contained a single church, but forty-two saloons.[36] The Associated Charities survey, then, supported a growing movement for more specific tenement laws and their stricter enforcement. Good homes could provide a refuge from the evils of the tenement district environment.

This tenement house reform movement coincided with a political reform movement to bring "honest, efficient, and progressive government" to machine-dominated Cincinnati. Both movements accelerated after 1903 and appeared closely related. When the nonpartisan Citizens' party attempted to overthrow Republican Boss George Cox's dominance in local government, it established a weekly reform newspaper, the *Citizens' Bulletin*, which not only supported political reform, but strongly backed tenement betterment and other kinds of environmental reform. The paper clearly equated urban improvement with greater efficiency and rationalization of civic as well as physical structures. So did many of the political reformers who joined with tenement reformers and lobbied for stronger tenement codes and their enforcement to improve both the physical and social conditions of the unstable basin tenement districts.[37]

Social reformers and philanthropists, however, remained at the forefront of the movement. For instance, on March 6, 1903, the Monday Evening Club, an organization composed of such do-gooders, prepared a campaign to improve the city's tenement code. It specifically called for more stringent hygienic and sanitary requirements for future tenement construction.[38] That same summer, the Associated Charities, assisted by the United Jewish Charities, the Union Bethel, the Elizabeth Gamble Deaconess Home, the Glen Industrial Home, the Mennonite Mission, and others, formed a bureau of inspection to cooperate with the health officer's inspection of tenement houses. It drew up a manual of instructions for the volunteer inspectors and held several meetings with health officials to plan an inspection strategy. Although the voluntary inspectors did remedy some sanitation problems, they complained that ineffective tenement regulations impeded their work.[39]

The increased public agitation for better tenement control influenced city council's decision to appoint a tenement house code committee to draft acceptable legislation. Council's committee, composed of Charles A. Tocker, chief building inspector; Richard Murphy, plumber; Samuel Hannaford, architect; and W. D. Breed and C. M. Hubbard, both of the Associated Charities, was to consult with a variety of other local citizens before it wrote the proposed law. Soon after the appointments, the local chapter of the American Institute of Architects informed council that the entire building code needed revision. In response to this declaration, council replaced the original tenement code committee with a board of architects designated to draw up a new building code including stricter tenement regulation. But that committee failed to act, in part because of pressure from other architects and builders who feared that too much regulation might overly increase future building costs. After several years of delay, Councilman Michael Mullen, long an important member of the notorious Cox machine, introduced a tenement code to council in 1906. Despite the support of more than forty educational, philanthropic, and business groups in the city, council failed to act. Rather, it yielded to a request by a committee of architects to review the proposed tenement code.[40]

Only after three more years of delay, again caused by builders, realtors, and others who opposed tenement regulation, did council finally enact a new building code with satisfactory tenement regulation. Shortly after council passed the ordinance, on May 10, 1909, the *Charities' Review* hailed the new law. It would not only assure "adequate light and air and proper sanitary appliances in future tenements," the magazine observed, but require existing tenement owners to make needed improvements meeting new minimum requirements to protect the health and morality of those "who must live in tenement houses."[41] Reformers particularly rejoiced about the new requirement that mandated separate water-closet space for each dwelling unit in the tenement. In addition, the new law made tenement house owners responsible for the cleanliness of their properties and liable to a fine if they did not properly maintain them. Finally, the new tenement code designated several sanitary inspectors as tenement house inspectors to help enforce the code. Never before in the city's history had council created positions specifically to police the city's tenements.[42]

Although the new tenement code did improve the physical condition of existing tenements, as well as prevent construction of very bad tenement buildings, it had a more negative impact too. According to the Cincinnati Real Estate Board in 1917, "Very few tenement houses have been erected in the basin of the city" after the adoption of the code because it had "increased the cost of building of this property to such an extent that the rent received from such property does not pay a fair return on the investment."[43] Tenement regulation, then, helped eliminate the basin's worst housing, but did little to provide additional good housing for the city's working-class poor.

As a result, even though tenement regulation and model tenement building suggest a concern with the poor, such efforts did not always help the poor. Tenement regulation created new housing shortages while the "business creed" destroyed any chance of substantial model tenement building. By eliminating the darkest and dirtiest of Cincinnati's tenements, housing reformers hoped to prevent conditions which posed the greatest threat to family life. One of many strategies to improve the tenement district, tenement house reform became a popular cause simply because of its close ties to family life. If unsanitary and overcrowded tenements were identified as a major contributor to disrupted home life, then tenement reform seemed absolutely necessary. In their effort to promote more wholesome dwellings, middle and upper-class Cincinnatians from a variety of organizations banded together and worked out a tenement reform strategy. Indeed, their successes and failures ultimately led to the formation of the Better Housing League, and to the discovery of a citywide housing problem.

Redefining the Housing Problem: From Inappropriate Dwellings to Inadequate Community, 1910–19

> When I was here last year I witnessed a revolution. It is my privilege to travel pretty well all over the U.S. in the interest of housing reform, and I have never found any city that was so thoroughly aroused throughout the whole constituency as was the city of Cincinnati last year.
>
> —Lawrence Veiller, *Proceedings of the National Housing Association, 1913*

> Citizens of the right type cannot be made from children who sleep in dark, window-less rooms; in dwellings much overcrowded, where privacy is unknown, and water supply is inadequate; where filthy fly-infested privy vaults are shared by six or eight families; where lots are so overcrowded that there is no room for flowers, vegetables, or even a grass plot; and the children are forced on the street to play.
>
> —*The Citizens' Book*, 1916

Almost from its enactment on May 10, 1909, social and civic organizations voiced their displeasure over the enforcement of the tenement code which they had worked so hard to secure. For instance, C. M. Hubbard complained to the Associated Charities' Board of Trustees on March 7, 1910, that the building commissioner was very slow in carrying out the new tenement code.[1] Max Senior, founder of the United Jewish Charities, provided an even stronger indictment of the enforcement procedure during a talk at the City Club on April 15. Senior, a leading tenement crusader, complained that Cincinnati's two tenement inspectors sometimes failed to average two visits a day. To place this in the proper perspective he noted that New York City required its inspectors to make a minimum of thirty daily visits. Even more disturbing, Senior charged that those who evaluated the work of Cincinnati's inspectors declared it useless.[2]

The agitation for better inspection, and specifically the paper by Max Senior, led the newly created Cincinnati Bureau of Municipal Research to investigate the existing administrative procedures in the inspection of tenements. Its report, issued on April 20, 1910, to Mr. Scott Smith, director of public safety and chief administrator over the entire Building Department, included strong criticism of the system and made recommendations for its improvement.[3] Once again, the agitation for more and better tenement regulation coincided with a political reform movement aimed at bringing more efficient and cost-effective government to boss-ridden local government. And with the success of that movement in 1911, resulting in the defeat of Boss Cox's machine, council proceeded to reorganize tenement house inspection procedures.[4]

Under the reorganization, which newly elected reform Mayor Henry T. Hunt strongly endorsed, the tenement inspectors no longer reported to the building commissioner or functioned as a part of the Building Department. Instead, they would become an independent department reporting directly to the director of public safety, who also headed the Departments of Fire, Police, Charities and Correction, Smoke Inspection, and Building Inspection.[5] To oversee this reorganization, council used privately subscribed funds and brought in Robert E. Todd, a New York City tenement expert, to organize the new department. Under Todd, who acted as the chief housing inspector from February 15, 1912, to January 28, 1913, the department changed its procedure: instead of inspecting on complaint, the department instituted the systematic inspection of all tenements. In addition, Todd inaugurated new inspection and reporting techniques. Finally, council increased the size of the department from two tenement inspectors to a chief inspector, three deputies, and three clerical assistants. But these changes represented only one manifestation of an increased civic awareness and concern with the tenement problem.[6]

The Anti-Tuberculosis League, which participated in the reorganization of the Tenement House Department, proved another source (as well as symptom) of the new enthusiasm about tenement reform after 1910. Organized on January 31, 1907, by representatives of forty commercial, medical, and educational bodies to combat the city's high tuberculosis rate, the league focused on the horrible conditions found in the basin. Improving the city's health, though its primary concern, was not the league's only one. For according to these health reformers, "When you teach a man the principles that underlay the prevention of tuberculosis, you have taught him the dangers of excesses of all sorts."[7] Nevertheless, since most of the city's tuberculosis cases originated from the basin, the league soon joined with other environmental reformers to improve that area's living conditions. Specifically, it promoted "the construction of sanitary tenements, with abundant light and air" as well as "the establishment of playgrounds and other breathing spaces for the poor in the overcrowded districts." In its attempt to abolish "disease breeding slum localities," the league sponsored a tenement house survey in 1911 and lobbied strenuously for a more effective tenement house inspection procedure. Even more significant, it conducted a massive publicity and educational campaign to awaken civic consciousness of the tenement problem.[8]

The league initiated its survey to expose "the appalling conditions in the tenement houses" and to discover the causes for the basin's problems. It examined four separate residential sections representing the dwellings of 1,373 families and concluded that the tenement landlords' "absolute disregard of the law" represented one of the basin's greatest problems. In addition, the survey cited poverty and bad living conditions, drink and dissipation, and dark rooms as other sources of the basin's problems.[9]

Besides the tenement survey, the Anti-Tuberculosis League kept a close watch on the newly founded Tenement House Department and promoted laws to make its work easier. For instance, the league lobbied for the passage of a local ordinance to facilitate the vacation of tenements in violation of the law. The league pushed for this ordinance after its survey revealed that many of the worst tenements which consistently violated the city's tenement code returned a profit of 20 to 40 percent.[10]

The league's most important contribution, however, was in arousing citywide interest in the tenement problem. Fearful that public indifference prevented any successful resolution of the problem, the league joined with sixty-eight other organizations on June 10, 1912, to plan a strategy for a publicity campaign to educate and motivate citizens to support tenement reform. By showing how bad tenements adversely affected all classes in Cincinnati, reformers attempted to rally the city's diverse population together by identifying tenement reform as a common cause.[11]

As part of this strategy, Samuel P. Withrow, the superintendent of the Anti-Tuberculosis League, produced a twenty-minute motion picture entitled "Darkest Cincinnati," depicting the city's appalling tenement districts. The movie, which premiered at the Colonial Theater on Fifth Street, September 29, 1912, captured the city's horrid tenement conditions, and showed the high costs of them to the city, by interspersing shots of hospitals, clinics, and ambulances throughout the presentation. The film played to over 75,000 people at fifty-six theaters that fall.[12] That motion picture, as well as a map reproduced in the commissioner of buildings' 1913 annual report, clearly reflected the concerns of tenement reformers. The map of Cincinnati's social geography drawn by the Department of Charities and Correction clearly equated the city's disease, dependency, and crime with the tenement-filled basin. Data used for that map showed that 70 percent of the city's institutional population came from the "most congested portions of the tenement districts."[13] If citizens wanted to combat the problems associated with the institutionalized population, and thus create a more effective use of their tax dollars, then they were obligated to support tenement reform.

The Anti-Tuberculosis League also sponsored several meetings at the end of 1912 to "further impress the people of Cincinnati with the importance of housing reform." It held a banquet featuring Lawrence Veiller, a nationally prominent New York tenement house reformer, on November 29. Seven days later it joined with other civic improvement associations and hosted a rally at Music Hall to publicize the citywide dangers posed by the tenement housing problem. Over 2,500 attended the meeting, which had been strongly endorsed by reform Mayor Henry T. Hunt as a way to arouse public consciousness of the problem. According to Hunt, only through the public's participation could the "civic disease" and "social malady" caused by the tenement problem be eradicated. Keynote speaker Dr. Woods Hutchinson, a respected authority on hygiene problems, echoed the mayor's contention. According to Hutchinson, housing conditions were a community problem and should be effectively controlled by the community.[14]

Mayor Hunt, who joined Hutchinson and E. L. Hitchens of the Central Labor Council[15] as the evening's speakers, reaffirmed the need for an active housing movement which aimed "to secure a real home for every man, woman and child in Cincinnati." Toward this end, he announced the formation of a Housing Association which would "hold a quasi-official relationship with the city administration." He also proposed two specific remedies for the congestion and squalor found in the city's tenement districts. First, he recommended that council appropriate $250,000 for the improvement of the marshy Mill Creek Valley, an area Hunt likened to an open sewer. Once the necessary improvements were completed, the valley could provide an adequate site for permanent working-class housing. Second, the mayor predicted that the proposed rapid transit system loop around the city would allow the wage earners more freedom in choosing their housing locations.[16]

The enthusiasm generated by the public meetings in 1912 did not totally dissipate either. Although Hunt's Housing Association seems never to have functioned, the Chamber of Commerce pushed better housing through its Committee on Industrial Welfare and Housing, established in 1913. That year's *Annual Report* observed that the chamber planned to undertake a general campaign for better housing in the belief "that the work can be accomplished in this way more successfully than by the usual method of forming an independent association." According to the report, a number of other organizations interested in the housing problem had pledged their support to the chamber. Although the chamber successfully landed the annual meeting of the National Housing Association (NHA) in 1913, it appears to have failed in its effort to provide a central, coordinated, housing reform organization for the city.[17]

Only after the newly formed Woman's City Club took up the issue in 1915 did a permanent housing association become a reality for the city. The Woman's City Club was organized February 12, 1915, as a civic organization dedicated to studying and acting on municipal issues. From the beginning, its founders envisioned a club committed to serving the entire city. Toward this end, club members were encouraged to join subcommittees to examine discrete topics such as public education, housing, city planning, and public health. After studying such topics in depth, committee members reported their findings to the larger membership. This system gave club women a broad overview of the city's civic affairs and helped them decide where to act.[18]

More than 1,500 women, representing a wide variety of backgrounds, joined the club during its first year. Its leadership, however, came largely from married women whose husbands were either businessmen or professionals.[19] These women shared their husbands' views, which emphasized the interdependence of the whole city, and which sought to rationalize the city to make it more efficient.

Such an orientation better explains why that club played such an important role in housing reform. Shortly after the Woman's City Club's housing committee investigated basin tenement conditions, the women decided that Cincinnati needed a separate housing organization to deal with its tenement problem. As a result, Louise Pollak and Setty S. Kuhn, members of the housing committee, launched a series of discussions with prominent Cincinnatians about the possibility of forming such a group. The women also turned to Laurence Veiller, executive secretary of the NHA, an organization he founded in 1909.[20]

Ever since the NHA's 1913 meeting in Cincinnati, Veiller, who viewed tenements as a discrete problem, had urged Cincinnatians to create a distinct tenement housing association. His push for such an organization rested on his premise that housing was a full-time problem and required a full-time organization devoted entirely to solving that problem. As Veiller put it: "We must recognize that we are not sallying forth as amateurs on a pleasant holiday into sociological realms, but are embarked upon a movement . . . with the most serious consequences to the community."[21]

The women must have concurred, for on June 6, 1916, they inaugurated a campaign to raise $5,000, the amount Veiller claimed they needed to create a housing association. About the same time they secured the support of Max Senior, founder of the United Jewish Charities, and Courtenay Dinwiddie, secretary of the Anti-Tuberculosis League. After spending nearly a month canvassing for funds and discussing the nature of the proposed organization, local housing enthusiasts finally organized the Better Housing League of Cincinnati (BHL) on July 10, 1916.[22]

The ten present at the initial meeting, presided over by lawyer Alfred Bettman, appointed Bettman's aunt, Setty S. Kuhn, as temporary chairman of the board of directors. They also selected a committee to write a constitution and hired E. P. Bradstreet, a former Cincinnati newspaper reporter, as field secretary for the league at $125 per month.[23] Several months later they adopted a constitution which pledged "to promote better housing especially in the tenements of Cincinnati." At the same meeting, the league elected Max Senior president, A. O. Elzner vice president, and Setty S. Kuhn treasurer.[24]

As a culmination of the turn-of-the-century concern with proper dwelling units, particularly tenements, these housing reformers expended most of their energies on tenement law enforcement. Agreeing with Veiller's analysis that sanitary deficiencies were the root cause of bad housing, the league battled against unfit privy vaults and catch basins, along with dark halls and poorly lighted interior rooms, because such conditions caused social and health problems which threatened the stability of the working-class family.[25]

For example, the league conducted a vigorous campaign to increase the budget of the recently created Municipal Housing Bureau (a division of the Building Department) so it could employ additional tenement inspectors for its meager staff of four. Although council authorized the increase, it never occurred, according to the league's first report, because "the war and the City's straightened finances . . . defeated this movement." Despite this setback, the league continued to publicize the tenement problem and conduct investigations into Cincinnati's tenement districts. It disseminated its findings to a variety of civic institutions, including social welfare and labor organizations, as well as the metropolitan daily newspapers.[26]

Indeed, education rivaled regulation as the league's most important task. "Getting the facts before the people" would have a positive impact. For the league believed that "once the public knows the facts and desires a remedy, improvement will follow inevitably." Education, then, would "develop organized public opinion for a careful, practical plan of improvement."[27]

The league's educational emphasis did not stop with the general public, however. In response from complaints by the Cincinnati Real Estate Board that "ignorant" black tenants were abusing their rented housing, the league established a system of visiting housekeepers at the beginning of 1918. According to league publicity, the housekeepers taught "tenants how to live properly, to appreciate repairs and improvements that are made for them, to be fair with the landlord and to pay their rent promptly." This program, developed by Setty Kuhn, originally sought to combat the "tenant problem" in the rapidly changing West End, but soon expanded to serve landlords and tenants throughout the basin. Although the former paid a nominal fee for this service at first, the league absorbed the costs after 1918.[28]

Kuhn also helped the BHL devise and implement a systematic plan of working for better housing through the public schools. Thirty thousand copies of a pamphlet called *Home, Health and Happiness* were distributed by teachers to their pupils. In addition, each year the league sent speakers into the upper grades of all public schools in tenement districts to discuss the importance of cleanliness and neatness "in and about their homes." When students reached the eighth grade, they were asked to write an essay on the "Proper Care of the Home," with the five best receiving special recognition from the BHL.[29]

Mindful of the limitations imposed by regulatory and educational reform, the league attempted to organize the Better Housing Company in 1917. This action stemmed from a report by the building commissioner which noted that many tenements remained unrepaired because their owners simply could not afford their proper maintenance. In response to this situation, BHL vice president and architect A. O. Elzner proposed that the league organize a company to buy or lease some of the city's old tenement buildings. Once in possession of the tenements, the league could rehabilitate them into adequate dwelling units. In addition, by using proper managing techniques, the BHL would be able to maintain clean, sanitary, and livable conditions at a modest rent. Efforts to raise capital for this project proved unsuccessful, however, and the plan was shelved.[30]

Although the league failed in several of its earliest ventures, it nevertheless undertook several internal improvements which assured its permanence as a central housing reform body. First, on October 12, 1917, it joined the Central Budget Committee of the Council of Social Agencies, an organization composed of twenty-nine agencies which pooled their resources for joint consideration of individual budgets after conducting a single fund-raising drive. Thus the BHL freed itself from depending solely on its local membership to raise money from friends and relatives. Several years later, the Council of Social Agencies merged with the Cincinnati Community Chest and the league retained its membership in that organization.[31]

Just as important to the league's success was the employment of Bleecker Marquette on September 1, 1918, as the housing association's new executive secretary. A former French high-school teacher from Schenectady, New York, the twenty-five-year-old Marquette succeeded Frank E. Burleson, who resigned to join the Council of Social Agencies staff as associate director. Marquette, who had for the past three years worked with Lawrence Veiller as assistant secretary for the New York State Tenement House Committee, brought much knowledge and experience to the Cincinnati movement. Indeed, the employment of Marquette as a "high salaried executive" (his $5,000 salary doubled the amount the league's first head received) marked an important stage in Cincinnati housing reform.[32]

Marquette's credentials and his close association with Lawrence Veiller, the dean of restrictive tenement reform, suggest that the BHL brought in an expert to produce a housing strategy consistent with Veiller's. And under Marquette the BHL did continue to promote betterment through regulation, supervision, and education. But soon after his arrival, the BHL broadened its focus and embraced a community development strategy.

Traces of this new trend appeared in the BHL's first two published reports, appearing in 1919 and 1921. The 1919 report conceded that "our tenement situation in Cincinnati is so serious and pressing that in the past naturally most of our attention has been concentrated upon the tenement as the most acute phase of our problem." But it also recognized that "the time is at hand that the housing problem includes all classes of dwellings." For in Cincinnati, "as in every other large city we have conditions just as serious . . . in one and two family dwellings, as we have in tenement houses." As a result, the report recommended that the city revise its building code so as to cover not just tenements, but every type of housing in the city. Such action would ensure that "evils permitted to develop in the past may be made impossible in the future" and guarantee that "all new houses shall afford the necessities and conveniences essential to right living." The code revision, then, would prevent existing housing from deteriorating into the slum of tomorrow.[33] Although council delayed approval of such a code until much later because of strong opposition from local realtors, the BHL's report suggested that the local housing association would no longer focus exclusively on the city's tenement districts.[34]

Even more important, the league began to act as if good housing meant something more than well-built and sanitary dwellings. For example, it strongly endorsed the development of a city zoning ordinance "to protect future growth, not only of its residences, but its business buildings." Only by rationalizing the use of city space could the potential for good housing be secured. The league's second report reaffirmed this new concern with better housing for the entire city when it cautioned that "our greatest effort must be to make sure that the future growth of our city is along proper lines and that houses built from now on shall not be the type that deteriorate into slums." It also supported the city's nascent city planning movement by asserting that "without a city plan there can be no satisfactory solution to the housing problem."[35]

The new concern for citywide housing codes, zoning, and comprehensive planning, which gained the strong endorsement of the BHL by 1919, reflected a different definition of housing from that which marked earlier efforts. Early housing reform concentrated on preventing the worst kinds of housing in the congested tenement districts while the new housing emphasis promoted what reformers viewed as good housing throughout the city. Moreover, housing reform after World War I seemed to suggest a complex and tangled relation-

ship between the dwelling and its larger neighborhood setting. Earlier tenement reformers worked for safer and more sanitary tenements and focused
almost exclusively on the tenement districts. But the new housing emphasis
seemed antagonistic to tenement dwellings and the perpetuation of the tenement district altogether. Indeed, since the BHL predicted that "ultimately the
basin of the city will be devoted to business and industrial purposes," it did
not wish to see that congested residential area replicated throughout the city.[36]

Given the expectation that the city's natural growth would eventually de-
stroy the congested basin residential quarters, the BHL saw no reason to encourage model tenements, which had been a strategy designed specifically for
the city's congested areas. If tenements had been the logical consequence of
the old walking city, reformers argued, they were no longer needed in the
extended city characterized by plenty of open spaces and an efficient transportation system. In addition, under the new definition of housing which focused as much on the neighborhood community as it did on individual dwellings, large tenement houses seemed altogether undesirable. As a result, by
1920, reformers not only continued their opposition to unsanitary and structurally defective tenements but also began viewing all tenements as a problem
because their very nature undermined the characteristics of good housing.
After observing in the league's second report that "any city's greatest effort is
its homes," Marquette concluded that "tenement houses do not provide real
homes. No matter how well constructed they are not the best place for children to live in. They make home ownership impossible. What Cincinnati and
every other city in the country needs is not more tenement houses, but more
small homes, where each family may live unto itself with a place for the
children to play—a home which the family itself may own."[37]

The league's suspicion of tenement houses and its concern with better housing for all became evident when it created another housing company. BHL
Members W. A. Julian, Tylor Field, and Bleecker Marquette formed a company in 1919 to provide new housing for the unskilled wage earner, the group
most pinched by the war-induced housing shortage. These men anticipated
that the league's newly formed enterprise would build 100 low-cost houses
quickly and cheaply. Their undertaking would be different from the small and
fragmented private housing industry, the founders observed, because their
company would be able to secure the advantages of quantity buying, quantity
hiring of labor, the elimination of duplication of architects' fees, and a saving
on profit margin. After consulting with John Nolen, the prominent Cambridge, Massachusetts, planner, and George H. Schwan, a Philadelphia architect, the company decided to erect only fifty houses. And these would be
for workers with higher income, since the committee's survey clearly demonstrated "that it would be impossible to construct houses at that time in

reach of the ordinary workingman." Instead, the company would build better houses with the view of relieving "the pressure from the top." When this plan also seemed too expensive, the BHL dropped its building strategy.[38]

Throughout the short history of this building company, no mention was made of the possibility of constructing model tenements to alleviate the city's housing shortage. Such a response seemed inappropriate, according to the league, since tenements provided bad home settings. Furthermore, the BHL seemed unwilling to build in the congested basin since it appeared destined for nonresidential use. Additional business, commercial, and manufacturing concerns rather than model tenements seemed destined to replace the basin's dilapidated housing stock in the future.

Another housing venture undertaken about the same time by the newly formed Model Homes Company proved more successful. Its efforts suggested a broader definition of the housing problem than had been present earlier. Just as the BHL represented the culmination of turn-of-the-century tenement re-form agitation, the initial efforts of the Model Homes Company reflected the new community development strategy which would become the trademark of housing reform after 1920. Formed in 1914, the Model Homes Company was the brainchild of Jacob G. Schmidlapp, a wealthy philanthropist of recent German origin. Using some of the fortune accumulated from his liquor and banking businesses, Schmidlapp, a close friend of Andrew Carnegie, built ninety-six dwelling units for the poor prior to the founding of Model Homes.[39] Unlike earlier philanthropic builders, Schmidlapp shunned the tenement districts and erected his dwellings outside the basin area.

Schmidlapp first became interested in the city's housing problems, particularly those related to blacks, while serving as a trustee for the city's McCall Colored Industrial School. He decided to build model units, and in his search for a standard to imitate he considered but rejected the model tenement types employed by reformers Alfred T. White and E. R. L. Gould. Instead, he followed the lead of the more recently established Washington (D.C.) Sanitary Improvement Company, founded in 1907 by former U.S. Attorney General George M. Sternberg. This company built houses and small apartments for Washington blacks, rather than larger and less private tenement houses. Schmidlapp followed this example and constructed houses and small apartments outside the congested basin area. He defended this strategy and explained that "the best house for the wage earner is the same as the best house for yourself, and that is the individual house." Although he felt it impractical financially to build single-family houses, he attempted to duplicate the positive aspects of a single dwelling in his apartments.[40]

For instance, in his initial foray into model housing, using a special $25,000 fund that he had set aside and some blueprints from the Washington Sanitary Improvement Company, Schmidlapp built two-family houses with separate entrances and a backyard for the two families to share. Each flat, moreover, contained a bath, indoor toilet, and gas heat. When the venture proved too expensive he cut costs by modifying Sternberg's plans.[41] This, however, resulted in ugly buildings such as the "prison-like tenements on the southeast corner of Park Avenue and Chapel Street." But it nevertheless provided inexpensive sanitary dwellings (three rooms and a bath for $1.75 per week).[42]

Hoping to attract others to follow his example and build good and affordable working-class housing, Schmidlapp erected a number of two-family houses and larger apartments in the city neighborhoods of Walnut Hills, Hyde Park, Avondale, and Oakley, as well as in the incorporated city of Norwood, encircled by Cincinnati.

Sometimes his efforts were not welcomed. When Schmidlapp attempted to build housing for blacks in the already integrated neighborhood in Avondale, he met resistance. Although he planned to rent his Fredonia and Whittier Street dwellings to blacks, neighborhood pressure forced him to make the flats available to whites only.[43] And when Schmidlapp tried to build in Norwood, he faced uncooperative city officials. Like much of the rest of the Cincinnati metropolitan area, Norwood had experienced enormous change in a short period of time. Once an attractive suburb, dubbed the "Gem of the Highland," Norwood experienced rapid industrialization at the turn of the century. Nevertheless there had been little construction of housing for the workers employed there. Instead, laborers traveled from their homes in the congested basin. Because of this, Schmidlapp decided to build there, a decision which some Norwood officials strongly resisted. According to Schmidlapp, officials overcharged him for building permits and overassessed his land for tax purposes. Furthermore, one of Norwood's officials allegedly told Schmidlapp's assistant that "we don't want your rattletraps; build 'em on East Walnut Hills."[44]

Notwithstanding these problems, Schmidlapp attracted some other investors and formed the Model Homes Company in 1914. Cincinnati businessmen who originally had been involved in model housing efforts through the Chamber of Commerce's Committee on Industrial Welfare and Housing, turned to the Model Homes scheme after their efforts failed. As a result, Henry N. Hooper, an architect who chaired that committee, joined with local businessmen Max Senior, William H. Alms, Sidney E. Pritz, and Schmidlapp to incorporate the Model Homes Company on January 30. Other prominent Cincinnatians also bought stock in the company. They included Frederick A. Geier, machine tool industrialist, and C. J. Livingood, acting as the executor of the Thomas Emery, Jr., estate. Although the company raised the necessary $500,000 (of which Schmidlapp provided $150,000) by the end of that year, building did not commence until 1915.[45]

If Schmidlapp's early efforts marked the culmination of the model tenement house emphasis of the turn of the century on building safe and sanitary dwelling units, the Model Homes Company's first venture, Washington Terrace, represented a new direction in local housing reform. For Schmidlapp did not want merely to provide shelter, but to encourage the needy "in every way we can toward a better life." As a result, the large-scale housing project planned for black families was based on a "community plan." Under that plan, Washington Terrace offered its 600 tenants not only safe and sanitary buildings, but also a cooperative store, recreational facilities, an assembly hall for meetings of religious, educational, or community value, and an environment enhanced by architectural and landscape features. Furthermore, in an attempt to foster group spirit, the company created community clubs for both men and women. These clubs, according to Schmidlapp, "would have the responsibility of caring for the place and for the conduct of its members." All the tenants at Washington Terrace were expected to join a club. This massive reconstruction of the tenants' physical and social world, according to the community's founder, would result in "racial and civic opportunity and a stronger economic position." Freed from the dangers of social disorganization, physical disease, and neighborhood deterioration, the tenant could better learn the middle-class values of hard work and participatory democracy.[46]

Indeed, four years after he opened Washington Terrace, Schmidlapp declared his experiment in social engineering a success. He noted that only fifteen tenants had been arrested, amounting to one arrest for every forty individuals as compared to the citywide black arrest rate of one for every six individuals. In addition, Schmidlapp pointed to the project's low death rate, less than a third that for Cincinnati blacks as a whole. Finally, Schmidlapp argued that Washington Terrace promoted greater residential stability, observing that 51 percent of the original tenants still resided in the model community.[47]

Washington Terrace, then, signalled the first attempt by Cincinnati reformers to build housing for wage earners on a "community plan." More important, it suggests that "good housing" now meant something more than safe, sanitary, and homelike dwellings. According to the Model Homes formula, housing included a package of amenities such as play space, neighborliness, and shared commercial conveniences which combined to create a setting for group interaction and the development of a sense of community. Indeed, Washington Terrace differed from earlier tenement reform efforts in that it focused on a comprehensive and holistic approach to community development rather than solely on individual dwelling improvement.

Several consequences resulted from this redefinition of the housing problem. First, comprehensive metropolitan and neighborhood community planning became increasingly important elements in combatting bad housing. Second, the emphasis shifted from providing adequate dwelling space for the poor to providing appropriate community housing for the metropolis. As a result, housing replaced the poor as the central concern. Only such a shift can explain why the BHL, an organization established "for the purpose of improving in every practicable way the homes of the working men and of the poorer people of the city" could become so supportive of both comprehensive planning and the new town, Mariemont, developments which contributed little directly to the needs of Cincinnati's poor.[48]

PART II

Housing, Place, and Urban Cultural Problems

In 1916, Robert Park's seminal article "The City: Suggestions for the Investigation of Human Behavior in the Urban Environment" appeared in the *American Journal of Sociology*. That article argued that the city was more than "a congeries of individual men and of social conveniences." Rather, it was "a state of mind, a body of customs and traditions, of organized attitudes and sentiments." And just as the city possessed a unique culture, so did each of its neighborhoods. Indeed, Park believed that "every section and quarter of the city takes on something of the character of its inhabitants."[1]

By the 1920s, housing reformers appeared to work under similar assumptions. Unlike earlier tenement reformers, who had attempted to improve tenement districts by improving the dwelling unit of the wage earners, housing reformers abandoned their narrow focus on the current neighborhoods of the working classes, since they now feared that mere physical or social change in the tenement districts could not noticeably alter the mind, body of customs, traditions, attitudes, and sentiments emanating from those slums.

What they wanted to do was uproot and transport those located in a slum environment so they could develop cultural traits in accordance with the needs of the metropolis. Thus under the pluralistic vision of the 1920s the slum culture, but not black culture or other kinds of culture, was to be eradicated. Under this new emphasis, reformers focused on housing rather than dwellings, and encouraged a housing policy for the metropolis rather than just the tenement districts. Moreover, planning and zoning emerged as important housing tools.

Although much has been made about the diverging paths of the housing and planning movements, Cincinnati suggests another interpretation.[2] Here, planners like Segoe and Bettman participated in housing reform while

Bleecker Marquette, a houser, supported planning. The willingness of both sides to participate in each other's movement stemmed from shared assumptions about the nature of the metropolis and the need for a truly comprehensive approach to the physical environment. Certainly tensions arose because of differences in the specific focus of the movements, but by the 1920s both groups clearly shared common assumptions about how to solve the city's physical needs, assumptions very different from those they had held in 1900.

If Lawrence Veiller and tenement regulation symbolized the focus of housing reform during the Progressive Era, the Regional Planning Association of America (RPAA) and the community development approach to better housing represented the new emphasis of the 1920s. Created in 1923 as an informal network of specialists and generalists in the fields of housing, planning, conservation, and economics, the RPAA dominated much of the discourse on housing and planning in the 1920s.[3]

Members of this group advocated not only comprehensive regional planning as a solution to urban housing problems, but promoted a community development strategy emphasizing the neighborhood rather than the dwelling. Indeed, RPAA members planned two of the decade's most important community developments—Sunnyside and Radburn.[4]

Cincinnati experienced similar developments in the 1920s. Housing became an issue inextricably linked to neighborhood as well as regional planning. That decade saw the city adopt its first comprehensive metropolitan plan, and witnessed the development of Mariemont, an experiment in new town building. This broader definition of housing took place at the very time that a housing shortage in the basin intensified the city's tenement house problem. The unavailability of adequate shelter for blacks proved particularly bothersome. Ultimately, that shortage, as well as the new emphasis on community development, would force housing reformers to reevaluate their belief in local initiative and control, and push them to the federal government for help.

CHAPTER 3

Housing Reform and Comprehensive Planning in Metropolitan Cincinnati: The 1920s

Whether looked at from the point of view of the engineering problems, such as water supply, sewage, transportation, or as a commercial organism, or as a social unit, the political boundaries of the municipality seldom correspond to the realities.

—Alfred Bettman, "How to Lay Out
Regions for Planning"

Town planning is not merely the making of a general plan. . . . Town planning is more comprehensive, more complex. It embraces everything in the physical sense, but it is more than the sum of all.

—John Nolen, "Town Planning for Mariemont"

Many of the same civic organizations which pushed low-cost housing reform also supported Cincinnati's nascent city planning movement. Groups such as the Chamber of Commerce,[1] the Business Men's Club, the Federated Improvement Association, and the Woman's City Club decided that Cincinnati needed planning for its well-being and proper development.[2] Not only would planning encourage a more rational use of land, but it would prevent the development of slums. The Woman's City Club, responsible for the formation of the Better Housing League, worked particularly hard to encourage city planning. Its City Planning Committee, formed April 14, 1915, explained that "Intelligent City Planning is founded on the idea that in every well planned city there can be no such thing as overcrowding, bad housing, unsanitary conditions as to sewage, or streets too narrow to shut out the light."[3] Other groups also tied comprehensive planning to better housing and supported the efforts of the United City Planning Committee (UCPC) in securing a city plan.

Formed in 1915, the UCPC owed its existence to Alfred Bettman. Born in

Cincinnati in 1873 to Rebecca and Louis Bettman, German Jews, Bettman earned a law degree from Harvard in 1898 and became involved in local reform politics soon after his return to the city. As part of the reform effort which defeated Boss Cox's political organization in 1911, Bettman became the city solicitor. There he improved the city's budget-making process and developed an interest in rational land use. Although turned out of office on the defeat of the reform coalition in 1915, Bettman headed up the planning movement which led to the formation of the UCPC.[4] Bettman did not stop there, but authored a general city-planning enabling bill for the state's general assembly, and organized the UCPC into an effective lobby to secure its passage on May 27, 1915.[5] Despite the new law, which authorized the formation of city planning commissions, the machine-dominated city council, lacking funds and jealous of its legislative prerogative, failed to fund such a body until it was included in a new charter in 1918. Until that time, an unofficial planning commission advised local officials in regard to planning matters.[6]

With the new charter in place, council created a seven-member planning commission with the mayor as chairman. Other members included the director of public services, the president of the park board, and four other appointed citizens. The state law gave the commission exceptionally broad powers, such as permission to make a city plan which had the force of law. Only a two-thirds vote of council would permit a departure from any item on that plan. The commission also possessed authority to pass on all subdivision plats not only within the city but also up to three miles outside its boundaries. Finally, the law empowered the commission to care for and preserve historical landmarks and to oversee the location of public works of art. However, despite the appearance of broad authority, the city planning commission was quite limited in what it could accomplish because council refused financial support for a city plan.[7] As a result, the commission spent its early years passing on new subdivision plats and settling controversies between residential neighborhoods and commercial interests over the allowable use of urban land.[8]

That situation changed in 1919, when the UCPC broadened its membership to include thirty-two civic organizations and raised through private contributions the funding needed to develop a comprehensive plan and zoning ordinance. It ultimately collected over $100,000, which when supplemented by the $20,000 supplied by city council, proved enough to undertake the comprehensive planning effort.[9] In May 1921, the City Planning Commission contracted with the Technical Advisory Corporation of New York (TAC), the first private urban planning consulting firm in the nation, for a preliminary city planning survey at a cost of $14,000. That report, compiled under the supervision of George Ford and E. C. Goodrich, was issued during March of 1922. It examined the city's transportation circulation, public services, public and semipublic property, the regulation of private property, law, public administration, and finances. After discussing each of these components the report concluded that "no one element is independent of the others." [10]

The study also observed the city's bad housing conditions and acknowledged that "one of the most serious problems that confront the city is to attract the tenement dwellers into healthier homes, and as a palliative, let more light and air into the worst tenement blocks." It warned that blight, or the heavy depreciation of real estate, threatened the city, and suggested that Cincinnati should take careful stock of itself "to see if there is anything organically wrong that could be remedied, and to see where or in what way the functioning of the city could be improved as to correct the present retarding influences." [11] The commission apparently agreed, for on June 30, 1922, it hired the TAC to help the city make a comprehensive plan. [12]

Those who supported the development of Cincinnati by the use of comprehensive planning contended that the absence of a city plan contributed to the city's congestion and inefficient land use, which both discouraged new industry from locating in the city and promoted bad living conditions for wage earners forced to locate near their places of work. Indeed, many at the time identified Cincinnati's congestion as the city's most pressing problem. In response to the problem of congestion, the city plan urged that "decentralization of housing and of industry should be encouraged by every means." [13] Furthermore, most of the topics addressed by the plan, such as thoroughfare development, downtown traffic problems, transit and railroad development, waterways and flood control, as well as the placement of parks, schools, and public buildings, focused in one way or another on the issue of basin congestion. However these topics were not viewed as self-contained problems, but as closely interrelated issues needing comprehensive rather than piecemeal effort.

According to Alfred Bettman, recent "patchwork planning" projects would in themselves create new problems if not planned in conjunction with all the other city elements. He cited the courthouse, the proposed rapid transit system, and the Kessler plan for central mall and boulevard development as examples of patchwork efforts. The courthouse, Bettman observed, had been built without any plan for the protection of the area around it. As a result, Bettman feared it was "too late to develop the region in a way which will protect the public's investment and at the same time give opportunity for private development appropriate to the neighborhood." From this experience, Bettman concluded that some of the city's immediate needs, such as railroads and river terminals, highways, and better housing sites, were so interrelated that there was in fact a "close organic relationship between each city improvement and every other city improvement." [14]

The TAC's study also argued that the combination of planning and comprehensive zoning would help promote a more orderly and efficient use of land on the city's undeveloped fringes. Although the plan gave minimal attention to the housing of the poor, it provided a comprehensive prescription for better housing throughout the entire city, and suggested that Cincinnati be divided into fairly "homogeneous areas of good size." In addition, the plan included a model of good subdivision layout. Rather than abandon an emphasis on housing, it appears that Cincinnati planners expanded their concern from good housing for the wage earner to good housing for the entire metropolitan community.[15]

Furthermore, in Cincinnati, both housing reformers and planners embraced zoning and viewed it as a facilitator of better housing. Slums, such as those which existed in the basin area, would have little chance of developing in the future if the city were well zoned. By eliminating slums which produced "sickness, delinquency, crime, dependency, and bad citizenship," zoning was received as housing reform and heartily endorsed by better housing advocates. So when the City Planning Commission and the TAC introduced a zoning ordinance in 1923, it received widespread support from a variety of civic leaders and community organizations interested in a better-housed city. The ordinance, which divided Cincinnati into several types of residential, business, and industrial districts and prescribed acceptable land uses, made sense to many concerned with negative effects of congestion and disorder.[16]

For instance, the Public Health Federation supported zoning because it was "the only method [known] that will absolutely prevent the future development of slum congestion, and that will guarantee for all homes hereafter erected at least a minimum of light, ventilation, and play space."[17] The Better Housing League echoed these sentiments and went on to observe that zoning would be particularly helpful to wage earners attempting to maintain their own homes. By establishing locations exclusively for residential development, zoning would protect homeowners from the intrusion of commercial or industrial nuisances. And that would protect property values and promote appropriate family settings. According to the league, for years council and other governmental bodies had been flooded by petitions from homeowners requesting that certain industries be barred from their neighborhoods because of their threat to property values. The BHL noted that such spot zoning was fair to neither property owners nor industrialists because of its unpredictability. Comprehensive planning would solve that problem and provide for the wage earner the same protection against industrial intrusion that was enjoyed by the wealthier classes, whose new subdivisions were protected by local covenants. As a result, the BHL concluded that comprehensive zoning would do away with the injustices of arbitrary rulings and the disadvantages of poverty by establishing the "principle of protection to all residential neighborhoods, those of the family of small means as well as of the well-to-do."[18]

The league's enthusiastic support of zoning typified its new concern with the city's, rather than just the basin's, housing problems. Admitting that the "existing tenement situation is hopeless," league officials sought to protect future residential areas from such deterioration. Although his organization continued to battle the basin's "intolerable tenement conditions that are sapping the vitality, undermining the moral stamina, shattering the ideals of citizenship of many children who are doomed to tenement life," Bleecker Marquette admitted that tenement regulation and better housekeeping training were merely palliative. Reviewing the BHL's efforts over an eight-year period, Marquette confessed that "conditions are not materially better than they were when we started." [19] But because the city's zoning ordinance encouraged one and two-family homes, "the type of residence that tends to conserve and promote family life," Marquette believed that overall future housing conditions would improve. No longer would the city's ambitious wage earners be forced to live in squalid tenements in the city's basin area. Instead, they would live in detached homes with yards and gardens in proper neighborhoods. Such a setting would not only improve their health, safety, and comfort but would also foster "a higher type of citizenship by encouraging families to take a greater interest in their neighborhood and city." Better housing would also "keep many persons from breaking down under the nervous strains of city life and contribute to the efficiency and vigor of others." [20]

Housing reformers supported zoning, therefore, because it promoted good housing—single-family homes in stable neighborhoods—rather than merely eliminate the worst forms of bad housing—tenement dwellings in slum neighborhoods. Indeed, zoning limited areas where multiunit buildings could be constructed, protected all residential neighborhoods from the unwelcome intrusion of nuisances, and guaranteed better housing conditions and less congestion for the future. Such actions would help eliminate threatening settings which destroyed the moral and civic consciousness of the wage earner and his family. Housing reformers also believed that because zoning would rationalize the use of city space, builders would be more willing to undertake working-class housing in appropriate locations outside of the basin. [21]

When the zoning act passed by a unanimous council vote on April 1, 1924, it was seen, then, as a victory for the housing as well as the planning movements. For the Cincinnati zoning code, unlike the New York zoning law passed eight years earlier, made specific reference to different types of housing districts, and distinguished between single-family and multifamily housing. [22] The Cincinnati law created eight classes of districts, which determined the bulk and usages permissible on each parcel of land. Residential class A reserved land exclusively for single-family homes while class B permitted both two and four-family detached housing. Class C allowed the building of large multifamily dwellings. The zoning ordinance also created two types of business classes and three industrial zones. [23]

The zoning act suggested that its authors anticipated continued physical expansion for the city, and attempted to control that expansion in a way that might eliminate the city's basin tenement housing problem. Despite Cincinnati's relatively slow growth between 1900 and 1920 of 20 percent, and even though few new industries located in the basin during those years, Ladislas Segoe of the TAC oversaw the development of a city plan and comprehensive zoning law which looked confidently to Cincinnati's future.[24] Expecting that the basin's continued industrial and commercial development would one day clear the area of residential use, the planning ordinance zoned the entire area as nonresidential although over 120,000 people still lived there. The zoning ordinance also reserved 14 percent of the city's land for industrial use even though current usage for that purpose was at 1.6 percent. Moreover, the city zoned enough land for business use to serve a city five times the size of Cincinnati.[25]

From the perspective that Cincinnati was an expanding social system, both zoning and planning ordinances proposed solutions to the housing problem. Reacting to the congestion and mixed land use of the basin, the city plan, as well as the zoning ordinance, approved of and in fact committed the city to a strategy encouraging the decentralization of housing. This was critical since the congested basin, in the eyes of housing reformers, did not allow the development of a proper community setting. The only hope for this area, according to the plan, was that the "old tenement house" there was "gradually disappearing with the invasion of industry and business."[26] The seven-volume "Cincinnati Industrial Survey, 1925," sponsored by the Chamber of Commerce and also prepared by the TAC, came to a similar conclusion. It observed that the disappearance of between 1,000 and 1,500 tenements during the last decade was due to their displacement "by business and industrial establishments, to the wearing out of structures and to the fact that scarcely any apartments or tenement houses were built during the decade until quite recently."[27]

Because of this "natural slum clearance" within the basin, and because housing conditions there seemed so bad, the city plan offered few strategies for upgrading basin tenements. The plan sought to solve the basin's housing problem by "relieving pressure from higher up" so the city's ambitious wage earner could leave the slum environment. The authors of the city plan put it bluntly.

> In other words, as fast as the families in better circumstances move out of the older tenements and houses, they will become available for housing the lower wage earners. This means that it is not feasible now to give any consideration as a part of the city plan to providing housing for the low-wage earners, and that attention should be concentrated now on the amelioration of living conditions in the older parts of the town by zoning protection and by the provision of parks, playgrounds, community centers and open spaces.[28]

The main problem threatening Cincinnati, then, according to both planning and housing reformers, was that of congestion, which had developed because of the absence of earlier comprehensive planning. As a result, the competition of people, industries, and businesses for space in the city's basin resulted in bad housing conditions for those residents forced to live in inexpensive housing. The city plan blamed inadequate transportation facilities and the improper distribution of industry for forcing almost 30 percent of the population to live in one-nineteenth of the city's area. This seemed needless since three-fourths of the city's land still remained available for residential use.[29] Other planning matters, too, according to housing reformers, such as flood control and the placement of parks and playgrounds, affected the city's housing conditions.

Recognizing a complex and tangled relationship between the different parts and elements of the city, Cincinnati's comprehensive plan suggests that its authors assumed that Cincinnati was actually greater than the sum of its parts. Accordingly, civic improvers no longer believed that they could simply improve one aspect of urban life without also and simultaneously adjusting a variety of related areas. The housing reformers' strong support of the plan implies that they agreed with such a vision and equated the health of the housing stock with the proper development of the city as a whole.[30] Unlike the actions of tenement reformers twenty years earlier, which focused solely on the city's tenement districts, the housing reformers of the twenties not only enthusiastically supported housing measures such as comprehensive zoning and citywide housing codes, but they also vigorously endorsed a city plan which offered few immediate remedies to the tenement problem. Rather it provided a general prescription for the physical and social improvement of the entire city.[31]

Although the city plan in its final form contained legal jurisdiction for Cincinnati and the three-mile unincorporated area surrounding it, planners during the twenties were quick to point out that political boundaries did not delineate the real community. In its first chapter, "Community Development," the city plan observed that the proper unit for planning was metropolitan Cincinnati, "that is, the whole surrounding region that is directly tributary to the city." And this unit, according to the plan, included the population of counties within a fifty-mile radius of the city.[32]

In another chapter, the plan's authors made the point more adamantly. "In studying the Report," they declared, "it must be surely evident that the Comprehensive Plan cannot be cut off sharply at the purely arbitrary political boundaries of the city. The physical, the economic and the social problems of Cincinnati," they continued, "extend beyond those imaginary lines, just as though they did not exist. The problems of the whole tributary region are one, and in any study must be treated as one." As a result, they concluded that

TABLE 3-A. Population of Cincinnati metropolitan district.

	1910	1920 (% increase)	1930 (% increase)
Cincinnati metropolitan district (new)	***	630,896	759,464 (20.4%)
Cincinnati metropolitan district (old)	567,876	606,850 (6.9%)	***
Cincinnati	363,591	401,247 (10.4%)	451,160 (12.4%)
Outside Cincinnati (new)	***	229,649	308,304 (34.3%)
Outside Cincinnati (old)	204,285	205,603 (0.6%)	***

Note: The old metropolitan district measured both the central city population plus additional suburban areas within approximately ten miles of the municipal limits if the population density was at least 150 per square mile. The new metropolitan district measured the same unit plus all civil divisions that were either directly contiguous to the central city or were entirely or nearly surrounded by minor civil divisions that had 150 inhabitants per square mile.

Sources: Fourteenth Census of the United States, 1920: Population: Number and Distribution of Inhabitants, vol. 1, p. 63; *Fifteenth Census of the United States, 1930: Metropolitan Districts: Population and Areas*, p. 53.

"the City Plan is really a metropolitan, or regional or county plan, and to a certain extent, especially in matters of circulation, includes the adjacent area on the Kentucky side of the river as well." Statistical data and the Census Bureau's new interest in measuring the metropolitan district (see table 3-A) confirmed this observation.[33]

The Chamber of Commerce–sponsored industrial survey came to the same conclusions about metropolitan growth when it observed that "industrial development here is absolutely a regional matter and not at all a municipal matter." From this point of view the report continued, "It is not too much to say that the industrial program of Cincinnati is also the industrial program of Covington and Newport [Kentucky], to say nothing of many other (mostly smaller) municipalities; and it should be sponsored by the commercial organizations of all of the incorporated places involved."[34] This last observation paralleled a recommendation made by the city plan which called for "the common planning of the whole region and tributary to Cincinnati" by a regional or county planning commission.[35]

Despite such recommendations, no such commission appeared in Greater Cincinnati until 1929, even though the Ohio General Assembly enacted legislation in 1923 to permit the formation of regional planning bodies. Although Alfred Bettman was the chief architect of that law, local jealousies of the region's smaller units outweighed their nascent metropolitan consciousness and delayed the creation of a formal regional planning body for Greater Cincinnati.[36] Nevertheless, a new town planned for the Cincinnati area did in fact reflect the new metropolitan consciousness, and deserves to be examined for what it can tell us about the emerging metropolitanism of the 1920s.[37]

On April 23, 1922, the *Cincinnati Enquirer* announced that Mary Emery, a wealthy philanthropist, would soon develop a model town for workers just east of the city. Located near the main line of the Pennsylvania Railroad on 365 acres overlooking the Little Miami River, the town would be designed by one of the nation's leading planners, John Nolen. The *Enquirer* reported that the new town would "furnish better housing for the people" and would "illustrate intelligent and sane town planning, by following a preconceived plan along scientific lines, including proper road building, harmonious house construction and the relation of homes to industrial areas and public service facilities." According to Charles Livingood, Emery's close associate and project overseer, the new town would be "an antidote for the growing disadvantages of city living, without the inconveniences of the country."[38]

John Nolen, the town's planner, echoed these sentiments. Mariemont would be more than merely a place of residence for those who did not want to "live under the shadow of the factory." Mariemont would furnish shelter, observed Nolen, but it would also provide for a variety of the family's social needs. Schools would be built for children, while provisions for recreation, commerce, and entertainment would be established for all to enjoy. Mariemont was conceived and planned, observed Nolen, "in definite terms of community life to be shared by everyone."[39]

And by arranging the neighborhood housing around a town center which included a town hall, library, theater, inn, and shopping center, the community offered citizens a central focal point where they could congregate and interact. Because this center would be carefully planned with relation to the whole, Nolen believed it would contain none of the congestion which often made such centers "hopeless and unattractive."[40] Not only would the community center differentiate Mariemont from some of the other developments on the city's fringe, but so would its population composition. For Mariemont would contain a variety of housing, from multiunit dwellings to expensive single-family houses. According to the town's founder, such an arrangement would provide particular benefit to the town's working-class population who could model their lives on their more successful neighbors.[41]

The town's plan, as well as the rhetoric of the town's promoters, suggested that they wanted to provide residents with something more than safe and sanitary dwellings. Rather, they wished to cultivate a sense of belonging and involvement in Mariemont's residents, and combat the "bifocal" existence perpetuated by typical suburbs of that decade.[42] Unlike those suburbs, which did little to promote community, Mariemont, according to its advertisements, was developed as a "small self-contained community" capable of producing "local happiness." According to the Mariemont formula, only by treating a variety of closely related human needs could housing reformers actually resolve the housing problem.[43]

Despite their emphasis on Mariemont as a self-contained community, the town founders also emphasized its relationship to the larger whole. For instance, promotional material stressed Mariemont's convenient location near the area's factories and workplaces. According to the sponsors, Mariemont was only a few minutes away from the industrial suburbs of Oakley and Norwood. In addition, they noted that once the city completed its proposed subway system, Mariemont would be within a half-hour ride "to all parts of Cincinnati." Finally, the town promoters observed that Mariemont's streets were laid out to blend with Cincinnati and the rest of the metropolitan region. Under the roadway plan, some arteries would lead to the "hill-top" suburbs while others, such as the state highway route which ran east and west through the town's center, would connect Mariemont directly to "the heart of the metropolis."[44]

Mariemont's founders, then, did not establish the model town as the antithesis of city life but as a synthesis of the better features of urban and suburban life to produce a metropolitan mode of living. And even though Mariemont's plan adopted certain aspects from the design of English garden cities such as Letchworth, it was developed for different purposes. For Letchworth, the company's prospectus observed, had been developed by Ebenezer Howard "to stem the tide from country to city and to counteract the growth of larger cities." Mariemont, the prospectus continued, would attempt no such thing, for "cities have been growing rapidly and steadily for a century and there seems to be no prospect that the tendency will change in the near future." Therefore, the prospectus concluded, "it seems more practical . . . to accept these conditions as facts and to see what can be done in connection with cities to provide better homes."[45]

Three years later, advertisements for the new town reiterated that Mariemont was developed as a part of the Cincinnati metropolitan region. The model town, according to the advertisement, would not attempt to compete with Cincinnati. Instead, its residents would be a part of the Cincinnati metropolitan area. As such they could "enjoy what Cincinnatians enjoy," cultural events, top-notch entertainment, excellent medical facilities, and broad educational opportunities. Nor would Mariemont be a parasite, since it would "furnish to Cincinnati a more pleasant place to live than in the crowded downtown districts." [46]

Mariemont, then, differed not only from earlier English garden cities, which attempted to combat urban growth, but also from earlier Cincinnati tenement efforts. Mariemont focused on community and metropolis while turn-of-the-century tenement reformers concentrated on dwellings and basin tenement house districts. Furthermore, the two housing betterment strategies treated the poor differently. Late nineteenth-century housing reformers seemed to accept the permanence of class differences and attempted to improve the conditions of working-class housing. For they viewed tenement reform as a way of improving the health, morality, and discipline of the working-class poor. Mariemont's founders, however, worked under different assumptions. They believed in a more fluid society where with the proper incentives and influences, slum dwellers could become socially and economically mobile.

The significance of Mariemont did not escape Cincinnati housing reformers who themselves had looked forward to the thinning out of the congested living conditions of the city's basin area. Immediately following the announcement of the proposed Mariemont project, BHL president Julian A. Pollak wrote Charles Livingood and congratulated him on the new town project. Mariemont, Pollak observed, should "hasten the movement away from congested tenements to the light and air of the suburbs." And because of its community building potential, Pollak concluded that Mariemont "should do more for the advancement and prosperity of Cincinnati than any other project that has materialized in years." [47]

Others around the nation also recognized the value of this model town. The *New York Times* hailed it as a "new experiment in town planning fit for the motor age" while the organ of the National Housing Association called it "America's outstanding garden city." [48]

Much of Mariemont's popularity was clearly linked to its ties to metropolitan and neighborhood community planning, themes which dominated the 1920s. Clarence Perry's monograph on the neighborhood plan in 1929 was probably the most precise articulation of this concern with local community but hardly the only one. [49] Indeed, since the Progressive Era many had identified the neighborhood as an essential unit in citizen making. Progressives from Jane Addams to Herbert Croly had argued that "active, popular participation created responsible and creative citizens." Wilbur C. Phillips, who devised the nationally watched Cincinnati Social Unit Organization in 1917, worked under similar assumptions. He wished to make the neighborhood into a "well constituted community within the larger city." By learning to function intelligently and democratically within the confines of the neighborhood, Phillips thought, citizens would be able to understand society and participate more fully in its operation. The Cincinnati Social Unit Organization focused its neighborhood program on the Mohawk Brighton area in 1917, and attempted to mobilize the entire community to pursue better health. Toward this end, it nourished an interaction between medical and social welfare personnel and the neighborhood citizens. Moreover, it gave local residents a say in the development of health programs for their neighborhood.[50]

Clarence Perry, however, approached neighborhood community from a different perspective. No longer confident that simple territorial closeness and organized activity from outside would promote community, Perry devised physical plans to develop a proper setting for neighborhood community. Perry, a member of the Regional Plan of New York Association, articulated his solution to the nation's newly defined housing problem most clearly in volume seven of the *Regional Plan of New York and Its Environs* in a work entitled "The Neighborhood Unit." According to Perry, "The underlying principle of the scheme is that an urban neighborhood should be regarded both as a unit of a larger whole and as a distinct entity in itself."[51] His neighborhood unit, which allegedly would strengthen the family and create better citizens, consisted of six elements which he thought would foster a communal spirit. They were: a limited geographic size, distinct boundaries (bordered by thoroughfares), green and open spaces, certain institutions such as an elementary school to serve as a community center, a small commercial section for the unit's residents, and an internal street system designed to facilitate circulation within the unit and discourage its use by through traffic.[52]

While Perry's plan may have been unique in its precision and influence, it should be viewed not as a cause but as a symptom of the new definition of housing, which focused no longer solely on the dwelling but on the larger neighborhood. For according to Perry, "You can bring sky-light into a tenement home by rebuilding it, but to give it genuine sunshine you are compelled to do something to the surrounding structure. To afford greater safety in the street, to provide the conditions conducive to moral living," Perry concluded, "it is not enough to change the dwelling; its environs also must be modified."[53]

The President's Conference on Home Building and Home Ownership, which met in Washington in December of 1931, enunciated a similar concern with creating large-scale, low-cost housing projects based on community building principles. At the conference, thirty-one committees reported on their inquiry into the nation's housing experience. President Herbert Hoover had called the conference during the depression to better mobilize the existing housing movements. He also hoped that "a new state of thought and action" might emerge from the conference. Over 3,700 attended the conference and heard the work of 500 committee members. They pointed out that the most important defect in the nation's housing was "the building of desultory unrelated individual homes instead of homogeneous communities."[54]

For as we have seen, the housing problem of the 1920s was not merely a problem of unsanitary individual dwelling units, but a problem of incohesive and antisocial neighborhood settings. According to one common view articulated at the conference, part of the trouble with big city slum neighborhoods was that they were too heterogeneous; residents had little in common. Because of this, diverse populations of whites and blacks, or the "deserving" and "undeserving" poor, shared the same space but had little on which to build a sense of community. To remedy this defect, participants at the president's conference emphasized the need for "homogeneous communities." [55]

Many Cincinnatians, including Alfred Bettman, Bleecker Marquette, Murray Seasongood, Walter S. Schmidt, and John W. Wyman, participated in the work of the conference's committees. Schmidt, president of the Frederick A. Schmidt Real Estate Company, played a prominent role in the committee on large-scale operations. Its final report concluded that "in the modern complexity of urban life, the home neighborhood must provide more than mere shelter." The committee on housing and the community offered a related theme, noting that "housing is no longer concerned with the house alone but with the home in its neighborhood setting." [56]

To further emphasize this fact, the first volume of the report on the president's conference on housing, entitled *Planning for Residential Districts*, spent over thirty pages exploring how best to encourage the development of neighborhood units. Neighborhoods were important, according to the report, because they provided "something between the family and the great metropolitan city." As a result, neighborhood units "may be fostered as an appropriate introduction to training in citizenship." [57] Those interested in the low-cost housing problem, then, turned to developing model neighborhoods because they could offer the sense of community and interdependence that reformers thought was missing in the slums. And once the lessons of neighborhood citizenship were learned, they could be applied to the metropolis, leading to what Alfred Bettman termed "a civic consciousness of the organic nature of the problem of region and an interest in and enthusiasm for the development of the region." [58]

The intense emphasis on neighborhood community in the 1920s, then, should not be construed as a new parochialism, but a technique for achieving just the opposite—metropolitan consciousness. True community, according to reformers, could best be developed among people with shared interests. And homogeneous neighborhoods could help create a shared civic vision for the metropolitan whole among the city's various classes and ethnic groups. As a result, reformers identified traditional heterogeneous urban neigborhoods as problematic and concentrated on encouraging homogeneous units throughout the city.

The president's conference on housing, the *Regional Plan of New York and Its Environs*, Mariemont, and Washington Terrace built by the Model Homes

Company during the teens all reflected the increasing preoccupation with developing neighborhood community through large-scale, low-cost housing projects. Cincinnatians participated in this nationwide identification of good housing with good neighborhood and set their energies toward laying out the proper type of large-scale housing developments that would bring about the sought-for sense of local community. Their efforts suggest agreement with the observation made at the president's conference on housing that "every objective cherished by the leaders in social progress is forwarded in one way or another, when the local community is promoted." [59]

Mariemont's importance went beyond its commitment to developing a localized community within a metropolitan setting. It also represented the accepted means of carrying out such an effort. For the model town, whose projected cost was $2 million, would not be a philanthropic undertaking but a business venture to demonstrate that private enterprise could supply housing for wage earners and still earn a profit. According to the developers, "The only solution to the housing shortage in America is cheaper quantity production and a limitation of the excessive profits being demanded by home builders." [60] And the Mariemont Company hoped to show the feasibility of such a solution by building a model town "that could be duplicated wherever initiative, capital and social planning could be combined to support the building of new towns and suburbs." [61]

Unfortunately for the Cincinnati metropolitan community, Mariemont did not provide additional housing for the city's wage earners. From the start, rents for housing in Mariemont were so high as to price out a large part of the city's population. Even the group housing constructed specifically for the lower-paid wage earners rented for sums well above their means. In November of 1923, a BHL rent survey had found that the average four-room flat rented in the city for $24.20 per month. The least expensive four-room apartment in Mariemont rented for $35.00 per month, a sum much too high for the typical basin dweller. [62] Moreover, the BHL found that the city's wage earners could not afford a house which cost more than $5,000, but advertisements in the *Mariemont Messenger* quoted a $9,500 starting price for houses there. [63] Perhaps this explains why the highly publicized project, originally promoted as providing housing for wage earners, faced such strong criticism in Cincinnati. Local antagonism became so great that in 1925 the BHL felt compelled to defend Mariemont. Its annual report observed that there had been "much misunderstanding about" Mariemont. Moreover, it reminded its readers that the model town's "value is far more appreciated elsewhere than in Cincinnati." Lauding the planning principles behind the new town, the BHL's report concluded that Mariemont would improve the city's present housing congestion by "helping to relieve the pressure from the top." [64]

Mariemont not only failed to provide new homes for the wage earner, but it apparently failed as a model for other subdivisions too. After observing that "a decided trend toward the development of real estate operations in the country" had appeared in the last three years, a 1928 BHL report warned that eight subdivisions "for colored occupancy" were "becoming a growing menace from the standpoint of health, housing and fire danger."[65] In a December letter to the county commissioners, the BHL acknowledged that the black subdivisions had been platted in accordance with the regulations of the City Planning Commission, but quickly pointed out that nothing else in the way of improvements had been done for them. Meanwhile, poor blacks with meager incomes built their houses in stages, producing both an unattractive landscape and unsafe living conditions. Because of these defects and the unplanned nature of the subdivisions, the BHL labeled as slums these areas north of Lockland, and pleaded with the county commissioners to improve the horrid conditions found there.[66]

Such action would not only safeguard the larger metropolitan community against additional slums, the league promised, but protect blacks from the pitches of unscrupulous realtors. According to Bleecker Marquette, speculators purchased farmland, subdivided it, and sold lots costing from $300 to $800 to house-hungry blacks. After spending an additional $3,000 on building the actual house, all these people had to show for their money was a poorly constructed dwelling on unimproved land. Unfortunately, Marquette continued, these poor blacks usually invested their life savings in such housing and were unaware that "if they [were] ever to have decent living conditions" they would be "saddled with the cost of installing water, sewers, gas, and also the cost of paving and sidewalks." As a result, the BHL head requested the commissioners to "find ways and means of providing such regulation as well as require subdivisions to provide sewers, water and roads before lots are offered for sale to the public."[67] It is in this context that the BHL supported the growing movement to create a local regional planning body. And in 1929, the BHL changed its name to the Better Housing League of Cincinnati and Hamilton County to reflect its concern with the larger geographical area.[68]

Other Cincinnatians also supported the regional planning movement because they too believed that unregulated suburban development threatened the whole metropolitan community. For instance, the Woman's City Club opposed unregulated development in Greater Cincinnati because "it creates bad spots all over the county and we already have enough of old bad subdivisions. The point we wish to make," the club's report continued, "is that rural development of an urban nature requires urban improvements. Without urban improvements . . . the county property deteriorates instead of improving, the values are low and it is extremely unfair to the whole community."[69]

The United City Planning Commission also strongly advocated regional metropolitan planning and favored regulating county subdivisions because it feared that unregulated developments threatened the Cincinnati area. And it explicitly identified the metropolitan region as a basic unit to be dealt with by noting that "the boundary lines of any particular problem do not correspond with the territorial boundary lines of any single city." As a result, the UCPC lobbied with local officials to create a regional planning commission as allowed under state law. It also supported new state legislation establishing even stronger regional planning laws.[70]

The Chamber of Commerce joined in the regional planning movement too. Its monthly publication, the *Cincinnatian*, probably best summarized the need for regional planning. Only planning could properly decentralize Cincinnati, the publication observed, and decentralization, it thought, was "the only hope of having livable cities in the future." The *Cincinnatian* concluded that regional planning would accomplish for Greater Cincinnati what city planning accomplished for the Queen City: it would provide a coordinated plan for "all the physical phases of the region" so that distinct business, industrial, and residential districts would be set aside and development allowed to "take place along orderly lines."[71] Realizing that regional planning was crucial for the proper decentralizing of Cincinnati, businessmen participated with both housing and planning activists to support regional planning.

Responding to the increased demand for metropolitan planning, the Cincinnati City Planning Commission, along with the Hamilton County commissioners and representatives of the suburban municipalities of Norwood, Silverton, and Cheviot, formed a regional planning body on March 21, 1929. The newly established Regional Planning Commission encompassed part rather than all of the metropolitan community, owing to state boundaries and local political jealousy.[72] It included a chairman selected from the county commissioners, and two representatives appointed by each planning commission of the cooperating municipalities. The commission decided to limit its initial planning program to land subdivision, recreation, and thoroughfare planning.[73]

Although the new Planning Commission functioned with limited powers, operated with insufficient funds (only $6,500 in 1929), and covered an area smaller than the metropolitan region, supporters of metropolitan planning claimed victory. For now a vehicle had been invented to permit city and suburban officials to cooperate and plan for the metropolis. Problems affecting both city and suburb could now be treated in a comprehensive manner.[74]

Regional planning, then, joined new town building and comprehensive zoning as solutions embraced by Cincinnati housing reformers during the 1920s. And all three approaches relied on assumptions quite different from those evident in 1900. At the turn of the century, reformers tended to focus on a particular problem area and acknowledge its connection to other problems in the urban system. But they never suggested the existence of a tangled bank of interdependence tying one problem to all others so intimately that only a systemwide solution encompassing all problems would suffice. In addition, they rarely suggested that the system with which they worked extended beyond the corporate boundaries of the city into its surrounding area. However this too changed. Just as tenement reformers finally concluded that the dwelling was too closely related to the larger neighborhood environment to warrant separate treatment, urban policymakers also agreed in the 1920s that the corporate city was too closely linked with its region to require separate treatment. Thus, Mariemont, located outside the city's corporate limits, and regional planning, dealing with a variety of physical elements, gained strong support from local officials as well as housing and planning activists.

CHAPTER 4

Reformers and the Decline
of the Filter-Down Theory

In spite of the fact that the year 1922 will show more construction than normal years, there is such a great accumulated shortage that this construction is having but very little effect on the general situation. No relief therefore is being afforded by this construction for the people of the tenement classes even indirectly.

—BHL, Oct. 10, 1922

The greatest problem today in housing, not only in Cincinnati but in every city in the country, is to find ways and means of building new homes for the mass of wage earners.

—*Ten Years of Housing Work
in Cincinnati*, 1928

The 1920s marked a watershed in the city's history not only in regard to changing perceptions about housing and planning problems, but in relationship to the city's general development. World War I had produced prosperous conditions for many of the city's industries. For instance the Lunkenheimer Company, one of the city's many machine tool manufacturers, tripled its sales between 1915 and 1918. Those profits helped Lunkenheimer expand its facilities after the war. Although labor unrest and recession temporarily retarded the growth of many Cincinnati tool manufacturers, by the mid-1920s they recovered and joined other Cincinnati concerns such as Procter and Gamble and Crosley Radio to provide Cincinnati with a healthy and dynamic economy.[1]

The 1920s also signaled the death of a vital German immigrant community. Although Cincinnati experienced the anti-German sentiment which had swept the nation since 1917, at least one historian has argued that the German community in Cincinnati "was moribund before the war had even begun in Europe." More than 125,000 Cincinnatians identified German as their native tongue in 1910, but the traditional pockets of ethnic community such as the Over-the-Rhine neighborhood in the basin suffered rapid loss of German population and a decline in its role as a center of German population prior to World War I. As early as 1910, German-Americans were distributed widely throughout all of Cincinnati's wards.[2] Although Olivier Zunz has raised new questions about the persistence of ethnicity which are beyond the focus of this book, sufficient evidence exists to suggest that the nineteenth-century German neighborhood communities were rapidly disintegrating.[3]

Of course, many German-Americans as well as other Cincinnatians benefited from the new housing opportunities offered by improved transportation facilities. Not only did the city have an adequate streetcar system which opened up previously inaccessible housing areas, but by the 1920s many Queen City residents benefited from the relatively low cost of Henry Ford's mass-produced Model T. As a result, automobile registrations would rapidly increase in Cincinnati after 1920. That year, one out of every fourteen persons in the Cincinnati area owned an automobile. By 1940, one out of four area residents owned an automobile. The combined impact of public transportation and the automobile also helps explain the rapid expansion of metropolitan Cincinnati from 330 to 520 square miles between 1920 and 1940.[4]

Such patterns of growth and physical expansion during the 1920s fit in neatly with national urban trends during the era. But the city's development in other areas seems to contradict traditional knowledge, which usually claims that World War I ended reform and ushered in a more hedonistic and individualistic "jazz age."[5] For Cincinnati experienced not only unprecedented political reform, but also massive planning and housing activity during the 1920s.

As we have seen, the city's planning and housing movements in the 1920s seemed less preoccupied with the poor and more with providing standards that would benefit an entire metropolis. Despite this broader commitment, old problems such as deteriorating tenements in the basin area and a continuing housing shortage for local blacks would dominate much of the BHL's attention during the decade. Moreover, the persistence of such problems during the 1920s helped lead the BHL to reevaluate its approach to the housing problem, which combined a strategy of housing codes, zoning, comprehensive planning, tenant education, and an adherence to the filter-down theory of housing. By 1929, the league questioned whether such efforts were sufficient, since the shortage of adequate housing for the working class remained.

From its beginning, the BHL combined a concern with tenant education with its crusade for better tenement regulation. By the 1920s, this instructional emphasis became a major part of the BHL program. In part, this reflected the wish to ready tenement dwellers for the better housing the league hoped they would one day inhabit. But by the 1920s, the expansion in tenant education also represented one of the few positive contributions the BHL could make, given their definition of the problem.

World War I seemed to have produced a crisis reminiscent of earlier

TABLE 4-A. Residential construction in Cincinnati, 1915–30.

Year	Value of residential construction
1915	$ 6,607,548
1916	6,561,239
1917	3,494,239
1918	668,659
1919	3,400,000
1920	4,600,000
1921	6,385,500
1922	11,451,000
1923	13,546,500
1924	13,881,360
1925	13,985,275
1926	13,850,639
1927	18,485,884
1928	21,615,735
1929	12,956,660
1930	10,031,167

Source: "Application for Low Rent Housing Project," submitted by the Cincinnati Metropolitan Housing Authority, September 1936, to the Federal Emergency Administration of Public Works, Rowe Papers, CHS.

days—a shortage of adequate dwelling space (see table 4-A). The moratorium on house construction combined with an influx of black migrants during the war resulted in increased congestion and deterioration in the basin. And after the war ended, the problem remained. Bleecker Marquette, writing in 1921, pointed clearly to the extent of the postwar housing crisis when he observed that "one of the striking results of the lack of home construction during the war period has been to change the emphasis from the problem of getting rid of slum conditions to that of providing decent shelter for the middle classes—though it has in no way minimized the problem of the slums."[6] Although the shortage eased for the middle classes by 1923, conditions for the poorer classes had not improved at all. In fact, the executive secretary of the BHL noted in 1923 that "during the past two years we have actually gone backwards in housing in this city." The migration of blacks intensified congestion within the already crowded black neighborhoods and the city's financial problems impeded its efforts to maintain even minimal living standards in some sections of the basin. For example, financial cutbacks reduced the housing inspection staff from four to two.[7]

The city's Housing Bureau, charged with enforcing housing regulations, suffered the same fate as other city departments during the twenties because of a municipal financial crisis. Ohio's Smith Act of 1911 was most frequently cited as the reason for Cincinnati's financial woes. That law limited the city's taxing power to ten mills per dollar of assessed real-estate valuation and allowed other limited increases in this rate by referendum only. Both government officials and outside observers agreed that this law generated too little money to run effectively a city of Cincinnati's size.[8]

Although many of the city's problems in the 1920s appeared linked to the state's taxation laws, reformers pointed to the city's Republican organization run by George Cox's successor, Rudolph K. Hynicka, as the real problem. Under Republican Mayor John Galvin, the city started construction of the Cincinnati Railroad Transit System in 1920. This system, planned since reform Mayor Hunt's administration, proved a financial fiasco, since council consulted old fiscal data. Indeed, by 1923 with the city verging on bankruptcy, officials halted construction and abandoned $6 million worth of terminals, stations, and graded rights-of-way.[9]

The subway proved not to be the only casualty of the Smith Act and inefficient local government. Between 1917 and 1924, council cut the Police Department by 23.5 percent. The Fire Department experienced a similar reduction in personnel, and cutbacks in other services accelerated the city's physical deterioration. Not only had the city's canal become polluted, but its courthouse was dirty and the city's streets were in a sorry state. One observer from the New York Technical Advisory Corporation thought the situation so bad in 1925 that he feared Cincinnati was "confronted with the possibility of a more or less complete breakdown in municipal functions."[10] Such a situation helps explain why city officials failed to commit many resources to the housing problem in the 1920s.

The financial crisis also helps explain the political reform movement which roughly paralleled the planning and zoning movements. Boss politics, according to the reformers, equaled parochialism and selfishness, and was inconsistent with a vision which pictured the city as an organic whole. So was a city government which included a thirty-two seat, ward-based city council. Unhappy with such a government, Charterites under the leadership of Charles Taft and Murray Seasongood implemented a city manager/proportional representational form of government, and helped elect sympathetic leaders to the nine-seat council. The Charterites controlled council until 1937 and remained an important element in local politics into the 1960s.

Segoe, Marquette, and Bettman joined the Charter cause, which sought to affect government the same way they sought to affect the environment—by promoting programs which encouraged order and cohesion. Just as the city's slums brought on a crisis which threatened the city as a whole, so had the imperfect nature of the city's government structure. Moreover, according to the views of Bettman, Marquette, and Segoe, both areas needed strong leadership from civic-minded professionals and businessmen, rather than the much more limited direction offered by parochial interests such as real-estate agents and ward politicians. Only then could the city as a whole benefit.[11]

Contrary to the city's experience, the BHL faced no crisis in leadership and actually found itself in much better financial shape than earlier, thanks to the Community Chest. After joining this centralized fund-raiser and coordinator for the area's charitable, civic, philanthropic, and public agencies which managed most of the community's social and health needs, the league's budget increased from $4,000 in 1917 to $14,300 for the 1922–23 fiscal year. With the additional monies, the league enlarged its visiting housekeeping staff from one to six.[12]

The league used its housekeepers to initiate a systematic educational program that would inform the tenants of their rights and responsibilities as well as instruct them in the fundamentals of good housekeeping. Each housekeeper regularly visited housing in an assigned district. Those districts included the Central City; the "Negro West End;" Walnut Hills and other outlying black residential areas; the North Central City; Mohawk Brighton; and the East End.[13] Besides their educational activities, the housekeepers kept a sharp eye out for housing defects and attempted to remedy any tenement house code violations through the cooperative efforts of the landlord, tenant, and City Housing Bureau. Along the way, the housekeepers accumulated some impressive numbers. Between 1917 and 1927, they made 57,123 visits and oversaw 19,031 repairs, along with 39,078 paint, paper, and cleaning improvements. They also "bettered" the housekeeping practices of 3,492 families and removed more than 5,550 fire and health hazards.[14]

The housekeepers' enthusiasm occasionally caused trouble for the league. On April 5, 1919, W. P. Dabney, editor of the *Union*, a black newspaper, charged that one of the league's black housekeepers, Mrs. M. E. Wilson, had misguided some black tenants. According to Dabney, Wilson, a "wolf in sheep's clothing," advised some tenants of a building he owned on the East Side to move to a flat in the West End. Arguing that his 412 McAllister Street building was in good condition, the newspaper editor wondered if the housekeeper's instructions were part of a larger scheme to move all the city's blacks into the West End. Marquette strongly denied any such plot, and responded that Dabney's building threatened the health and safety of its occupants.[15]

Ten years later, William Devou, owner of many basin tenements, sued the BHL for $50,000 over an incident involving a housekeeper. Devou, a wealthy, seventy-two-year-old eccentric who lived in the West End, charged that a visiting housekeeper deprived him of his livelihood when she advised a family to move from one of his unsanitary tenements. Devou's suit climaxed a feud between the tenement landlords and housing reformers that had been underway since at least 1911. For years the two parties had warred over the enforcement of the tenement code. Devou's suit against the league appeared merely to be his latest ploy to disrupt the work of housing reformers in the city. Eventually the case was dropped. Despite these occasional challenges to the league's housekeeping system, it generally received praise from both realtors and social reformers.[16]

The league supplemented its visiting housekeeping program with a good-housekeeping apartment. Spending only $50 a room, the league converted a typical three-room tenement found in the black West End to a model flat. On January 16, 1920, the league opened the flat to the public and conducted classes there in housekeeping, sewing, and cooking.[17] That same year, the league participated in a program with the Travelers' Aid Society, the Board of Health, and the Americanization Committee to aid immigrants newly arrived in the city by teaching them both American and urban ways of living. In 1924, the league participated in a similar program for southern black migrants cooperating with Community Services, the Board of Health, the Travelers' Aid Society and the Negro Civic Welfare Association.[18]

The black migrant program represented only part of the increased attention black housing received in the 1920s. Confined to limited residential areas within the city, particularly the once aristocratic West End (Fifteenth to Eighteenth wards) where their population had nearly doubled from 8,647 to 17,207 between 1910 and 1920, blacks experienced further deterioration of already bad housing conditions.[19]

Even before World War I, Cincinnati contained one of the larger black populations among northern cities. The 1900 U.S. Census found 14,476 blacks in a city of 325,902. In 1910, that figure had jumped to 19,639 blacks, or 5.4 percent of the total population. During the next twenty years, Cincinnati's black population grew approximately two and a half times to 47,818. Meanwhile, the city increased by 24.1 percent, from 363,591 to 451,160. As a result, in 1930, blacks composed 10.6 percent of the city's total population.[20] And as we have seen, much of that population concentrated in the lower West End, resulting in the city's first large-scale ghetto (see map 4-A). The limited resources of black newcomers as well as white antagonism toward them clearly limited their housing opportunities. Meanwhile, many of the housing units available for black occupancy near the river were cleared for large business houses and clubs. This combination of prejudice and private redevelopment led the BHL to conclude in 1922 that "the situation among colored families is almost desperate."[21]

The overcrowding lured greedy speculators to the West End, where they traded and bought tenements, raised rents, and reaped the economic benefits while blacks suffered. Rents, which tripled in some instances between 1918 and 1922, produced doubling and tripling up in some West End flats and some truly extraordinary cases of congestion. A housekeeper for the league re-

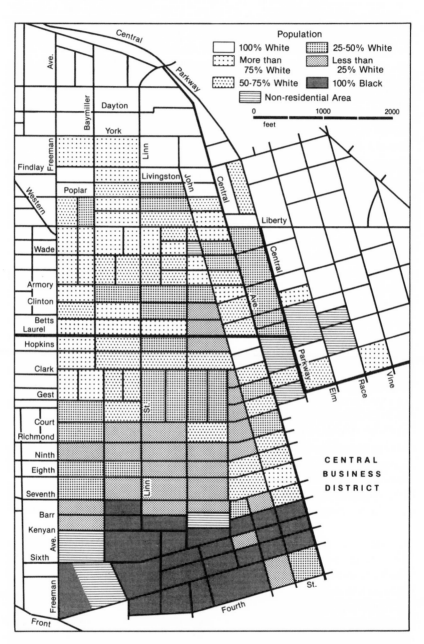

Map 4-A. Blacks in the West End, 1930 (Stanley M. Rowe Papers, The Cincinnati Historical Society, Cincinnati, Ohio 45202)

ported in 1923 that twenty persons lived in a three-room flat at 1131 Hopkins Street, and that another twelve-room tenement at 324 George Street contained ninety-four occupants. Later, when Dr. Haven Emerson of New York visited the West End he told the Public Health Federation that "you could not produce a prize hog to show at a fair under conditions that you allow Negroes to live in in this city. Pigs and chickens would die in them for lack of light, cleanliness and air." [22]

The situation deteriorated so badly that a pamphlet by the BHL in 1922 reported that "housekeepers, for the past year and a half had to devote the greater part of their time in finding flats for homeless families." Acknowledging that no one built specifically for the tenement population anymore, the BHL concluded that the only way to help the needy wage earner was by "relieving the pressure from the top." [23] Yet the "filtering down" system appeared not to be working, either, for 1922 was a banner year for housing, with over 1,760 housing starts. Nevertheless the city was haunted by the "paradoxical fact," the league explained, "that the situation for tenement people is worse instead of better." Refusing to read too much into this lack of progress, Marquette believed that the current housing boom provided for those families of moderate means that had been forced to double up because of the wartime housing shortage. Eventually, Marquette predicted, the benefits of the latest housing activity would filter down to the city's neediest residents in the basin. [24]

Meanwhile, housing conditions for blacks continued to degenerate. In January of 1924, the Community Chest asked the directors of the BHL to create a relief program in response to the black housing situation. The league complied and created a special committee on black housing on February 4, 1924. [25] That committee formulated a program and attempted to initiate it on April 21, 1924, by holding a large public meeting. At the gathering, the committee showed a motion picture on the horrible West End housing conditions "to arouse public opinion to the serious plight" of those suffering from the housing shortage. Following the movie, Marquette called for a citywide response to the basin's housing crisis, arguing that "the problem has gotten beyond us [the BHL]." Toward this end, he outlined a six-point program suggested by the committee. [26]

First, he asked the Community Chest to increase its contributions to the BHL so the league could enlarge its visiting housekeeper staff from six to fifteen, thereby providing for the "cleaning up and keeping in reasonable repair the tenement houses in the West End of the city." Toward the same end, he requested that Cincinnatians pressure their local government officials to increase the number of inspectors in the City Housing Bureau from two to six. For a more permanent solution to the problem, Marquette called on the area's capitalists to invest $500,000 in the Cincinnati Model Homes Company so that it could build additional housing for the city's wage earners. Along the same line, the league advocated an increase in Building and Loan Association deposits so that more money might be available for housing. Finally, the league announced that in an effort to promote more and better low-cost housing, it would award a $500 prize for the best house built for under $5,500 before December. The response to the contest typified the response to the whole better housing proposal—lack of participation. Despite the prize offering, only one legitimate contestant entered the housing contest and that entry was promptly rejected for shoddy construction. The league kept its money.[27]

The failure to raise new capital for the Model Homes Company particularly distressed league members, who firmly believed that "the present situation" could not be "relieved materially without the constructing of more homes." Although the Model Homes Company had provided more than 400 homes between 1914 and 1919, including the only new low-cost housing for blacks, it remained practically dormant after the World War.[28] Part of this had to do with the lack of strong company leadership after Jacob Schmidlapp died of a heart attack on December 18, 1919.[29] But the higher postwar building costs provided an even greater barrier. In 1925 it cost $3,750 to build the same flat constructed in 1915 for $1,400.[30]

When the company did construct an "experimental" three-unit building in 1923, the consequences of high building costs became very evident. Washington Terrace, the company's first project, built in 1915, charged blacks as little as $11 per month for a four-room flat. Eight years later a four-room flat in the new building cost tenants $35 per month, a rate much too expensive for most of the city's blacks. Even then, the building returned only a 2-percent profit to its investors.[31]

Several years later the company experimented with another approach to relieving the black housing shortage. In 1926, company officials acquired a tenement on Carr Street in the West End, remodeled it, and rented it to blacks. According to the 1927 annual report, this ten-unit dwelling proved only a "limited success." The Carr Street units suffered from "excessive vacancies." Model Homes officials explained this by reasoning that blacks wanting and able to afford their company's accommodations simply did "not want to live in the West End Bottoms."[32] The ambitious poor wanted out of the basin slum and would not be satisfied with just better dwellings—they wanted better neighborhoods.

Unable to build for blacks, and unwilling to remodel more basin tenements for needy blacks, Model Home Company officials believed that an additional influx of capital might allow their company to build housing for better paid white wage earners, who by vacating their old neighborhoods would indirectly help resolve the black housing shortage. Unable to attract the needed capital, this attempt to solve the housing shortage by private enterprise failed like all the other efforts.[33]

Meanwhile, some realtors attempted to implement their own solution to the black housing shortage, drawing a strong rebuke from the BHL in 1924. When several local real-estate agents bought up tenement houses in the white Mohawk Brighton residential district and started selling or renting them to blacks, the league's board of directors called it a "momentous problem." Fearful of the "outbursts of violent feeling and bitterness" such blockbusting prompted, the board instructed its housekeepers to dissuade their black clients from moving there. Then the league's leadership discussed how best to solve the black housing problem and concluded that it was "by finding room for the expansion of the colored people of this city without this scattering in neighborhoods." [34] Such actions underscore the limits of the BHL's willingness to help the city's blacks. It appears that the BHL never even considered integration as a viable response to the black housing shortage. Outward residential mobility still depended on the availability of expanded black neighborhoods. But as we have seen, the league opposed the type of housing blacks were erecting in the suburbs during the 1920s because it failed to conform to the league's definition of good housing.

Until such housing could be found for blacks, the BHL focused on improving conditions in the congested West End through its emphasis on regulation and education. For instance, in a special program for the West End, the BHL sent three of its black visiting housekeepers to work with some caseworkers from the Associated Charities at the newly established Shoemaker Health and Welfare Center. By joining forces to create the Family Service Department at the Shoemaker Center on 667 W. Fourth Street, the league attempted to alleviate some of the area's suffering through a systematic and coordinated effort. The league also loaned its assistant executive secretary, Ethel Ideson, to the center, where she supervised all the housekeeping instruction given by the caseworkers. [35] The cooperative effort aimed to improve the family life of blacks living in the 1,897 dwellings located in Wards Sixteen through Eighteen. It attempted to ease the area's congestion, better its bad housing, and "eliminate the poor sanitary conditions festering in the district which impeded the inhabitants' effort to get forward in their struggle for normal life and decency." [36] The league also hoped that with the aid of the Shoemaker Center it could help reduce black Cincinnatians' death rate, which was more than double that of whites. [37]

Various BHL reports indicate that local housing reformers were both optimistic and pessimistic about the housing problem in the late 1920s. As early as 1926, the housing shortage had eased enough to permit the league some hopefulness. That year, Bleecker Marquette observed that a "marked improvement" in tenement houses had occurred. He also concluded that "at no time in the city's history has greater progress been made" in bettering local housing conditions. [38] During the next four years the minutes of the BHL brimmed with reports of accomplishment by the league's housekeepers and the city's Housing Bureau. For instance, the 1930 annual report revealed that the league's housekeepers had made 8,202 visits during the previous year and had given 2,781 housekeeping lessons. They had also helped adjust rents for 285 families and helped 125 families find better housing.[39] Such statistics imply that the league had created an effective visiting housekeeping system which positively affected the living environment of the West End.

Despite the apparent success of the BHL, one specific difficulty re-mained—meeting the demand for good low-cost housing. Some develop-ments followed the pattern the league had anticipated. The basin's industrial and manufacturing sections were expanding and eliminating basin housing, thus creating a "natural slum clearance." What the league had not expected was the failure of the filter-down system to provide adequate replacement units, particularly for black Cincinnatians. As a consequence, tenants forced to relocate from unsanitary and structurally unsound tenements scheduled for demolition merely moved to nearby unsanitary or structurally unsound tene-ments, or they doubled up with friends. At first, the league dismissed the shortage of good housing as only a temporary aberration due to the war's negative effect on private construction. But by 1928, the BHL grew increas-ingly impatient with the lack of good housing for wage earners. The filter-down system seemed not to be working and new ways to create an adequate supply of low-cost housing were needed. According to the league's 1928 an-nual report, the private speculative builder had failed to build for the needy working class, and private industry had "proved itself unequal to the task of providing new homes for the mass of the population."[40] The next year's report repeated the same theme and concluded that "without question, the great challenge in the field of housing is how to build satisfactory new houses at prices our families of moderate means can afford."[41]

The title of its 1930 annual report, *Housing: Forward or Backward?*, re-flected the uneasiness of the BHL. Although it gave impressive accounts in improvements brought about by the league's visiting housekeepers in regard to sanitary improvement and tenant education, it also sounded pessimistic at times. For instance, instead of anticipating the positive effects its actions would have on the city's housing conditions, it reflected on what could have been, had the city "seventy-five years ago [been equipped with] a modern housing law, an up-to-date building code, a zoning system and a plan to guide and regulate construction."[42]

The adherence to the model of a dynamic and outward-growing city, seg-regated by function, class, and race, limited the league's definition of and solution to the housing crisis. When the war-related housing shortage checked urban expansion and failed to provide the necessary housing units for the working poor, philanthropic and limited dividend building companies were asked to fill the void. Another option was the more expensive town project such as Mariemont, which could ease "the pressure from the top." [43] One strategy failed for lack of investors while the filter-down system no longer seemed to work either. Consequently, Cincinnati housing reformers in the years 1927–29 continued to be confronted by a serious housing problem which demanded innovative approaches by private capital. But as Thomas Philpott has pointed out elsewhere, "Private enterprise proved incapable of solving housing problems even during periods of prosperity." [44]

Not only did the BHL and private capital fail to resolve the city's housing shortage, but housing reformers actually contributed to the black housing shortage by supporting tenement regulations which discouraged the building of additional dwellings for the needy. As a result, black neighborhoods in the basin continued to experience unprecedented congestion and deterioration. Such conditions led a frustrated Bleecker Marquette to conclude in 1929 that during the past twenty-five years, "little progress . . . has been made in getting rid of what is commonly called slum conditions." [45] Although real progress probably had been made in eliminating some of basin's worst tenement conditions, the black housing shortage as well as the changing definition of the housing problem from inadequate dwelling to insufficient community made conditions in the basin appear even worse. Simply put, the perceived housing problem required resources unavailable to those attempting to resolve it. The BHL, for example, had insufficient capital either to clear the basin slums or to build new housing. All it could do, according to Marquette, was make sure the city government did everything possible "to stimulate the construction of low-cost houses of a desirable type." In addition, the league would educate the group of tenants that had developed "the slum concept." The league would combat this loss of community consciousness developed from years of living "in ugly, unsanitary, congested buildings, with all sorts of handicaps." By demonstrating better housing skills, the league would not only help individual families but also make the tenants more conscious of how their actions affected others. This program then would educate families on how to "make the best of bad living conditions" and also "prepare them for better houses in the future." [46] But until these families actually moved from their slum environment, the strong influence of place on the slum dwellers would limit the impact of the league's teaching.

The league's main strategy for eliminating the city's slums was also closely tied to its metropolitan strategy of comprehensive zoning and planning. That is, the league attempted to raise basin housing conditions to some bare minimum, but acknowledged that only time and the outward expansion of industry and business would eliminate the city's worst housing conditions. To prepare for that day, the league fostered a preventative strategy for the entire metropolitan community. This would guarantee a proper community setting for housing and discourage future slums. The underdeveloped suburban fringes of the Queen City, then, were to play an important role in the ultimate solution to the city's basin tenement problem. For only after the whole metropolitan region was opened up and regulated for better housing would each family have "the kind of home that American standards require." Only after such housing became available and the poor "educated to the point of appreciating such a home" did Marquette believe that "many of our most disturbing social problems would be solved." [47] Despite this well-conceived housing strategy, housing reformers by the late twenties grew increasingly impatient with the lack of any real housing progress and questioned both their definitions of and solutions to the low-cost housing problem, a process which would ultimately lead them to the federal government for assistance.

CHAPTER 5

Promoting Good Housing: Large-Scale Slum Clearance and Urban Reconstruction, 1929–33

> While we have been eliminating [tenements] at a rate of about 100 a year, and while as the years go by they will wear out more rapidly, nevertheless there is no reason for believing that it will take less than forty or fifty years for this problem to solve itself by a gradual wearing-out process. We can hasten it along somewhat by vacating and condemning these buildings as they become totally unfit for habitation. Industry and business will no doubt continue to displace others. This is a slow process at best, but perhaps the only practical course open to us.
>
> —Better Housing League, 1929

> It is a forlorn hope that much more of this section will be used for business or industry. City studies confirm this. Either the basin will be reclaimed by modern housing development or the downward trend will continue.
>
> —Better Housing League, 1933

Although Cincinnati housing reformers had supported efforts throughout the late nineteenth and early twentieth centuries to demolish old and decrepit tenement houses threatening the city's health and physical safety, they did not pursue massive slum clearance and the building of large-scale housing projects in the inner city until the late 1920s. Indeed, *The Official City Plan of Cincinnati*, issued in 1925, pointed back to the turn-of-the-century mode of thinking, which looked to the "natural" forces of the city's commercial and industrial expansion to eliminate the city's worst housing.[1] It observed that the old tenement houses would eventually disappear "with the invasion of industry and business," and suggested that "an earnest, sincere attempt to plan for orderly development of the city during the fifty years to come," must assume that the entire basin would be devoted to commercial and industrial activities.[2] According to the plan, 67,000 persons living in the 2.3 acres of the West End would eventually be forced out of their tenement houses into secondhand housing outside the basin area by the expanding commercial and industrial sectors. In anticipation of this expansion, then, the City Planning Commission in 1924 zoned enough basin land for commercial activities to "provide for the needs of [a city of] nearly five times the present population." It also zoned the industrial districts "for expanding the present industrial holdings at least ten times." [3]

By the end of the 1920s, however, Cincinnatians lost confidence in the "natural" method of slum clearance and started discussing how best to replace the city's slums with housing. For instance, Bleecker Marquette acknowledged in the BHL's 1928 annual report that slum clearance and housing redevelopment "would offer a much quicker solution and would be a great boon to the city's health and general welfare." [4] And in 1929 Commissioner of Health William H. Peters observed that "nothing short of a huge development will relieve the situation of the West End within a reasonable time, a consummation that we look forward to devoutly." [5]

Along with their changing conception of urban expansion, reformers attached a different meaning to the word "slum" in the late 1920s than they had in 1900. The turn-of-the-century definition of the term, which was used infrequently by Cincinnatians, emphasized physical conditions and the character of the population in this undesirable part of the city. Slums, the dictionary noted, were "foul back streets" with "a degraded and often vicious population." [6] By the late twenties, however, the slum was defined as a force rather than a condition. That is, the heterogeneity of peoples, housing, and land uses found in slum areas was believed to promote social and psychological disintegration and disorganization because such areas lacked "an established culture pattern which would serve as a guide for the overt acts of the community." As a result, groups, individuals and families lost "their identity" and "the various social patterns tend to blend into a mixture without any purposeful objective." So many elements of slum areas needed readjustment to promote a healthy community that total clearance and rebuilding of the place seemed an expedient alternative. [7]

Despite the apparent attractiveness of slum clearance, housing reformers realized that some sort of governmental assistance would be necessary before large tracts of land could be assembled and demolished within the city's congested slum areas. The need for such aid dimmed the enthusiasm of some local reformers. In 1928 Bleecker Marquette, who strongly opposed direct federal aid to the housing problem, thought the prospect of government-assisted slum clearance quite remote. "We know," he wrote in the BHL's annual report, "that our old tenements will be worn out and gone before public opinion of America reaches the point where it would support such a proposal." [8]

Nevertheless, housing reformers in the late 1920s continued to discuss slum clearance, usually with reference to the need for local governmental assistance to carry it out. For example, Lawrence Veiller, the well-known New York housing reformer, met with Cincinnati housing reformers on November 25, 1929. At that conference he suggested that the city could buy blocks of slum land in the West End, demolish the buildings there, and create a municipal park in the center of each block. Then, the city could sell the unused land to limited dividend corporations for the construction of low-cost housing.[9] Nothing ever came of this proposal, however. Only after the nation's economy faltered in the Great Depression, did large-scale slum reconstruction become a reality for the Queen City.

Although a diversified industrial base and an ambitious, locally sponsored public works program cushioned the early impact of the depression on Cincinnati's workers, the city nevertheless suffered greatly from the nation's economic calamity. Between May 1929 and May 1931, the city's unemployment rate more than tripled to nearly 19 percent. And by 1933, 30 percent of the city's workers were unemployed while another 18 percent managed to cling to part-time jobs. Blacks faced much worse conditions. By 1933, 54 percent of all black laborers in Cincinnati were out of work.[10]

Responding to the unemployment problem more than to the housing crisis, Congress approved the Emergency Relief and Construction Act during the last year of the Hoover administration. That law authorized the Reconstruction Finance Corporation (RFC) "to make loans to corporations formed wholly for the purpose of providing for families of low income or for reconstruction of slum areas."[11] To qualify for those loans, housing companies had to be "regulated by state or municipal law as to rents, charges, capital structure, rate of return, and areas and methods of operation." In addition, the loans needed to be "self-liquidating in character."[12] Soon after the bill passed, housing reformers from both Cleveland and Cincinnati lobbied for a state housing law which would permit local housing companies to receive federal loans. They achieved their goal when House Bill No. 8 passed the Third Special Session of the 89th Ohio General Assembly and became law on January 3, 1933.[13]

Ohio's housing law, modeled after New York's state housing law of 1926, set conditions under which the limited dividend housing companies might construct projects. It established a seven-member State Board of Housing authorized to recommend and approve areas within which limited dividend housing companies might construct projects. Furthermore, the board could study housing conditions throughout the state to determine Ohio's low-cost housing needs. Finally, the board could grant the power of eminent domain to the housing companies to help them assemble land more easily. Unlike the New York law, however, the Ohio State Housing Law did not grant tax exemption to low-cost housing companies.[14]

Nevertheless, several Cincinnati groups expressed interest in limited dividend slum clearance and low-cost housing at this time. The Model Homes Company, the Schwartz Reality Company, and the Ferro Construction Company all proposed large-scale developments for the West End. The Ferro project, pushed by the company's president, Tylor Field, proved the most ambitious one. As both a Charterite city councilman and president of the Better Housing League, Field had shown interest in the city's low-cost housing problems since at least the teens. And now, like many of his contemporaries, Field believed that only large-scale slum reconstruction could resolve the city's housing problem.[15]

Although bad housing conditions existed elsewhere in the basin, Field and other reformers identified the West End as the city's neediest slum. That area had experienced the most spectacular deterioration of any place in the city between 1890 and 1930. Its once posh mansions, now converted into tenement houses, attracted the city's unskilled wage earners because of their convenient location near the factories of Mill Creek Valley.[16] In addition, some of the cheapest accommodations in the city could be found there. This combination particularly attracted urban newcomers, especially blacks and southern whites. In 1890, native whites, Germans, and Irish made up the majority of West Enders. By 1930, few foreign born remained, and American blacks replaced them. A comparison of the Fifteenth Ward in 1890 with census tract 3 in 1930 documents the nature of the population changes (see table 5-A and maps 1-A and 5-A). In 1890 the ward's population of 9,350 contained 6,819 native whites (72.9%), 2,289 foreign born (24.5%), and 242 blacks (2.6%). In 1930, the slightly larger census tract contained 9,845 residents. Of that population, 5,007 (50.9%) were black, 4,253 (43.2%) were native white, and 585 (5.9%) were foreign born. The physical deterioration, the substantial demographic changes, and the social problems that the rapid changeover produced, helped make the West End Cincinnati's most notorious slum.[17]

Before Field or any other Cincinnati group submitted plans to the RFC to redevelop a part of that area, Congress enacted legislation in the opening months of President Roosevelt's administration for meeting both the unemployment crisis and the housing problem. Under terms of the National Industrial Recovery Act created June 16, 1933, the Public Works Administration created a Housing Division "to promote the program of low cost housing and slum clearance projects." To achieve this goal, Congress authorized the Housing Division to continue Hoover's program of loans to publicly regulated housing companies for construction, reconstruction, alteration, or repair of low-cost housing and for slum clearance. Those loans were now fixed at 85 percent of the project's total cost and charged a 4-percent interest rate for thirty years. In addition, the law permitted the Housing Division to provide grants and loans to states, municipalities, and other public bodies. The origi-

TABLE 5-A. Population trends in the West End, 1890 and 1930.**

	Total population	Native white	Foreign	Black
1890 Wards				
Ward 15	9,350	6,819	2,289	242
Ward 16	9,930	7,015	2,282	633
Ward 17	10,165	6,912	2,469	784
Ward 19	8,202	5,539	2,074	589
Ward 20	9,347	6,698	2,059	590
Ward 21	10,267	7,710	2,395	162
Ward 22	12,462	9,300	3,028	134
TOTAL	69,723	49,993	16,596	3,134
1930 census tracts				
Tract 3	9,845	4,253	585	5,007
Tract 4	9,061	2,646	222	6,193
Tract 5	12,960	1,182	154	11,624
Tract 8	4,461	2,203	306	1,952
Tract 1	7,437	3,246	238	3,953
Tract 2	8,430	5,951	510	1,969
TOTAL	52,194	19,481	2,015	30,698

**This is only a rough estimate of the same West End area and is used to show trends rather than give accurate numbers. To compare the areas see maps 1-A and 5-A.

Source: Report on Population of the United States at the Eleventh Census, 1890, p. 547; Fifteenth Census of the United States, 1930, Metropolitan Districts, Population and Area, p. 54.

nal plan of the Housing Division, however, focused on furnishing loans to housing companies.[18]

Encouraged by Alfred Bettman, chairman of the City Planning Commission, and Clarence A. Dykstra, the city manager, Field continued to develop his slum clearance project. The proposed West End project, planned by Ladislas Segoe, was to be a "civic enterprise of broad scope, with speculation and excess profits entirely eliminated." Located just north of Lincoln Park Drive, the main approach to the recently completed Union Terminal, the project site was bordered by Linn Street on the east, Armory Avenue on the north, and Cutter Street on the west.[19]

According to Segoe, that site was "without question the most suitable location for a slum clearance and low-cost housing project for white people in the basin area." It would not only replace a congested tenement district exhibiting one of the city's highest tuberculosis and infant mortality rates but also eradicate an area known for its crime and juvenile delinquency. Furthermore,

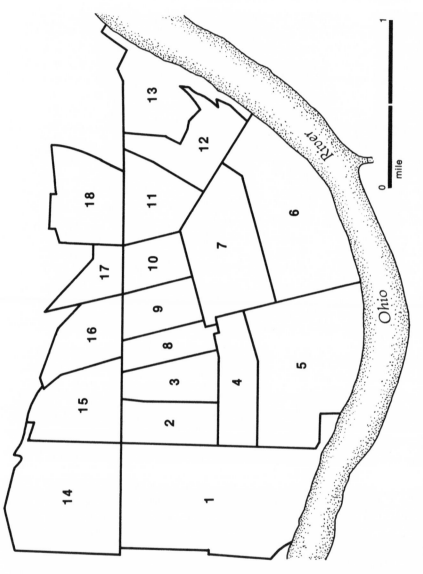

Map 5-A. Census Tracts of Cincinnati Basin, 1930 (Census Tract Files, Archives and Rare Books Department, Universities Libraries, University of Cincinnati)

the twenty-two-block site offered sufficient space for the development of a self-contained neighborhood unit and a more stable community.[20]

Indeed, the Ferro Construction Company planned to replace the old buildings with a "complete neighborhood community," which would contain "a center for business such as grocery stores, barber shops, a branch bank, as well as provisions for amusement and a few offices for doctors, dentists and lawyers." The living quarters, some to be provided with auto garages, would include both three and four-story walk-up apartments for approximately 3,200 families. The total cost of the project, for which Ferro Concrete Construction would act as agent and general contractor, was placed at $15,920,000.[21]

The application for a loan from the Housing Division of the PWA to build the project was first submitted August 16, 1933, and then resubmitted on October 25, 1933. According to the proposals, the Cincinnati Housing Corporation, incorporated under the recently passed Ohio State Housing Law, would acquire land and construct and maintain the housing project under the supervision of the Ohio State Board of Housing. The corporation, which would pay a 6-percent dividend after the entire loan was paid back, had an impressive board of directors. They included William Cooper Procter, chairman of Procter and Gamble; John J. Rowe, president of the First National Bank; Howard S. Cox, president of the Union Central Life Insurance Company; George Dent Crabbs, an official in the Philip Carey Manufacturing Company; Arthur Espy, executive of the Southern Ohio Savings Bank and Trust Company; Maurice J. Freiberg, president of the Freiberg and Workum Company; and John Omwake, chairman of the board of directors of the U.S. Playing Card Company. Other board members would be nominated by the mayor, the Health Board, the Recreation Commission and the Better Housing League. Besides having the planning services of Ladislas Segoe, the project's promoters also employed Alfred Bettman as legal adviser. In addition, Field hired the architectural firms of Samuel Hannaford and Sons, Tietig and Lee, and Potter, Tyler and Martin.[22]

Not only did some of the city's best architects and planners help design the project, but the city closely cooperated with the Ferro Company and pledged 13.3 acres of its land in vacated street and recreation areas. City Manager Dykstra lobbied with the PWA for the project, emphasizing that it was in response to studies made by the BHL, the City Planning Commission, and the Building Department.[23] All these groups concluded that the West End needed redevelopment.

Only the report of Myron Downs, who had replaced Segoe as the city planning engineer, seriously questioned the technical aspects of the proposed slum clearance and rehousing project.[24] Because the Ohio State Board of Housing required that the City Planning Commission report on seven phases of any limited dividend housing project before it, Downs responded with a written analysis. It examined the relationship of the Ferro project to the city's zoning regulations, thoroughfares, public transportation, public recreation facilities, schools, flood control measures, and community development plans. Although Downs approved of the way most of these elements were treated, he found problems with the community development plans. He criticized the placement of the project's C-shaped residential buildings because he feared they reduced ventilation and encouraged unnecessary congestion. Furthermore, he argued that the street system encouraged too much vehicle traffic in front of the public school.[25]

City Planning Commission Chairman Alfred Bettman, however, reminded Downs that "there should be a great deal of leniency regarding average population intensity when a project is truly slum clearance in its nature and of the neighborhood unit type, as developments of this nature should be encouraged and not subjected to the detailed standards of the zoning ordinances provided that the layout as a whole represents progressive standards in the developed portion of the city."[26] Bettman's observations apparently influenced the Planning Commission, for its final report offered no fundamental objections to the plan.

Despite the Planning Commission's approval, the project's sponsors failed to build because they could not raise the necessary 15-percent equity to obtain a federal loan.[27] And even if this had been done, Ferro would have been hard-pressed to supply homes for the area's neediest. The high land costs ($2.44 per square foot) and the low land coverage (less than 40 percent) required by good housing principles pushed the rents skyward. Indeed, Field estimated that a three-room apartment in his project could rent for no less than $25.50 per month, a figure much too high for most of the West End's residents.[28]

Other less ambitious projects ran into similar types of problems. Six of the eight applications for limited dividend money proposed to build housing on vacant land, since slum clearance projects took more capital and time to complete. One such proposal from the architectural firm of Rapp and Meacham called for a 292-apartment project renting at $8 per room per month. It initially received a favorable reaction from federal housing officials. But this effort, planned to be built outside the basin on the old Bellevue Incline House site, was eventually rejected because of the equity problem.[29] Federal housing officials rejected the Lane Gardens limited dividend project, the best-conceived vacant land housing proposal, for the same reasons.

Lane Gardens, initiated by the architectural firm of Tietig and Lee, along with the Penker Construction Company, would have erected housing on the site of the former Lane Seminary located less than three miles northeast of the downtown business section on Gilbert Avenue between Chapel Street and Yale Avenue. The nearly $2.5-million project would house 556 families in well-built, fire-resistant buildings that would cover only 27 percent of the building site at a rent of approximately $9 per month per room. Such a project would allow the more fortunate poor to escape the slum conditions of the basin. Furthermore, the housing site contained a playground and was located near a large commercial center as well as school and church facilities. The prospectus for Lane Gardens also noted that its officers would employ a resident manager to oversee the project.[30]

The PWA Housing Division officials were so impressed with the Lane Gardens proposal that they approved a $1,980,000 loan to the developers on October 23, 1933, contingent only on their raising the necessary 15-percent equity.[31] Unfortunately for the Cincinnatians, this requirement proved impossible to meet. Although the architects, Penker Construction Company, and two other sources secured $220,000 of the needed $370,000 equity money by September 22, the other $150,000 was never forthcoming. Despite their efforts to supply the equity in forms other than the required cash, the Lane Gardens Corporation failed to meet the Housing Division's requirements. As a result, on February 9, 1934, the federal government's Special Board for Public Works rescinded its financial allocation to the local housing corporation because it had failed to fulfill the conditions necessary to receive its loan.[32]

The failure of the Lane Gardens project reaffirmed the local housing reformers' suspicions that private and philanthropic ventures were unable to meet the city's housing needs even with low-interest loans. Just as slum clearance and rebuilding required large outlays of capital that the private sector was either unable or unwilling to provide, the large-scale vacant land housing developments thought necessary to provide the right kind of setting for good citizenship also required large outlays of capital. As a result, no limited dividend slum clearance or vacant land project was implemented in Cincinnati at this time. Evidently clearance and building for wage earners were not sound business practices.[33]

The limited dividend projects did not fail because of insufficient planning data, however. Local governmental agencies undertook a variety of housing-related studies in 1932 and made them available to all limited dividend housing corporations. The City Planning Commission provided much of the new information. That agency, formed in 1918, had spent its first decade planning for the future growth of the city.[34] Only in 1932, when it decided that the basin slum problem would not be remedied by the "natural" forces of growth did it turn its attention to the investigation and replanning of that area.[35]

Under the direction of its planning engineer, Myron Downs, the City Planning Commission initiated in 1932 a survey of the North and West Central basin area. It examined the area's overcrowded conditions, its lot valuations, its land use, and its water and sewer facilities. Apparently this was not enough to satisfy Bleecker Marquette, who wrote Alfred Bettman that every phase of the basin's slum characteristic should be analyzed to help foster the future redevelopment of the area. According to Marquette, some of the necessary information could be found in the U.S. census data for Cincinnati, which had been collected and assembled for small geographic units in 1930 for the first time.[36]

Cincinnatians had contributed $1,500 to a local committee for the creation of permanent census tracts because they believed that the current collection of data on a ward level was "purely arbitrary," largely ignoring "natural areas and boundaries." Designated tracts contained approximately 5,000 residents, and, whenever possible, their boundaries were determined by "topography, natural boundaries, and homogeneous development."[37]

In addition to the census tract data and the findings of the City Planning Commission, Marquette thought that additional housing-related information could best be collected by sending field workers into the West End. Marquette admitted that such a study would be costly, but believed it necessary because of the "large investments of money . . . represented in the properties involved." Marquette argued that "not only the city but the property owners and the financial agencies who have mortgages in these properties would find it in their interests to determine by a searching study what is happening in these areas and if the studies confirm the belief of many, that the trend is in the direction of further deterioration, then to determine whether it would be for their best interests to enter a plan of development by which these areas might be redeemed."[38]

Bettman concurred with the need for a comprehensive survey, observing that there was a need for "discovering what have been the forces and factors which cause the district to be as it is and what are the elements of a replanning." Bettman recommended that such a survey might best be conducted by a group of "an unofficial nature, which by reason of its financial facilities and its community contacts, could be more successful in putting the survey through." No such organization materialized, however, so the Hamilton County Department of Welfare and the BHL joined with the City Planning Commission in a series of studies of not only the physical but also the social and economic conditions of the basin, particularly the West End.[39]

The County Department of Public Welfare's *Survey of Housing Conditions in the Basin of the City of Cincinnati* typified the new concern with the slum by local government officials. That department, assisted by the BHL and the City Planning Commission, embarked on a comprehensive survey of five sample census tracts (3, 4, 10, 15, and 16) in the city's basin beginning on August 9, 1933 (see map 5-A). The findings from the survey, according to Marquette, would guide "those who are planning the kind of housing developments that are being encouraged by the federal government."[40]

The housing investigation, which used sixteen men and took four weeks, particularly explored the area's physical and economic status. For instance, it found that 66.6 percent of the dwellings were only in "fair condition" (structurally safe but in need of repair). Of the 4,666 buildings investigated, 10.1 percent were deteriorated and structurally unsafe. The survey also found that of the 9,864 families interviewed, 3,249 of them (32.9%) paid between $5 and $6 rent per room. Another 1,517 (15.4%) paid under $4 per room per month. Of the 9,751 families responding to the survey's income question, 4,701 (48.2%) earned a weekly income of between $5 and $20. An additional 1,155 (11.8%) reported no income.[41]

These findings, along with social data which showed that the western part of the basin led the city in crime, sickness, juvenile delinquency, and unemployment convinced planners and housing reformers that this area was an unredeemable slum. As a result, the City Planning Commission decided to draw up its own redevelopment plans for the West End and part of the neighboring Over-the-Rhine district. Since the commission identified this area as a hopeless slum, it called for the razing of 145 blocks in the north and west central basin district. And the plan, drawn up principally by Myron Downs, called for more than simple replacement housing for the city's aging tenements (see map 5-B).[42]

Downs's plan proposed the development of sixteen superblocks. Not only would they help relieve the area's congestion and provide its inhabitants with more light and better breathing space, but the superblocks would promote a setting where residents could develop a real sense of community and group interaction. To facilitate the proper type of community building, Downs arranged the superblocks around small centers or schools, places that people of the immediate neighborhood would frequent. This would encourage the area's residents to become better acquainted. In addition, each superblock was bordered by main thoroughfares to create a sense of self-contained local community within the larger metropolis. These blocks contained plenty of open space for recreation and provided areas for churches and other meeting places.[43] The City Planning Commission's redevelopment plan, like the Tylor Field proposal, borrowed from the neighborhood plan concept and attempted to achieve the same type of community development in the central city that Mary Emery's Mariemont had promoted in suburban Cincinnati. Both endeavored to foster a "small self-contained community" capable of producing "local happiness."[44]

The North and West Central Basin District Plan suggests more than merely a commitment to the neighborhood unit idea. It suggests that the Planning Commission had abandoned its vision that the commercial and industrial sector would expand throughout the entire basin. Indeed, by the early 1930s, others echoed this sentiment. For instance, when Bleecker Marquette spoke before the Housing Institute in November of 1933, he predicted that "[t]here

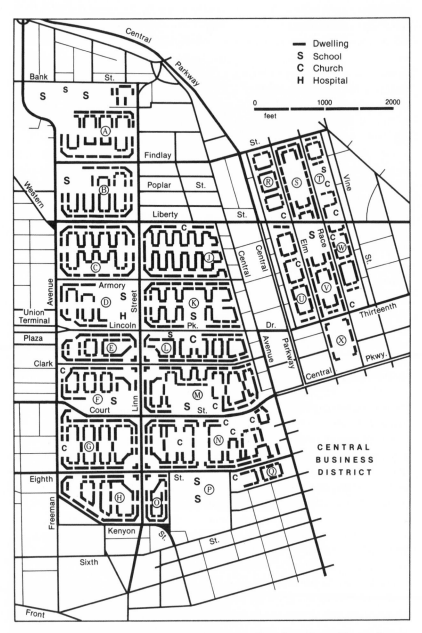

Map 5-B. Proposed Basin Redevelopment Housing Plan (Rowe Papers, Cincinnati Historical Society)

is little reason to believe that there will be extensive development of business or industry in the basin." Hence, with this potential "natural" slum clearance opportunity removed, the only real solution to the slums was to "tear down these areas and rebuild them along modern, well-planned lines, providing ample space for light and ventilation in the buildings and adequate recreation facilities for the population."[45] The City Planning Commission Redevelopment Plan proposed to do even more. It hoped both to rebuild the slum areas and to rehabilitate their residents through the promotion of community housing developments.

Not all of the north and west central basin was deemed appropriate for residential use (see map 5-B). The city's worst slum area, the lower West End (census tract 5) was not included in the residential plans because it was more industrial in nature than the rest of the West End. The railroad yards and the factories there would simply be too costly to relocate elsewhere, so the commission decided the area's primary use should be industrial-commercial. But it did not suggest what would happen to the predominately black population of nearly 13,000 living in the city's most substandard housing.[46]

In addition, the plan omitted the area east of Linn Street and north of Poplar Street because it contained a large number of packing plants and other objectionable industry. Land west of Freeman Avenue was also deemed inappropriate for community development because of its industrial nature and its susceptibility to flooding. Likewise, planners believed that no large-scale developments should be planned for the East Side of the basin because of that section's rough geography and the constant threat of flooding. Indeed, the commission apparently thought that the parts of the basin not included in the redevelopment plan should remain open primarily for industrial and commercial use.[47]

The North and West Central Basin Redevelopment Plan signaled a new approach by civic leaders in handling new inner-city housing problems. In the previous era, they had been content to regulate tenements and improve transit and sewer systems in the hope that the "natural" slum clearance of an expanding city would eliminate any real problem areas. By the thirties, government officials joined with housing reformers and recognized that those "natural" forces promised no remedy because of the city's slow growth. As a result, those officials developed a plan that called for the eradication of the city's slums and blighted areas through demolition and the construction of self-contained neighborhood community developments.[48]

Before the plans of the City Planning Commission could be implemented, however, massive amounts of capital were needed to acquire and clear the slum land to permit its redevelopment as residential community neighborhoods. By December of 1933, local housing reformers realized they had little chance for securing federal loans for limited dividend housing projects, so they pursued another alternative offered by the PWA.[49]

Besides loans to limited dividend housing corporations, the PWA authorized its Housing Division to make loans with outright grants of up to 30 percent of the total cost to states, municipalities, or other public bodies which engaged in low-cost housing or slum redevelopment. Since states and municipalities seemed reluctant to take on the additional financial burdens of housing construction, reformers figured that other public bodies, such as housing authorities, could be created to secure the federal grants. As a result, Cincinnatians began looking into the possibility of state-enabling legislation for housing authorities when the possibility of limited dividend projects lessened.

Members of the Citizens' Committee on Slum Clearance and Low Cost Housing, originally established to encourage the building of limited dividend projects, voiced some of the earliest sentiments favoring direct government action. Organized on July 20, 1933, by Mrs. Alvin Lehman, chairman of the housing committee of the Woman's City Club, the Citizens' Committee served as a clearing house of information for potential limited dividend developers. In addition, it provided free publicity for them. Finally, with the prodding of Alfred Bettman, it became a lobby group to ensure the complete cooperation of local political bodies with limited dividend slum clearance and housing developers. And Bleecker Marquette, who now favored federal help as the only viable remedy for the city's housing problem, supported the new group too. Although the city already had the BHL, Marquette believed that the challenge of unifying and carrying out housing projects would be a full-time job requiring the attention of a new organization. The BHL, Marquette observed, engaged in too many housing activities to give slum clearance its full attention. Moreover, he feared that the league might alienate some of its financial supporters if it led the movement for government-aided slum clearance and low-cost housing.[50]

By October, some of the organization's members had given up on the loan program. For instance, committee members Frederick W. Garber, Charles F. Cellarius, and Stanley Matthews, all architects involved with the planning of limited dividend slum clearance and housing projects, concluded that

> our studies in the planning and possible rebuilding of such areas as the West End convince us, however, that a commercial venture, where of necessity there must be some return on the private equity and where a government grant is not possible, must result in a scheme where the new population will be considerably greater than the present population and where the building coverage, as related to the area of land, will be considerably higher than is desirable for good light and air, open space and recreational activity.[51]

Because Cincinnatians were committed to large-scale community development for the inner-city housing needs, in addition to costly slum clearance, they turned to the federal government for help in their slum rehabilitation efforts. The vehicle which permitted Cincinnati housing reformers to create a housing agency was established when the Ohio State Legislature passed the nation's first housing authority law on September 5, 1933. Although Ernest J. Bohn, Cleveland housing reformer, was most responsible for the law, Cincinnatians such as Bleecker Marquette and Alfred Bettman also contributed to its passage.[52] In recognition that the housing problem affected more than just the municipality, and that it should be remedied on the metropolitan level, the initial legislation authorized the State Board of Housing to create county housing authorities whenever it determined "that there is a need for such . . . in the county." The authority would be a body corporate that could sue and be sued. Furthermore, the bill permitted the authority to borrow money from the federal government to clear slums, and to build and operate low-cost housing. Finally, it granted the power of eminent domain to the local authorities, stipulating, however, that it "shall be exercised only with the approval of the State Board of Housing."[53]

Despite the fact that new authorities would be corporate bodies responsible for their own debts, and despite the provisions in the bill which clearly acknowledged that the State Housing Board would assume any debts by an authority which ceased operations, county officials throughout Ohio objected to the concept of a county authority because they feared that their governments might be saddled with the authority's debts if the housing ventures failed. As a result, state legislators amended the bill so the authority would encompass "two or more political subdivisions but [be] less than all the territory within the county." Furthermore, the bill was renamed the Metropolitan Housing Authority Law.[54]

Only after the creation of the housing authority law did Ohio housing reformers secure federal grants to engage in slum clearance and low-cost community housing developments. The final decision to form a housing authority in Greater Cincinnati came after Robert D. Kohn, head of the PWA Housing Division, contacted Bettman in late October 1933, and urged him to encourage local reformers to apply for a federal grant. Kohn thought Cincinnati's chances of receiving federal housing money good because the PWA considered Cincinnati "a safe and desirable city" for public housing.[55] Bettman agreed and started the process which ultimately led to public housing in Cincinnati. On October 31, he requested the Citizens' Committee on Low Cost Housing to appoint a subcommittee that would initiate procedures for securing a local authority. At the very next meeting of the Citizens' Committee, reformers passed a resolution requesting the State Board of Housing to declare that Cincinnati and its outlying area needed a metropolitan housing authority. Three weeks later, the Citizens' Committee submitted to the State Housing Board a petition signed by twenty residents of the city and its suburbs, requesting an authority.[56]

The State Housing Board responded on November 22 by creating the Cincinnati Metropolitan Housing Authority, for the territory including the city of Cincinnati and the townships of Sycamore, Springfield, and Columbia. With this announcement, the Citizens' Committee on Low Cost Housing recommended citizens of the metropolitan area to fill the five-member board. Under the state law, Cincinnati's mayor would appoint two members, while the probate court, the county commissioners, and the common pleas court would select one member each.[57] The Citizens' Committee recommended its president, Stanley M. Rowe, president of Shepard Elevator Company; Setty Kuhn, philanthropist and founder of the BHL; Charles H. Urban, lawyer and former county commissioner; William Procter Matthews, former executive of Procter and Gamble; and Alexander Thomson, manager of Champion Coated Paper Manufacturing Company. The Citizens' Committee lobbied with the appointing officials for their recommendations and through these efforts secured the selection of four of their choices. Only Setty Kuhn's nomination was rejected, but she became one of the original members when Alexander Thomson refused to serve on the authority. The other member, John L. Spilker, chosen by the probate court, worried some of the city's housing reformers because the realtor and past president of the Ohio Real Estate Board had made some unsympathetic remarks about public housing before his appointment. But Spilker appeased local housers when he met with Bleecker Marquette and convinced the BHL head that he agreed with the goals of the federal housing program.[58]

The authority's organizational meeting convened on December 9, 1933, and promptly selected Rowe as chairman.[59] Along with the five appointed members, Myron Downs, planning engineer; Bleecker Marquette, BHL executive secretary; C. A. Dykstra, city manager; and Alfred Bettman, head of the City Planning Commission, attended most of the early meetings. With no budget for administrative expenses, the CMHA secured office space and supplies from the City and Regional Planning Commissions, and the BHL furnished secretarial help.[60]

The CMHA was able to submit a preliminary housing proposal to Washington five days later on December 14 only because the City Planning Commission's planning engineer, Myron Downs, had already prepared a redevelopment plan for the city's West End. Authority members requested $22 million to redevelop areas in the West End designated as blocks C, D, E, J, K, and L (see map 5-B). Some of the money would help build a vacant land low-cost housing project for blacks north of Cincinnati near suburban Lockland, another indication that housing officials viewed the housing problem in metropolitan terms. Since the proposed community projects for the basin would not house the same number of families they displaced, officials turned to vacant land projects to provide for those unable to find accommodations in the basin. Moreover, officials believed that vacant land projects could be developed more quickly to demonstrate both the economic and social fruits of the federal government's new housing program.[61]

From the beginning, however, the main emphasis of the proposal, in the words of Bleecker Marquette, was on a "redevelopment plan for that part of the basin district which may be salvaged for residential use."[62] That focus reflected the concern of both the City Planning Commission and the CMHA with the West End's high congestion and poor ventilation, and with the apparently disorganized state of its population. The remedy to the housing problem of that area, according to Marquette, was "fire-proof apartment houses, not massive structures but designed in many separate units, with generous spacing and grouped around a sizable park and recreation area." So the CMHA proposed buildings between two and four stories in height, and covering no more than 30 percent of the land. In addition, the apartments would be no more than two rooms in depth, which would guarantee good cross ventilation. And they would be equipped with all the "essential conveniences": indoor toilets, bathtubs, heat, electricity, and hot and cold water. Finally, schools, a small commercial area, and other services would be provided to encourage group interaction and the feeling of community.[63]

The CMHA's proposal, like the earlier limited-dividend proposals, justified the need to rebuild the West End by emphasizing the economic and social chaos of the area. It used statistics on crime and delinquency to support the reformers' argument that slum settings adversely affected the behavior as well as the health of slum dwellers. Moreover, the proposal showed that the city spent proportionately more on services for the basin slum area (i.e. health care, police, fire) than for any other area of the city.[64]

Soon after the CMHA submitted the proposal, it sent representatives to Washington, where they met with Robert D. Kohn on December 28. Kohn informed them that he had allocated $10 million to Cincinnati for slum clearance and low-cost housing. He quickly added, however, that the CMHA needed to revise its proposal before money would be granted. As the proposal now stood, rents would probably be too high and the vacant housing site near Lockland was inappropriate.[65]

Shortly after this session, on January 11, 1934, the CMHA appointed Frederick W. Garber as the chief architect for the West End project. Garber and his staff began working on a more detailed proposal for resubmission to the Housing Division of the PWA. The architects, according to the *Enquirer*, were equal to the task because "for a period of many months . . . [they have] been studying the housing situation in Cincinnati and have been working on plans for bettering the present conditions," a reference to their earlier participation in the limited dividend proposals.[66]

While the architects revised the proposal for slum clearance and relocation housing, the CMHA submitted to the Housing Division of the PWA on April 3, 1934, a plan to acquire land for the project. The CMHA also recommended that William S. Edgemon, an assistant city solicitor and author of the plan, head the operation. The Housing Division agreed to the proposal and on April 11 appointed Edgemon the federal land appraising official.[67]

On that same day, the CMHA submitted its revised application. It asked for an allocation of $8,825,200 to clear the slums and build low-cost housing in West End blocks D, E, F, and K (see map 5-B). The request also included plans for a million-dollar vacant land relocation project for Beekman Street near Mill Creek Valley. Immediately upon receipt of the application, federal officials contacted the CMHA, and informed anxious CMHA members that they would be granted only $6 million. According to Kohn, the smaller allocation had been ordered by PWA head Harold Ickes, who feared that Cincinnati was receiving a disproportionate share of the housing money.[68]

With assurances that a lesser project would be accepted, the impatient CMHA recommended to the Housing Division that ten men be hired to help Edgemon appraise the needed real estate. This was done on May 14, and the realtors immediately began appraising the cost of seven West End blocks (C, D, E, F, J, K, and L) (see map 5-B). After completing the appraisals, Edgemon received permission on October 9, 1934, from the PWA to begin securing options on the property in blocks D, E, and K.[69] The city's first slum clearance project was underway.

PART III

Government and the Housing Problem

Traditional knowledge asserts that the PWA housing projects were highly centralized efforts, planned and built by a Washington bureaucracy. Only after the 1937 Housing Act, the story goes, was the program decentralized enough to allow local housing agencies substantial participation.[1] Although the Housing Division of the PWA built Cincinnati's first slum clearance project, it never could have succeeded without the full cooperation of the sponsoring CMHA.[2] As we have seen, Laurel Homes originated from the studies of the City Planning Commission and the efforts of the Better Housing League. Only after the local housing enthusiasts submitted a concrete plan for housing improvement and showed their willingness to cooperate fully with the federal government did the city land one of the twenty-seven slum clearance projects built by the PWA.[3]

Much of the literature on early public housing emphasizes the economic rather than the social focus of the program. For instance Charles Abrams observed in 1969 that it was not until 1937 that public housing shed its emphasis on providing an economic stimulus and acquired a social purpose.[4] While the legislative intent of public housing may have been so, the rhetoric of the PWA Housing Division suggests a social as well as an economic focus in that program. And in Cincinnati, businessmen and middle-class housing reformers shared a concern over the social as well as the economic consequences of the city's slums.[5]

The Cincinnati experience, then, offers an alternative explanation of the origins, focus, and implementation of public housing. Despite the claims of at least one historian that the federal government imposed its plans on reluctant cities during the Great Depression, Cincinnati appeared to initiate its own public housing projects.[6] Working closely with the city council, the PWA

Housing Division and later the United States Housing Authority, the CMHA achieved the purposes for which it had been founded, to bring public housing to Cincinnati. It probably would be incorrect to characterize relationships between the CMHA, local, and federal government as always cordial, since the very definition of the housing problem in the 1930s raised a number of controversial issues and demanded a type of federal intervention unprecedented in American history. Land accumulation, costs, tenant selection, placement, and relocation, along with general administrative decisions, created conflict between the bodies. In addition, the CMHA, the city council, and the federal housing agencies relied on different criteria and approached the housing program from different perspectives. The changing relationship between city council and the CMHA illustrates this point. While both agreed on the general ideals of slum clearance and low-cost housing, and enthusiastically supported the initial program, tensions soon developed. As federal officials forced the local government into making a number of financial concessions at a time when controversy surrounded the public housing program, council attempted to wrest control of the federal projects away from the local housing authority. As a result, the years after 1935 were marked by conflict between council and the CMHA over the nature and direction of local public housing. Local housing and planning professionals such as Bleecker Marquette and Myron Downs, who advised and directed the CMHA, had one set of criteria while the city's councilmen had another. One group wanted to implement professional norms and principles, while the other wished to govern the whole city and retain political office.[7]

Moreover, the federal government's preoccupation with its broader program of economic recovery created real tensions for those who defined public housing primarily in social terms. For money was often shifted from the slow-moving housing programs to other programs that could provide quicker economic stimulus. A growing fiscal conservatism by Congress would also place severe constraints on the nation's first permanent public housing program, created in 1937.

Nevertheless, local reformers, city council, and federal housing officials agreed that large-scale, community-oriented public housing projects would better improve the social, economic, and cultural fabric of the metropolitan community and sought to compromise their differences to bring better housing to the metropolis. Unfortunately, those compromises sometimes caused new problems and failed to alleviate the needs of the poor.

CHAPTER 6

Implementing the Plan: Cincinnati, the CMHA, and Laurel Homes

Progressive and well-governed Cincinnati has been an outstanding example of the right kind of co-operation with the Government in slum clearance. . . . The Cincinnati project rests on the firm foundation of local interest and support. The city has not accepted it as the product of a distant and unfeeling bureaucracy; it has entered into it as a joint enterprise of local and Federal government that are pulling together in perfect harmony.

—Harold L. Ickes, September 26, 1935

Despite the Housing Division's approval, demolition on the Laurel Homes public housing site did not commence until February 14, 1936, more than sixteen months after Ickes authorized the project. And even then, the first tenant did not move in until August 22, 1938.[1] Some of the delay stemmed from the inexperience of both local and federal officials in administering such a program. In addition, an adverse court decision in 1935 on the constitutionality of federal condemnation proceedings for public housing probably delayed the project for more than a year, and a terrible flood in 1937 interrupted construction for several months.[2]

The federal government during Franklin Roosevelt's presidency placed more emphasis on providing jobs than on a comprehensive low-cost housing program during these depression-riddled years, and therefore sacrificed public housing money to other public relief projects that would better alleviate the agony of unemployment. This explains why FDR impounded $110 million of the Housing Division's $135 million on December 28, 1934, and transferred it to the Federal Emergency Relief Administration for direct relief. Cincinnati suffered from this transfer, since it had been allocated money but had not signed a binding contract for slum clearance and public housing. As a result, no funds were forthcoming and the city had to wait until April 8, 1935, when the Emergency Relief Appropriations Act set aside more money for low-cost federal housing projects.[3] This represented only one of many fiscal problems the developers of Laurel Homes faced. For instance, the CMHA saw its own plans change when it failed to meet a Housing Division collateral requirement.

The CMHA originally planned to build Laurel Homes with grants and loans from the federal government. But the Housing Division of the PWA ruled that "it was unable to find any satisfactory way by which security [could] be offered to a local authority unless such authority has funds with which to purchase real estate." Because the CMHA relied on small loans from the county commissioners as its only source of income, it failed to meet the PWA requirement. As a result, the Legal Department of the Housing Division of the PWA informed the CMHA that the federal government would "proceed with the acquisition of the real estate in the case of Cincinnati and perhaps begin construction before the enterprise can be turned over to the local authority."[4] Cincinnatians greeted that decision regretfully, since they had hoped to keep the development and implementation of public housing in the hands of local officials and housing reformers, those who had vigorously pursued and made preliminary plans for its execution.

Giving up its formal power over the building of the project, however, was not tantamount to giving up its activity and involvement with the issues of low-cost housing and slum clearance in Cincinnati. It is true that once the PWA accepted the CMHA's application for a project, the local authority formally relinquished the building of the project to a group of federal officials in the PWA Housing Division. But except for Ernest B. Johnson, who was appointed project manager of Laurel Homes in June of 1934, most of those directly involved in the planning and building of Laurel Homes were Cincinnatians recommended to the Housing Division by the CMHA. William S. Edgemon, the federal land appraising official, also served as the city's assistant city solicitor. And the Housing Authority selected the project's architectural staff, which included local architect Frederick W. Garber as chief architect, and members from the following firms: Charles F. Cellarius; Samuel Hannaford and Son; Potter, Tyler and Martin; and the firm of Standish Meacham and Walter H. Lee. The CMHA thus chose the designers and the sites.[5]

In addition, the CMHA became the leading advocate and defender of federally built public housing. Washington officials wished to avoid local controversy as much as possible and instructed the CMHA to mediate local differences over slum clearance and public housing. As it turned out, the CMHA worked hard in this role of mediator since a number of controversies appeared concerning the location, cost, and purposes of public housing. One of the first and most heated involved the land acquisition procedures used by the federally employed real-estate agents.

Problems in amassing large areas of land in the West End appeared soon after PWA head Harold Ickes ordered the securing of options in the area designated for slum clearance and public housing. The realtors attempted to obtain options in blocks D and E but discovered that their appraisals based on the 1931 tax duplicates were totally unsatisfactory to many property owners (see map 6-A). The initial decision to make offers 10 percent below the appraised value, as well as the rude methods of some realtors, produced widespread protest, the first organized opposition to the slum clearance project.[6]

Property owners complained that the 1931 tax appraisals were unfair because Cincinnati had revised property values downward three times since 1927. Therefore, they argued that the PWA was taking unfair advantage of them during a period of temporary distress. Since the 1931 tax appraisal in some cases listed property value at 50 or 60 percent of the 1927 appraisal, many refused to sign options and protested the government's unfair prices. The Harry Blum residence, located at 923 Armory Street, typified the differences between the final government asking price and the owner's price. According to the 1931 tax duplicate, the Blum property, which was mortgaged at $7,000, was worth $4,280. The PWA offered $4,325, but Blum valued his property at $12,000. Such price differences were common throughout the area and resulted in the creation of the West End Property Owners Association, formed primarily by the property owners of the D and E blocks.[7]

Speaking at a West End Property Owners Association meeting on November 12, 1934, Robert Lawrence Pastner, secretary for the organization, told the 700 present not to sign the options to sell being offered by Edgemon. Instead, Pastner, whose parents owned a home in the area scheduled for clearance, urged the West End residents to contact Cincinnati Congressman William Hess and protest the decision to undertake slum clearance in their neighborhood. Pastner charged that the CMHA chose the site which bordered the approach to the Union Terminal simply to make the area more attractive, and not because it was a horrid slum.[8]

Many property owners, homeowners, residents, and businessmen with shops in the ill-fated area followed Pastner's advice. In an attempt to prevent the destruction of 1,012 dwellings (including 268 homes owned by the occupants), they not only wrote to Hess, but also petitioned President and Eleanor Roosevelt. For example, Adelaide Myer's letter to the first lady protested that "many of the homes which they expect to take are in first class condition, having baths, garages and the best plumbing conditions and the people owning same are not slum dwellers at all, but it is a good neighborhood and they are very fine and intelligent people."[9]

The combination of the low offers being made to landowners and the supposed preoccupation of the CMHA and the federal government with beautifying the city at the expense of the area's residents and businessmen led the West End Property Owners Association to demand at a December meeting that the CMHA hold public hearings on the slum clearance project. At that

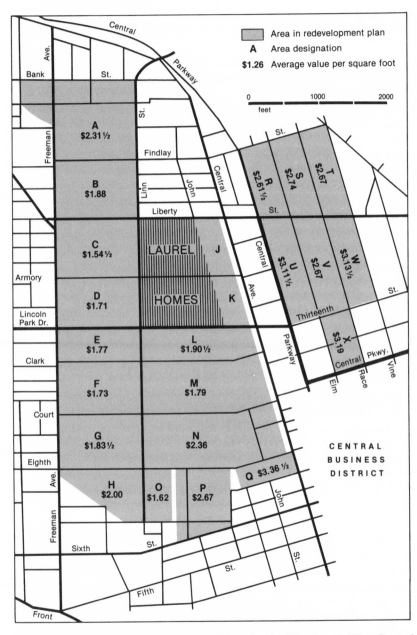

Map 6-A. Average Assessed Property Values in the North and West-Central Basin Districts, 1930 (Rowe Papers, Cincinnati Historical Society)

same meeting, residents and businessmen of blocks D and E emphasized that their neighborhoods were not slums and that their forced removal was unjustified. Wendell B. Campbell, president of the Model Homes Company, supported the association and predicted that the slum clearance project in blocks D and E would not eliminate a slum, but create one by bringing into the area a lower class of people.[10]

When the CMHA did hold a public hearing, it heard a repeat of the charges made earlier. Moreover it became clear that a number of owners were not going to sign their options and were prepared to fight the whole process, so the PWA Housing Division decided to relocate the proposed clearance site to north of Lincoln Park Drive. And when the CMHA discovered that land in nearby blocks J and K could be acquired for approximately the appraised price, it requested on February 26, 1935, that the Housing Division of the PWA build in these blocks (see map 6-A).[11]

According to estimates from the 1930 census, approximately 5,824 people lived in that area in two, three, and four-story red brick tenement and storefront houses with ornate fronts. The typical building in the area contained three stories and was three or four rooms wide. The rear rooms opened to the small backyard, usually cluttered with sheds and outhouses. The middle rooms were much gloomier since their windows faced nearby tenements with only a narrow yard or court separating the buildings. Seventy-five percent of the flats had toilets in the yards or hallways while 70 percent of the flats had a sink as their only "sanitary equipment." Furthermore, the area contained little play space (one acre of recreation space for every 42,000 people) and was spotted by a variety of small businesses, mostly grocery shops, restaurants, and confectioneries. The slum site also contained seven churches, the Ottoman Manufacturing Company (store fixtures), the City Ice and Fuel Company, and a fire department warehouse.[12]

Native whites and blacks predominated in the area. Of the 3,195 block-J residents, 2,394 (74.9%) were white (see map 6-A). However 1,980 blacks (56.1%) lived in block K. Approximately 91 percent in blocks J and K rented their dwellings. Finally, the area suffered high rates of infant mortality (108 deaths per 1,000 live births), high tuberculosis mortality (285 deaths per 100,000 residents), and much crime (15 arrests per 100 residents). All this suggests that by 1930s housing standards, the J and K site was a problem area.[13]

In addition, land appraisers encountered less hostility in this area than they had in the original site, suggesting that blocks J and K could be obtained much more easily than the original site blocks D and E. This was very important, for the federal government wished to avoid the real threat of a court fight over condemnation proceedings, particularly now that the PWA Housing Division had decided to acquire the land, build the project, and then lease it to the CMHA.[14] A Louisville U.S. District Court ruling on January 4, 1935, that the federal government had no right to exercise eminent domain in its slum clearance and housing projects, gave further incentive for the Housing Division to avoid a court fight over condemnation proceedings.[15]

Even after the Housing Division approved the site switch, some land acquisition problems continued. For instance, Edgemon failed to secure options on about 13 percent of the needed land in blocks J and K. Although local officials wanted the Housing Division to initiate condemnation proceedings despite the Louisville ruling, the federal government delayed any action pending the outcome of its appeal of the Louisville decision. When on July 15, 1935, the U.S. Circuit Court in Cincinnati upheld the lower court's ruling against federal eminent domain for housing, it created two problems for federal and local officials.[16]

First, it forced the Federal Land Acquisition Division to negotiate with each property owner. This slowed the acquisition process and raised the cost of acquiring land. Indeed, on hearing of the court's decision, the PWA forwarded Edgemon an additional $80,000 to buy off reluctant property owners. Second, the ruling created long delays in the clearing of titles for the acquired slum land. The title clearance problem proved a particular nuisance because of the unusual number of disputable ownership claims for property found in slum areas. As a result, title clearance took three months to a year after negotiations for the land had been completed. Before the federal court ruling in 1935, the Housing Division had planned to clear titles more rapidly through friendly condemnation proceedings which required the Housing Division to deposit the price of the land in escrow and secure the title, leaving any disputes over land ownership to be settled after the purchase. But with the court ruling, friendly condemnation was no longer possible. Sometimes uncontested titles also slowed up the process of land acquisition, particularly when held by out-of-state residents.[17] Because of all of this, land accumulation for Laurel Homes was a long and difficult task. According to William Edgemon, "Every type of encumbrance imaginable was held on the Laurel Homes parcels." This helps explain the delay between successful optioning of the land and its actual acquisition by the federal government.[18]

Other obstacles also inhibited the construction of Laurel Homes. The Broadway House Wrecking and Material Company of Cleveland, Ohio, delayed work by several months when it failed to produce the needed bond for its demolition of the Laurel Homes site. Only after the CMHA readvertised bids and contracted the job to the Cleveland Wrecking Company of Cincinnati for $44,000, did actual work get underway on February 14, 1936.[19] About eleven months later another problem arose in the form of a destructive flood. The high waters of the following January came to the edge of the northwest corner of the project and caused considerable delay in construction.[20]

But it was not these problems as much as the new relationship between Washington and Cincinnati which most taxed the CMHA. The ambiguous partnership between the federal government and local officials occasionally created tensions and misunderstandings despite the general consensus about the need for slum clearance and public housing.

From the beginning, local officials had supported reformers' efforts to secure public housing for Cincinnati. During the preliminary planning stages, Stanley M. Rowe, head of the CMHA, consulted with City Manager Clarence A. Dykstra and the heads of council committees most likely to be involved with public housing issues (the finance committee and the public institutions committee). He found that these officials appeared ready to cooperate with the authority in its slum clearance and low-cost housing endeavors. Indeed, because of the efforts of the City Planning Commission and the BHL, local officials seemed well-educated about the city's housing problems and quite ready to participate in a federally assisted housing program.[21]

Furthermore, the press of "conservative" Cincinnati readily embraced public housing as a solution to the city's housing problems. All three of the daily metropolitan newspapers initially endorsed the slum clearance and low-cost public housing scheme. For instance, the *Cincinnati Enquirer* on August 4, 1934, editorialized that unlike other New Deal recovery programs, the basin slum clearance project would have a long-term effect since it would help remedy the "demoralizing conditions under which many families have lived." And this in turn would help "mend the fabric of family life" so as to prevent "delinquency and crime."[22] About a year later, when the city's first slum clearance project appeared threatened, the *Cincinnati Times-Star* argued that the West End project represented "a golden opportunity for Cincinnati." It emphasized how the project would provide employment and be of great "social value" to the city.[23] The *Cincinnati Post* also supported the idea of slum clearance and large-scale public housing. In early April 1934, its editors ran a series of articles, entitled "Where the Other Half Lives," which explained why federally sponsored slum clearance seemed necessary.[24]

Nevertheless, tensions developed between local and federal officials when the latter failed to deliver its promises. As early as December 14, 1933, even before the CMHA submitted its first slum clearance proposal, local housing reformers discussed the possibility of having the city purchase open spaces of more than 11.5 acres in the housing project so that vacant land would not be charged against the project's rent. During a CMHA meeting on January 11, 1934, housing officials again discussed the possibility as a way to keep rents down.[25] By July, this became a condition in order for the city to receive a $6-million slum clearance and low-cost housing project for its basin. Federal housing officials stipulated that before work could be approved for the basin, city council had to commit approximately $1 million to acquire twelve acres of land around the proposed site for the development of parks and play-grounds.[26] Federal housing officials demanded the local contribution because of the excessive property values of the proposed slum clearance site. Usually, land for slum clearance projects constituted about 25 percent of the cost for the entire project. But in Cincinnati, the proposed land costs amounted to 33 percent of the estimated total costs. Myron Downs, secretary of the City Planning Commission, explained this abnormality by estimating that Cincinnati land values were two to fifteen times higher than in cities of similar size.[27]

On August 3, 1934, city council voted on what City Manager Dykstra identified as the "most important matter considered by Council since he came to Cincinnati in 1930," an ordinance stating council's willingness to spend up to $855,850 for parks and playgrounds along with another $144,150 for relocating streets, sewers, and water mains for the slum clearance project. Council, composed of five Charterites (the local reform association) and four Republicans, approved the appropriations 8–0. As a result, Cincinnati secured one of the earliest commitments from the PWA Housing Division for a slum clearance project. Only one councilman, Charterite Charles O. Rose, who abstained from the vote, refused to commit such money because he believed that the project did "not seem feasible or workable on the information which is now available."[28] Other councilmen also expressed doubts but nevertheless supported the pledge of appropriations because they believed it a worthy experiment which at least offered the possibility of jobs and better housing.

Cincinnati, then, became one of the first cities in the nation to allocate large sums of money to help facilitate federal slum clearance because land values on the proposed site were sufficiently high to preclude the federal program otherwise. A proper housing environment in the thirties meant low-density community developments with plenty of open space. Such a setting resulted in higher costs because vacant land did not bring in revenue. In an effort to retain both low density and low rents, council agreed to share the cost of land and recreational facilities.[29]

Council also readily agreed to its million-dollar contribution because it believed that federal slum clearance and public housing would revitalize an area that had contributed little to the local treasury and had drained the city's social services. At the time it voted to contribute to the project, council assumed that the housing project would pay taxes. In fact, a memorandum from the CMHA to council on June 1, 1934, stated this view and predicted that tax returns from the completed housing project would approximate $20,000 a year in excess of current tax revenue from the area.[30]

However, soon after council committed itself to contributing to the federal housing project, both local and federal housing officials reevaluated Cincinnati's slum clearance project and decided that full taxation might result in rents outside the range of many tenement families. On August 28, 1934, A. R. Clas, assistant director of the Housing Division, wrote to the CMHA and suggested that the city's slum clearance project could probably be speeded up if Cincinnati's city council would accept something less than the full tax rate for the project. Several days later, Charles H. Urban, vice chairman of the CMHA, wrote City Manager Dykstra and warned him that if the project paid full taxes, the minimum rent of $8.50 per room per month would be too high for most of the basin's residents to pay. As a result, he forwarded the Housing Division's request that a service charge in a smaller amount be considered by the local government.[31]

The tax issue became more complicated a month later, when on September 29, 1934, John W. Bricker, Ohio's attorney general, ruled that properties of the state's housing authorities under the Ohio Housing Authority Law were untaxable. Soon after this decision, on October 10, the comptroller general of the United States, John Raymond McCarl, ruled that the Housing Division of the PWA could pay neither taxes nor a service charge in lieu of taxes on its Ohio properties.[32]

Federal officials eventually responded to these rulings by proposing a 5-percent service charge in lieu of taxes (to be authorized by Congress) on the income from the project's rents. Stanley Rowe passed this information to council on September 26, 1935. He estimated that the service charge would amount to approximately $20,000 per year. Although Republican Councilman Willis Gradison objected and contended that the project should pay the equivalent of full taxes, council nevertheless formally authorized the drafting of an ordinance for the issuance of $500,000 in bonds for the project's parks and playgrounds. Several days later, at a council meeting on September 30, 1935, the CMHA reevaluated its estimates and concluded that Laurel Homes' annual gross income would produce a 5-percent service charge of $16,862, approximately $3,000 less than the earlier projected figure. Moreover, the service charge would bring in $2,000 less than the amount then being collected in taxes from that area. Presentation of these new facts probably dimmed some of council's enthusiasm, yet with the prodding of the CMHA, the lawmakers agreed to uphold their part of the public housing arrangement as outlined in the 1934 resolution.[33] And on February 13, 1936, council passed a bond ordinance for $200,000 to provide additional money for the slum project's parks and playgrounds.[34]

The tax problem, however, was far from settled in Cincinnati. While federal housing officials sought to secure local legislation permitting city council to accept a 5-percent charge in lieu of taxes, Councilman Gradison, head of council's powerful finance committee, attempted to force Washington housing officials into paying the equivalent of full taxes on its slum clearance project. When this did not work, he delayed council's approval of an ordinance vacating some streets for the project until he was reassured by Housing Division officials that the federal government really intended to make some type of payment "in lieu of taxes" to the local government. Even with these assurances, Gradison voted against vacating the streets when the resolution came before council on April 8, 1936.[35]

In spite of Gradison's opposition, council voted to vacate the necessary streets by an 8–1 margin. And with the passage of the George-Healy-Russell bill on June 29, 1936, Congress finally permitted the federal government to pay a 5-percent service charge on the total income of its housing projects in lieu of property taxes.[36] However, council's apparent acceptance of the Housing Division's service charge proved only temporary, and within eighteen months, a new battle raged over what the federal government should pay the city for its public housing property.

When the slum clearance housing project neared completion in the early months of 1938, federal housing officials reiterated their plans to lease the Laurel Homes project to the CMHA. Before this transfer could occur, however, city council had to agree formally to the 5-percent charge in lieu of taxes. And when those negotiations revealed that the service charge would return only $13,000 for the city, county, and school district to divide, the already controversial tax issue became more inflamed.[37]

Fearing that council would balk at the service charge proposal, the CMHA issued a memorandum to council which explained and justified the low service charge. The CMHA tried to explain why the project would pay about $4,000 less in "taxes" than had been estimated on September 30, 1935, and approximately $25,000 less than council had originally been promised in 1934. The CMHA blamed both court rulings and administrative decisions by the Housing Division for the government's decision not to pay the equivalent of full taxes on the Cincinnati slum clearance project. For instance, the court's ruling against federal condemnation procedures had raised the cost of land acquisition. And the Housing Division's recent decision to build fewer housing units at the Cincinnati site had decreased the amount of service charge payable to the local taxing bodies.[38]

According to the CMHA memo, the Housing Division's willingness to commit more money to the local project than originally planned countered the decrease in service charge payment. Not only had the Housing Division increased its original allocation from $6 to $7 million, but it converted what had been a 70-percent loan for the project into a grant as a way of insuring low rents.[39] The CMHA also argued that council's yearly contribution of $10,724 would certainly be justified by the social improvement that the new project would bring to the basin. Therefore, the CMHA claimed that the $6,224 lost in tax revenue and the $4,500 spent on debt service for park bonds were substantially less than the money the government had spent on city services for this slum area before clearance. Having made its point, the memo urged council to approve the service charge at its meeting on March 16, 1938.[40]

Council, however, used that meeting as a forum to attack the federal government's handling of the Laurel Homes slum clearance and low-income development. Republican Councilman Gradison accused federal housing officials of breaking their earlier promises, while Charterite Mayor Russell Wilson raised questions about government waste in building Laurel Homes. Wilson reminded housing officials that they had originally proposed to build a 1,600-unit project in Cincinnati for $6 million, but now were spending $7 million to construct only 1,000 units. Wilson deplored this cutback, which meant fewer good homes for the basin and a smaller service charge for the city. After voicing its frustrations, council postponed a vote on the agreement to accept a $13,000 service charge and instructed City Auditor Henry Urner to check the proposed operating expenses of Laurel Homes to find if the project could return more money to the city treasury without forcing up rent schedules.[41]

Several days later, Urner reported to the council finance committee that after examining the CMHA's budget for Laurel Homes he agreed that the federal government could not pay a higher service charge without increasing rents. At the same time, he admitted that it was impossible for him to judge the accuracy of estimates made by federal housing officials, since there were no guidelines in the newly passed Housing Act or in federal housing bulletins.[42]

Others, however, were not so reluctant to evaluate the housing project's proposed operating budget. For instance, at a public meeting on Laurel Homes held April 4, W. B. Campbell, president of the Model Homes Company, compared the proposed budget of Laurel Homes with some of his company's housing projects and concluded that Laurel Homes' administrative, operational, and maintenance costs were all too high. Furthermore, he argued that with less extravagance the government could afford to pay the city the equivalent of full taxes and still maintain low rents. To achieve the necessary cutbacks, Campbell recommended that a group of experienced real-estate operators and engineers examine the operations of the CMHA and set limits on the project's budget.[43] Albert H. Mayer, representing the Real Estate Board, also questioned the Laurel Homes budget and charged that it was "padded and fallacious." Only after the city's elected representatives took charge of public housing and the management of tax revenue, he argued, would conditions improve.[44]

Not everyone at the public hearing held by council's finance committee opposed the small service charge or emphasized the government's extravagance in building and maintaining Laurel Homes. Rather, some argued that the social benefits of the project far outweighed the expenses incurred by the city. Typifying this view, Ellsworth Bundy, a prominent labor leader, and Theodore Berry, a prominent black leader, urged council to accept the 5-percent service charge immediately, because of the social gains that Laurel Homes would bring to Cincinnati.[45]

Despite the public hearing (or maybe because of it), council's finance committee made no final recommendation to council on how to vote for the service charge ordinance. It did, however, suggest that perhaps $10,000 to $30,000 could be cut from the CMHA's proposed budget for running the project.[46]

Although some observers at the time noted that the tax payment issue was a ruse used by long-time opponents of public housing to defeat it in Cincinnati, city council members appeared to be generally concerned about protecting their city's financial well-being. The controversy over the service charge occurred because some members of council simply believed that the federal government had poorly handled the low-income housing development in Cincinnati and wished to register their unhappiness. Whatever the case, when council finally voted on the issue April 6, it accepted the 5-percent service charge by a vote of 8–1.[47] That vote suggests strong support for slum clearance and low-income housing that neither partisanship nor administrative differences with the federal government could thwart. Only Willis Gradison voted against the public housing issue, having campaigned for election to council on a platform of watchfulness over local governmental spending.[48] The CMHA had apparently done its job well and maintained the support of city council.

The Cincinnati Metropolitan Housing Authority did more than merely defend the PWA Housing Division. When increased costs for building materials led to cost overruns of over a half million dollars, the Housing Division officials reduced the number of housing units they would build. Local housing authority members recognized great irony in this situation. Federal officials had taken a slow and careful approach to planning and implementing the Laurel Homes project to hold rentals down. Yet the delays ultimately resulted in higher costs as the price of building goods soared. The Housing Division could reduce costs either by raising rents or by reducing the size of the project.[49]

Housing officials chose the latter approach by eliminating plans to build stores and garages, the community building, and seven apartment dwellings. This decision, which reduced the number of families to be housed from 1,279 to 925 and eliminated a number of community facilities, brought an immediate protest from the CMHA.[50] According to CMHA head Stanley Rowe, the "omission of the Community Building breaks down the plan for a well-integrated neighborhood development where important character building and educational work essential to the full success of a slum clearance project could be carried on." [51] The cutbacks threatened the community emphasis of the entire project, for under their original strategy, housing reformers would segregate a section of the "deserving poor" into a neighborhood unit which included community buildings, schools, and local commercial centers. These "extras" would produce a proper residential setting and promote cohesion and a sense of community among the project's residents. Here they would develop the patterns of living and the outlook on life deemed necessary to participate fully in the mainstream of American life. Without the building of local places where residents could meet, interact, and participate in their neighborhood's affairs, community would be hard to create. [52]

Not content with the revised plans, local housing officials continually pressured Washington to secure community facilities and the lost dwelling units. Soon after receiving local protests, PWA officials reinstated several of the apartment dwellings, but refused to include the community building. Nevertheless, CMHA members continued to lobby for the community building and submitted a separate application for one during the spring of 1936. Although this was turned down, the CMHA eventually got its building in 1939 under new opportunities offered by the Housing Act of 1937. [53]

CHAPTER 7

The Consequences of a Community Strategy: From Housing the Poor to Providing Better Housing

An area becomes a community only through the common experiences of the people who live in it, resulting in their becoming a cultural group, with traditions, senti- ments, and memories in common——a focus of belief, feeling and action. A commu- nity, then, is a local area over which people are using the same language, conform- ing to the same mores, feeling more or less the same sentiments, and acting upon the same attitudes.

—Harvey Warren Zorbaugh, *The Gold Coast and the Slum*

Laurel Homes did absolutely nothing toward clearing a single slum. . . . [Its tenants] are people with steady jobs, fixed incomes, and a good reputation for paying rent, and have moved into Laurel Homes from private owned property not in the slums, the owners of which pay full taxes.

—Mayor James G. Stewart, 1938

Laurel Homes was never meant for the city's neediest. From the be- ginning, Cincinnati reformers had decided that public housing would be most helpful to the city's struggling wage earners, threatened by or already infected with the social malaise of the slum. Laurel Homes, however, would be more than merely "middle class housing for working people."[1] Instead of supply- ing middle-class-like housing, public housing officials erected community de- velopment projects meant to transform the cultural setting of the basin's wage earner from one of heterogeneity, disorganization, and decay to one of ho- mogeneity, organization, and amelioration. Anomic families would be trans- formed into good citizens.

Laurel Homes, then, was more than merely environmental reform. The physical setting played a critical role, but the process of community organiz- ing seemed the key to cultural transformations desired by housing reformers.

So when the Housing Division hired J. S. Raffety as project manager, it gave him other responsibilities besides collecting rents and supervising maintenance. He was also charged with overseeing Laurel Homes' development as a community.[2] Actually, federal officials wished to develop two communities within Laurel Homes: one for whites and one for blacks, since each race would occupy separate buildings within the project. Toward this end, they hired two management aids, Verna Greene and Ernestine N. Rothass, to oversee tenant relations in the segregated project. In time, these women became part social coordinators and part troubleshooters. Sometimes they advised the project's organizations; other times they helped solve tenants' family and personal problems brought on by financial needs and marital misunderstandings.

In addition, they enforced a variety of rules made to promote the development of the right type of environment. When tenants moved into Laurel Homes, they received a handbook which welcomed them into a "neighborhood of homes." To preserve that neighborhood, tenants were forbidden to conduct any type of business from their apartments. Moreover, only natural family groups could move into the project; single-person households were not allowed.[3]

The tenant codebook also stressed other important ingredients believed necessary for a good community. It urged tenants to "make friends with your neighbor, avoid gossip or acts that may cause people to gossip." Finally, the codebook introduced the tenant to the recreational and community facilities of Laurel Homes, all "to help create a fine neighborhood." Confident that their efforts would be successful, the housing authority advised the Laurel tenants to "cooperate with the management and you will help keep the wheels of this community turning smoothly."[4]

Other evidence of the concern with creating community surfaced after Laurel Homes opened. Shortly after tenants moved in, they were urged to join a number of newly formed clubs and other cooperative efforts in both the black and the white housing sections. Mothers' clubs, music clubs, handicraft clubs, credit unions, boy and girl scout troops, bridge clubs, and smokers' clubs typify the assortment of organizational activities in the project.[5] Tenants also published their own community newspapers with the encouragement and scrutiny of the management. *The Laurel-Ville-Life*, published by and for the black residents of the project, received particular praise from federal officials for its quality and newsworthiness.[6] An article in the March 1939 issue of the paper also suggests how concerned the management was in maintaining the proper type of neighborhood. It emphasized that the Laurel Homes management provided recreational programs for the residents only and blamed the discontinuance of weekly dances for Laurel's black residents on the fact that too many "outsiders were coming in."[7]

Until the rest of the basin was redeveloped, officials wanted to prevent the surrounding slum from seeping into Laurel Homes in any form. This included the surrounding residents too. The project's security guards zealously kept out all "outsiders" who attempted to walk through the project. The guards particularly protected the white section and harassed blacks who passed in front of white's homes. One guard compared his job to that of the rangers in the earlier days—"We are keeping Indians away; or, using another expression, we are keeping the slime from pushing in."[8] Although publicly, officials claimed that they wanted their projects to blend in with the surrounding neighborhood, their actions suggest otherwise.

By concentrating on the proper arrangement of space, that is, the development of a neighborhood unit plan, and by facilitating a number of face-to-face encounters within the project in order to promote group and organizational activity, housing authority members believed they could create the type of neighborhood environment necessary for proper child rearing and citizen making. Furthermore, they argued that the very nature of the Cincinnati basin, with its numerous buildings and alleys as well as its intermingled business, industry, and housing units serving a heterogeneous clientele with diverse interests and little in common, prevented the creation of a proper neighborhood setting no matter how well constructed some of the housing units appeared to be. Therefore, local reformers decided that the best treatment of the old slum was to uproot the population from the neighborhood, demolish everything, and redevelop residential communities open only to the deserving poor.

Within two years of Laurel Homes' opening, J. S. Raffety announced that the project's strategy worked. According to the Laurel Homes' manager, "We have learned by two years' experience that our citizenship program, together with the advantages of ventilation, sanitation and other better living conditions offered at Laurel Homes can definitely make for rehabilitation and character building."[9]

The comprehensive community development strategy which clearly dominated the actions of housing reformers in the 1930s seemed to be working. According to the city's official housing policy, written in 1936, "Skilled large-scale management, social control, and the provision of suitable community facilities are all vital to all types of housing developments . . . whether on vacant land or slum clearance areas."[10] Safe and sanitary dwellings alone simply could no longer provide the solution to the housing problem.

At no time was this point more thoroughly documented than in the spring of 1939 when the Federal Housing Administration (FHA) built prefabricated, scattered-site low-cost housing in Fort Wayne, Indiana. That endeavor, which gained nationwide attention, came about after the Fort Wayne Housing Authority failed to secure money from the United States Housing Authority (created by the 1937 Housing Act) to pursue slum clearance and low-cost housing.

Wishing to alleviate the city's housing shortage, the Fort Wayne housing officials turned to the FHA's insured mortgage program for help and developed a temporary solution. Using blueprints for prefabricated housing developed at Purdue University, the authority proposed to place fifty small, three-room houses throughout the city and rent them for only $2.50 per week. The housing authority could charge low rents because labor paid by local Works Progress Administration funding built the houses. Moreover, the authority acquired property for the housing by purchasing deteriorated dwellings from local landlords for one dollar, demolishing the substandard vacated houses, and replacing them with new prefabricated ones. Any time the owner wanted to reclaim his cleared lot, he could do so by returning the dollar. This method of land acquisition gave tax relief to those landlords unable to rent their poorly maintained houses during hard times. Under its prefabricated housing venture, the Fort Wayne Housing Authority built forty-five dwellings by February 1, 1939, using a $45,000 FHA insured loan from three of Fort Wayne's financial institutions.[11]

Encouraged by the outcome of this temporary housing program for relief families, any city's neediest, FHA administrators toured the country trying to encourage other municipalities to copy the Fort Wayne effort. The FHA experiment gained favorable publicity in Cincinnati when the *Cincinnati Enquirer* published an article on February 22, 1939, about the undertaking. Coming as the last part of a four-part series about Cincinnati's slum clearance and low-cost housing projects, the article suggested that the Fort Wayne undertaking provided a more effective and cheaper model for meeting the city's low-cost housing needs than the USHA-sponsored projects in progress in Cincinnati. Apparently, some Cincinnatians agreed. Soon after the article appeared a few local officials, led by Omar H. Casell, city welfare commissioner, lobbied with the CMHA to duplicate the Fort Wayne effort.[12]

Despite the real need for adequate shelter for many of the city's neediest residents, a problem that scattered prefabricated housing could meet, housing boosters such as the BHL joined with the CMHA and strongly opposed the prefabricated scattered-site idea. On March 3, 1939, Stanley Rowe, president of the CMHA, explained to the *Cincinnati Enquirer* why he opposed scattered sites for low-cost housing. "No planning would be possible in these conditions," he contended, and "housing could not be developed in neighborhood units with relation to parks and playgrounds and schools." He also observed that "spotting better homes among old buildings in substandard neighborhoods doesn't improve the neighborhood and is an inefficient way of raising the general standard of housing conditions."[13] Soon after Rowe's statement, the CMHA officially voted to oppose the Fort Wayne strategy, because housing "is not the matter of the house alone, but also the environment."[14]

Bleecker Marquette echoed Rowe's sentiments. Marquette claimed that prefabricated houses on scattered sites simply did not permit "following good city planning principles." He also argued that such a housing effort did not "make for well rounded neighborhood development and the participation of tenants in forms of community activity which will tend to build character and to lessen delinquency." [15]

If the Fort Wayne scheme seemed unacceptable to Cincinnati housing reformers because they thought it contrary to good housing principles, it nevertheless seemed attractive from the cost standpoint. Because community housing projects demanded large tracts of land, this added time and considerable expense to the project. As a result, when Laurel Homes opened its doors, many basin residents could not afford the rents. An August 1933 rent survey covering 10,842 families in five basin census tracts found that only 8 percent of the white population and 3.5 percent of the black population paid $7.00 or more per room per month for housing, the proposed rent for Laurel Homes. [16]

Nevertheless, the CMHA justified its high rent and argued that another 6 percent of the whites surveyed, along with an additional 15.5 percent of the area's blacks, paid at least $20 a month for flats and could probably afford some CMHA low-cost housing if they moved into smaller accommodations. It also observed that housing rentals were unrealistically low because of the depression, and predicted that rents in the basin would rise after the economic recovery to figures comparable to predepression rentals in the basin. Those had averaged $6.40 per room per month, a figure closer to the Laurel Homes' rental. [17]

Within this context of high rents, the barrage of criticism from realtors made some sense. They agreed that parts of the West End were deteriorated and needed reclamation, but opposed the city's public housing project which failed to house the neediest and appeared to draw from a pool of tenants who could afford private housing. As a result, realtors saw their livelihood threatened and became the most vocal, but not the only, critics of Cincinnati public housing.

Many property owners in the city's basin area also opposed the CMHA's public housing program because it had not scheduled the worst slums for clearance. Most of the poorest residents lived in census tract 5, located in the lower West End (see map 5-A). Although that predominantly black area (95.5 percent) led the city in crime, dwelling violations, and public relief, the City Planning Commission had not called for its clearance and redevelopment in its West End Plan of 1933. Both reformers and planners decided against slum clearance redevelopment there, in part, because that area's mix of industrial, commercial, and residential areas made it too expensive to obtain and clear the land. And since good housing principles demanded self-contained neighborhood projects segregated from commercial and industrial concerns, reformers could not merely replace dilapidated dwellings with new ones.

Furthermore, in justifying the decision not to build in census tract 5, the reformers identified that population as the so-called undeserving poor. According to Stanley Rowe, many "habitual slum dweller[s]" who were "ignorant and shifting" lived in census tract 5. Even worse, Rowe confided, they were "incapable of rehabilitation and a serious liability to our community." By building north of this stinkhole, Rowe claimed that the CMHA was protecting the rest of the city from the expansion of this degraded area. And finally, Rowe noted that those in census tract 5 could not afford public housing, so if that area was cleared, its residents would scatter northward where they "would create another area similar to the one in which they now live." [18]

The new definition of good low-cost housing in Cincinnati, then, excluded the city's neediest. Now, the emphasis was on housing—the process of providing an appropriate setting for the development of beneficial cultural traits—rather than on the poor and their need for adequate shelter. Furthermore, public housing modeled the type of neighborhood settings that housing reformers hoped would be duplicated throughout the metropolitan community for all the city's residents. Local promoters of the community housing strategy had received an additional boost when the Resettlement Administration in the mid-1930s decided to build a new town on Cincinnati's outskirts.

When federal officials announced on November 25, 1935, their intention to build Greenhills in the Cincinnati metropolitan region, Cincinnatians saw a local precedent for this controversial and innovative approach to community building. Mariemont, which had been developed during the twenties, as we have seen, offered neighborhood and regional solutions to Greater Cincinnati's low-cost housing problem. In fact, its planner, John Nolen, now served as an assistant town planner for the proposed new town of Greenhills. And one of his assistants, Justin Hartzog, who had planned the parks for Mariemont, now headed the federal planning staff for Greenhills. [19]

Greenhills, however, would be more than merely an updated version of Mariemont. That project had been planned to accommodate between 1,200 and 1,500 families of mixed incomes on 300 acres of land. In comparison, the Resettlement Administration purchased nearly 39,000 acres and planned to build several large self-contained communities of 1,000 families each. In addition, the plan called for the integration of the rural and urban aspects of the region into a more cohesive whole through fostering farms and subsistence homesteads as well as neighborhood housing for the factory worker. To ensure the maintenance of this experiment in regional planning, Resettlement Administrators preserved a greenbelt of wooded and vacant land around the development to protect it from uncontrolled spillover from neighboring areas. [20]

Although the Suburban Division of the Resettlement Administration (RA) used money from the Federal Emergency Relief Act of 1935 to fund the greenbelt project, it meant to do more than supply temporary relief for those thrown out of work from the depression. RA officials hoped their greenbelt program would demonstrate the social and economic benefits provided by good planning—for both the local community and the larger metropolitan area. In addition, they planned Greenhills so that the new town's occupants could "enjoy the advantages of an urban community and at the same time have all the benefits of rural life." [21]

Unlike earlier federal efforts to promote low-cost housing in the Cincinnati area, the initiative for the Greenhills project came from federal officials, rather than from local housing reformers. The RA, formed by Roosevelt's executive order on April 30, 1935, surveyed the nation's 100 largest cities in order to discover the best locations for its experimental developments. Rexford Tugwell, who headed the RA, agreed with the findings of the Research Section of the RA's Division of Suburban Resettlement and selected the Cincinnati area for a project. The Queen City's "good industrial record, its favorable labor situation, and its low vacancy rate pointing to an immediate housing shortage" helped convince the RA chief to locate a greenbelt project nearby. [22]

While some critics of the project claimed that the federal government had arbitrarily imposed its new town on a reluctant metropolitan community, the actions of local housing officials and reformers suggest otherwise. In fact, the RA not only consulted and sought the advice of these people, but also met with local officials to gain their endorsements. For instance, after talking with federal officials, both City Manager C. A. Dykstra and City Planner Myron Downs agreed that Greenhills would indeed help eliminate the area's low-cost housing problem. [23]

Local housing reformers and area officials accepted and promoted the Greenhills project, in part, because its purposes coincided with their goals of creating good neighborhood housing and of encouraging orderly metropolitan growth so that future slums could not develop. Greenhills, which attempted to promote the positive features of both urban and rural life, would serve as a model for suburban development.

That the project's planners worked out of an office in Washington did not mean they ignored the peculiar features of the Cincinnati region or that they created standardized new towns for Greenhills and its sister greenbelt cities, Greendale, Wisconsin (near Milwaukee) and Greenbelt, Maryland (outside of Washington, D.C.). In fact, they were under specific instructions from the RA to fit Greenhills into the Cincinnati metropolitan region and to adapt the new town to local needs. To facilitate this requirement, the Resettlement Administration's Research Section undertook a series of investigations and surveys of the area's characteristics and the needs of its people. [24] Not only did the federal RA officials plan Greenhills "in relation to all existing topographic and regional considerations of drainage, traffic, industry, land use and recreation," but they also designed the project "with consideration of the way people [in the region] live, their habits, likes, [and] dislikes."[25]

For instance, the Research Section of the Suburban Division of the RA, headed by Warren Jay Vinton, undertook a field study of the "characteristics, customs and living habits of potential tenants of the Greenhills project" in order to help determine the "planning, design, construction and equipment of the dwelling units."[26] Planners worked from the assumption that the metropolitan region was a real social, economic, and cultural entity, not an artificial political unit like a city or town. As a result, they attempted to identify the region's important and distinguishing characteristics so that their project might better fit into Greater Cincinnati.

Albert L. Miller, the RA's regional coordinator, oversaw this task in Cincinnati. He consulted both surveys and local officials to assure the successful integration of Greenhills into the metropolitan community and publicized the benefits of this approach.[27]

According to Miller, Greenhills would contribute to a more cohesive metropolitan community by providing "new patterns of living in which the old lines between city and county are virtually wiped out." Farmers would supply the community with milk, vegetables, fruits, and meats while sharing the town's community facilities, thus making an environment, Miller noted, "in which farmers, industrial, and office workers are fellow citizens."[28]

The project would also demonstrate how to develop properly the outskirts of urban areas, which according to John Lansill, were rapidly being filled up with "jerribuilt shacks, misplaced factories [and] filling stations." By using careful planning procedures and working closely with the county's Regional Planning Commission, Justin Hartzog thought that Greenhills would be "protected from the dangers of isolation and stagnation by a planned integration with regional highway and recreational facilities."[29] And in a paper delivered at the American City Planning Institute, Hartzog suggested that if Greenhills were to have any national importance, "such influence [would depend] upon the degree of local success in aiding the future of the metropolitan pattern of Cincinnati."[30]

Besides improving the metropolitan community, Greenhills would, according to Hartzog, provide an appropriate setting for "well rounded community life . . . through its provisions for schools, stores, churches, playgrounds, and houses." Greenhills, then, would provide a good environment for a metropolitan region desperately in need of good low-cost housing.[31]

In fact, the planners' concern with creating appropriate neighborhood communities equaled their interest in planning for the metropolitan area. When planners developed the first (and only) town site, they proposed a setting not only of adequate dwellings, but of open space, sunlight, and pleasant surroundings for the "low-income families now inadequately housed in over-crowded industrial cities." Through skillful planning, they wished to provide a setting fostering primary relationships and an identification with the community.[32] Thus, they planned not only parks, playgrounds, and allotment gardens, but also a community center and other focal points to encourage face-to-face meetings and the interchange of ideas. The proposed community building was located in the town's center and fronted by a grassy commons. As the focal point of the community, it would house the entertainment and adult cultural center, along with educational facilities. And just northwest of the community center, planners proposed a business and civic center which would include a general store, a drug store, a barber shop, a post office, and branch banks, besides a small town hall which would house the management and service departments.[33]

Greenhill's officials not only attempted to encourage community through the development of community facilities but also constructed residential areas in a way to foster neighborliness. For example, they planned housing in a circular pattern with dwellings facing inward away from street traffic and toward the open spaces, gardens, and play spaces that they surrounded. These carefully developed "super blocks" were contoured to the land and surrounded by beautiful trees and wilderness, allowing for "an island of decent, peaceful homelife."[34]

In addition to paying careful attention to the physical layout of the town, federal officials gave attention to the human element too. They screened applicants wishing to live in the greenbelt town, making sure they met the selection criteria. In order to gain admittance, applicants filled out fourteen different forms. Only residents of the Cincinnati metropolitan area who maintained an income between $1,000 and $2,000 were eligible. Potential town residents underwent both a security and a credit check. Social workers also visited their current living quarters, and quizzed them on their attitudes toward financial obligations and their care of property. Martha Francis Allen, the federal official who oversaw the selection process, explained the tough requirements by noting that the government wanted only families "with a capacity for community citizenship."[35]

When Carlton F. Sharpe became Greenhills' first community manager, he also pushed the development of "community citizenship" by promoting associational activity. He apparently succeeded. Within two years of the town's occupancy, more than twenty community organizations appeared, including a Consumer Services Corporation to manage the retail stores in the shopping center. Furthermore, the RA encouraged the formation of a nine-member community council responsible for advising the federally appointed community manager in the governance of the town.[36]

Some close observers of the new town, such as Sharpe, believed that the community building efforts were successful. Evaluating the impact of the greenbelt town on its second anniversary, the community manager observed that citizens who were just "one in a thousand" in Cincinnati now participated in dozens of activities at Greenhills.[37] There can be little dispute over what the intentions of Greenhills' planners had been. They wished to foster a sense of localized community for low-income families within the larger metropolitan region. Such action, they hoped, would improve the social and economic well-being of the needy and create a model for emulation in the regional development of Greater Cincinnati.

Greenhills, as well as Laurel Homes, the city's first slum clearance and public housing project, were responses to the housing problem as defined in the 1930s. Bad land mix, deteriorated housing and a heterogeneous population had resulted in slum conditions and a "slum mentality." Carefully regulated land use, well-constructed dwelling units and a homogeneous population might result in a more productive citizenry. The Laurel Homes project attempted better housing by replacing the dangerous environment of the slums with a carefully planned neighborhood housing development. Greenhills, a more ambitious project, attempted to develop a larger part of the metropolitan area through neighborhood, town, and regional planning.

Both approaches, while different in particulars, shared the same ends—the bettering of the metropolitan community through the development of better housing. However neither served the neediest, since expenses involved in creating good housing pushed rents out of the range of most poor. Many of the indigent who had been displaced by Laurel Homes failed to meet the financial eligibility requirements. And when Greenhills opened up, most of its occupants were from the skilled or white-collar occupations.[38] Meanwhile, the poor remained in the decrepit basin, waiting on both local and national officials for help.

CHAPTER 8

Cincinnati's Vacant Land Project Controversy

> If we were visionaries we could be entirely consistent and recommend moving the population entirely out of the West End. But unfortunately it is necessary to sacrifice ideals for necessity. The basin cannot be abandoned. So even though we would prefer development of housing on vacant land, the second phase, building of apartments on the slum sites must be carried out too, as rapidly as overcrowding is relieved by these vacant land projects.
>
> —Bleecker Marquette, Oct. 4, 1938

> We have opposed suburban housing for the reason that 95% of the so-called "slum area" is colored and the suburban housing is represented as being exclusively for white persons. They will accept no one on relief in these projects. It can be easily seen that these suburban projects can have no effect on crime or health costs as only 5% of the occupants in the real slum area could get into the suburban projects if they otherwise qualified.
>
> —W. Ray Skivin, Nov. 1, 1938

Cincinnati, like other cities throughout the nation, experienced controversy over the placement of public housing projects.[1] But unlike Philadelphia, where John Bauman found conflict between so-called professional housers like Bernard Newman, who supported slum clearance projects, and so-called communitarians, like Catherine Bauer, who favored vacant land projects, Cincinnati housing and planning activists seemed in agreement that the city needed a balanced public housing program.[2] The lack of conflict is understandable if one remembers that both parties in Cincinnati not only embraced the community development approach to housing, but also accepted the close relationship between comprehensive planning and housing betterment. As a result, Alfred Bettman and Bleecker Marquette, individuals with very different backgrounds, agreed with the city's balanced public housing program. They supported, and the CMHA developed, slum clearance public housing projects only in parts of the basin conducive to large-scale, low-density, community development projects.[3] And since the community development slum clearance projects would house fewer residents than the number displaced, the two agreed that vacant land projects were necessary to house the excess population.

Controversy did occur in Cincinnati, however, when the federal government's first permanent public housing program developed building criteria which kept the CMHA from undertaking additional West End redevelopment projects. As a result, the CMHA turned to a vacant land strategy. This decision created a great furor among segments of the city's population. Indeed, the high costs of building slum clearance projects using the community development strategy, as well as the stringent requirements of the new federal housing program, resulted in conflict which clearly threatened the future of public housing in Cincinnati.

At first, local public housing supporters greeted the Housing Act of 1937 enthusiastically. Rather than question the stringent building requirements of the new program, they focused on the more prominent role it prescribed for the local housing authority. Instead of authorizing the federal government to build public housing, the law created the United States Housing Authority (USHA) and authorized it "to make loans to public agencies to assist the development, acquisition or administration of low rent housing or slum clearance projects by such agencies."[4]

Unlike the Housing Division of the PWA which it replaced, the USHA would not develop and construct the projects but merely lend money (up to 90 percent of building costs for sixty years) to local housing authorities. The USHA also made annual contributions available for local public housing authorities "to assist in achieving and maintaining the low rent character of their housing projects." In addition, the law required that the "political subdivision in which the project is situated shall contribute in the form of cash or tax remissions, general or special, or tax exemptions, at least 20 per centum of the annual contribution herein provided."[5] Although this provision eventually caused controversy in Cincinnati, particularly after the postponement of slum clearance and public housing for West End blacks, city council's finance committee showed an initial willingness to cooperate with the housing authority in any way "legally and financially possible." The CMHA gleaned from that December 8, 1937, meeting a commitment on the part of city council to meet its responsibilities with regard to public housing as defined by the Housing Act of 1937.[6]

Under the 1937 Housing Act, the three main participants—the local authority, council, and the federal government—remained. But now their responsibilities and duties changed somewhat. For instance, the new act assigned the local housing authority more responsibility in the building and maintenance of the project. Nonetheless the USHA, which was responsible for carrying out the 1937 law, retained much power over the final development of local housing projects. It still possessed the final say as to the project's location and type. For example, the USHA denied the CMHA its vacant land site for black low-income housing in an area north of suburban Lockland. And later, the USHA indefinitely postponed the CMHA's proposed slum clearance project for blacks in the West End despite the loud protests of the local housing authority and council.[7] The USHA also checked on the CMHA to insure that the local housing authority maintained federal standards and followed federal guidelines. Under the new law, the USHA still had final approval over architects' drawings and continually monitored the work of contractors. Another example of federal watchfulness occurred on November 11, 1941, when William E. Hill, regional racial adviser for the USHA, investigated the failure of local contractors to employ the percentage of black skilled mechanics specified by USHA regulations.[8] Although the 1937 Housing Act decentralized the federal slum clearance and public housing program by giving local authorities new responsibilities, federal officials through the USHA retained much of their power to shape and direct the final outcome of those projects. Indeed, for a while it appeared that federal regulations might prevent further slum clearance in Cincinnati.

Soon after Congress passed the Housing Act of 1937, the USHA appropriated $10.5 million for Cincinnati to help in that city's slum clearance and low-cost housing effort. Unfortunately for the Ohio River city, one provision of the law limiting the building costs of housing projects to $1,000 per room created an obstacle which inhibited and temporarily delayed the city's slum clearance efforts. In addition, the USHA required land costs not to exceed $1.50 per square foot. That requirement alone forced the CMHA to build its next two projects on vacant land because local housing officials could not meet the USHA's restrictions in the basin.[9]

Frustrated by these seemingly unrealistic cost limitations (land for Laurel Homes had cost $2.20 per square foot), local housing officials momentarily shelved a $3.4-million basin slum clearance project for blacks that it had planned for an area directly south of Laurel Homes. After five months of attempting to meet the rigid new requirements, the CMHA on the advice of federal housing officials turned its attention to building two vacant land projects.[10]

From the start, the CMHA anticipated using new federal money for building a vacant land project for whites at an Este Avenue location and a black vacant land project at a site north of the suburban town of Lockland.[11] Unfortunately for the city's black population, Washington housing officials disapproved of the north-of-Lockland site because of its distance from downtown as well as its lack of schools and utilities. As a result of this decision, and because of the widespread local prejudice against blacks which precluded the use of the Lane Seminary site on one of the hilltops looking over the basin, local housing authorities suspended their plans for a black vacant land project.[12] Instead, the USHA persuaded the CMHA to develop a second vacant land project for whites in North Fairmount on the city's near West Side.[13] On September 7, 1938, the USHA awarded the CMHA a $7,101,000 loan to build two vacant land projects, each to house 750 families.[14]

While local housing reformers heartily endorsed vacant land projects as an inexpensive way to develop a sense of neighborhood community, help correct bad housing conditions outside the basin, and provide needed replacement housing for those uprooted by basin slum clearance, some of the city's realtors, bankers, builders, and property owners viewed these developments with suspicion. Indeed, when the CMHA informed city council's public institutions committee on April 13 that it was postponing slum clearance and building vacant land projects, several groups voiced their strong displeasure. The CMHA's decision enraged the local Real Estate Board and the Savings and Loan Association, which consistently opposed public housing, and it also bothered some who had supported slum clearance. The former claimed that vacant land projects threatened land values and the private housing market even more than slum clearance did. The Hamilton County League of Building and Loan Associations and the Property Owners Association also took this stand. Their executive secretaries, W. Ray Skirvin and Randolph Sellars, had led a vicious but losing fight against Greenhills, the federal greenbelt town, during the winter of 1935–36. So when Skirvin learned that the CMHA intended to build two vacant land projects, he responded that such action was "a direct threat to home ownership in the two districts involved," and helped organize opposition to the projects.[15]

Others, because of either personal interests or philanthropic concern, also reacted to the apparent neglect of the basin's West End, the worst-housed area in the city. On July 1, 1938, the Realty Owners Association initiated a campaign to locate the next federal housing project in census tract 5, located in the West End, the city's worst slum area. Claiming that it could support "only properly located slum clearance," this association of basin property owners argued that redevelopment of tract 5 would not only revitalize that poorly housed area but also help the district to the east "now suffering blight from this slum area." Furthermore, it opposed any development of suburban projects since these would be in "direct competition with existing homes built by private enterprise and a hindrance to future building in these communities."[16]

The vacant land projects encountered further opposition from certain black organizations which believed that the redevelopment of the West End, the home of most of the city's blacks, should receive top priority from local housing authorities. That opposition grew even stronger after the Housing Authority announced in September that both vacant land projects would be for whites because of the problems in securing an adequate site on which to house blacks.[17]

During this time of controversy, the CMHA requested council to strike an agreement with the U.S. Housing Authority. In order to secure federal loans and grants necessary to build the two projects, local governments were obligated to provide free municipal services and tax exemption for the proposed projects. When city council held a September public hearing on this proposition, more than 400 attended and voiced opinions both pro and con. A petition from the committee on resolutions, representing a variety of real-estate and banking interests as well as some civic associations, opposed council's contracting with the USHA because it feared that council would be forfeiting some of its sovereign power, the right of taxation.[18] The Hamilton County League of Building and Loan Associations took up this same theme and protested that the city's contract with the USHA for tax exemption would create tax-free districts in the city and would set up the CMHA as a "Super Government" over the entire city. Furthermore, according to the league, that "Super Government [would] take orders from Washington because Washington [was] furnishing the money; and back of it all [was] a gigantic plan of regimentation."[19] Another group at the hearing, the West Side Real Estate Owners Association, claimed that it could secure slum land in census tract 5 for $1.50 an acre, thus meeting the USHA's requirements for slum clearance. According to the association, the CMHA had not tried hard enough in its search for available West End housing sites. Therefore, it too opposed the proposed contract between city council and the USHA.[20]

In an attempt to counter the opposition to the vacant land projects on account of the tax issue, CMHA director Stanley Rowe announced at the hearing that Nathan Straus, head of the USHA, agreed to pay the city a service charge of 2.5 percent for the two vacant land projects. According to Rowe, this would provide a revenue of $38,500, which was $1,400 more than presently collected from the sites. Rowe also reaffirmed the CMHA's commitment to a balanced public housing program and argued that vacant land housing projects were absolutely necessary to house those scheduled for displacement by slum clearance. Furthermore, Rowe reminded his audience that the USHA already had allocated money for a black slum clearance project in the West End and the current housing law was being amended to allow the CMHA to proceed with slum clearance in the near future.[21]

The CMHA's vacant land projects generated so much controversy in Cincinnati that the City Charter Committee felt it important to meet and clarify its position on the entire public housing matter. As a result, this political reform organization which had initiated the local good-government movement voted to endorse a public housing program "which has as its goal the destruction of slum dwellings—particularly in the basin—and their replacement with proper housing." It also supported vacant land projects for the relocation of tenants displaced by slum clearance. Councilmen Charles P. Taft, Albert D. Cash, Edward N. Waldvogel, and Russell Wilson, all Charterites, attended the meeting. The local Republican party, which also had four councilmen (the ninth member of council was an independent), generally attacked increased government spending and excessive federal involvement in local affairs, issues closely related to public housing. Despite the Republican criticism of the Charterites' social and economic programs as nothing but "extravagant promises of the campaign," at least one Republican council candidate, Charles Urban, strongly favored actions which would create a slumless Cincinnati.[22]

Council itself worked very slowly during the vacant land housing dispute. In part, this reflected the controversial nature of the issue but it also resulted from a new balance of power in council. The Charterites lost their majority in 1935 when independent candidate Herbert Bigelow won a spot on council. Despite this setback, Charterites had struck a bargain with Bigelow, who helped them elect a Charterite mayor and implement certain programs. That changed in 1937, when Bigelow ran for Congress and was replaced on council by another independent, Wiley Craig. This labor man struck a deal with the Republicans in return for labor representation on the Civil Service Commission. As a result, his deciding vote helped elect James G. Stewart as mayor, the first Republican since 1921 to hold that office.[23]

Although council's public institutions committee voted unanimously on October 6, 1938, to support the ordinance authorizing the USHA-council contract, Willis Gradison, head of the finance committee, asked that the ordinance be routed to his committee so it could search for hidden expenses. Soon after the finance committee got hold of the bill, it instructed the new city manager, C. O. Sherrill, to analyze the bill and report what it required of the city at the next council meeting.[24]

Council postponed any action at that meeting, however, when Sherrill failed to complete his report. Despite the CMHA's assurances that Cincinnati would be obligated to furnish no other services for the vacant land public housing projects than for any private subdivision, council refused to act until it received Sherrill's report. Issued on October 17, Sherrill's findings basically substantiated the authority's claims. The report estimated that the city would spend approximately $36,000 per year for highway maintenance, waste collection, police and fire protection, water works services, health services, and street lighting for the two vacant land developments.[25]

If Sherrill's report settled one controversy, it did nothing to resolve several other differences brought on by the vacant land proposals. For instance, when the CMHA announced in September that it would build no vacant land housing for blacks, certain influential black leaders protested. Republican Councilman R. P. McClain opposed the white vacant land housing projects and argued that he would support no public housing until the West End slum clearance project was underway. And Theodore Berry, head of the Community Chest's Division of Negro Welfare housing committee, agreed to support the vacant land projects only after housing officials assured him that the CMHA would shortly initiate slum clearance in the West End.[26]

Opposition came not only from real-estate interests and influential blacks, but also from specific neighborhood organizations. When rumors circulated that one of the vacant land projects would be located on the West Side, the Westwood Civic Association, the Westwood Improvement Association, and the Western Hills Business Men's Association all actively campaigned against the proposals.[27] This massive protest encouraged council to deliberate slowly on the contract, thus stalling the CMHA's public housing program for metropolitan Cincinnati.[28]

Council finally voted on the issue on November 20, 1938. At that time, public housing supporters argued that the Cincinnati lawmakers should pass the ordinance of cooperation as an emergency measure to thwart plans by the opposition to initiate a time-consuming referendum on the subject. In order to secure the necessary two-thirds votes for the emergency stipulation, Charterite Charles P. Taft, son of President William Howard Taft, introduced an amendment to the bill which stipulated that only $7.1 million of the allocated $13.5 million could be spent on vacant land projects. The rest would be spent on basin slum clearance for blacks. Apparently this amendment worked, for the ordinance received its necessary two-thirds support, 6–3, thus ending what the *Enquirer* described as "one of the most controversial issues considered in Council in recent years."[29]

Those voting against the ordinance, Republican Willis Gradison, R. P. McClain, and Mayor James Stewart, cited specific problems in the present program, and not philosophical misgivings about the general nature of slum clearance and large-scale, low-income housing development. When explaining his unhappiness with the local public housing ordinance, Gradison condemned the wastefulness and extravagance of the federal program. McClain, a black councilman, voted against the ordinance of cooperation because he disagreed with local CMHA priorities which resulted in low-cost housing for whites but not blacks. Finally, Mayor Stewart opposed the ordinance because of disillusionment with Laurel Homes. According to the mayor, the city's first public housing project had done "nothing toward clearing a single slum." Tenants of Laurel Homes, he declared, held steady jobs, paid their rent regularly and were not liabilities to the community in need of rehabilitation. The really needy ones, according to Stewart, had been shut out by the stringent occupancy requirements.[30]

When council passed the ordinance, the local fight over public housing turned to the courts as discontented citizens filed suits against Cincinnati's proposed public housing projects. For example, William J. Schultz sued to enjoin the city from employing the emergency clause. According to Eli G. Frankinstein, Schultz's lawyer, no emergency existed. The Ohio Supreme Court thought otherwise, denied the suit, and ruled that council could determine its own emergencies.[31]

Another suit brought by Walter K. Sibbald, however, held up construction of the vacant land projects for fifteen months. Sibbald contended that the proposed projects were neither low-rent housing nor slum clearance as authorized by the Ohio State Housing Act, and threatened to sue unless the city tested the law.[32] In order to avoid a lengthy case through the lower courts, the city agreed to test the validity of the act by taking the issue directly to the Ohio Supreme Court. To make this possible, City Manager Sherrill agreed not to sign the contract between council and the CMHA so City Solicitor John D. Ellis could seek a court-issued mandamus. On February 28, 1940, the Supreme Court decided the case of the *State ex rel. Ellis v. Sherrill* in favor of the plaintiff by a vote of 4–3. According to the court, the Ohio State Housing Act permitted the CMHA to use judgment and discretion. In reviewing the program of the CMHA, the court concluded that "on the whole" it offered "a carefully conceived and balanced plan to abolish selected slum areas in the city of Cincinnati and to provide low rent dwelling units within the municipal limits." Since the CMHA exercised judgment and discretion within the lawful limits, the court concluded, "no basis is afforded for judicial intervention."[33] As a result of that court decision, which forced Sherrill to execute the contract with the CMHA, construction finally commenced on the two projects.

Although the local housing authority differed with the USHA over cost limitation and site locations, the two groups fully agreed that the vacant land projects should be community developments containing not only new and sanitary dwellings but also low-density housing, open spaces, and recreational grounds. By building on larger plots of vacant land in relatively isolated areas within the city, CMHA officials believed they could both save money and develop distinct neighborhood units to improve working-class tenants. The cost differential between land in the basin and in the outlying areas was astounding. The land for Laurel Homes cost approximately $2.20 per square foot. The land for the proposed vacant land projects cost about two cents per square foot. Because of this, the two new projects were much more successful than Laurel Homes in limiting land coverage and density. While Laurel Homes covered 30 percent of the site, the two vacant land projects—English Woods and Winton Terrace—covered only 10 percent of their sites. The same held true for population density. Because of the basin's high land costs, developers found it necessary to build moderately large multistory dwellings which resulted in a population density of sixty-four families per acre. The two vacant land projects, by comparison, averaged twelve families to the acre. Indeed, their two-story row houses and large open spaces provided a more homelike environment. Low land costs also allowed the CMHA to purchase an extra 173 acres "for a protective belt" bordering the sixty-seven developed acres of Winton Terrace while it maintained forty-six undeveloped acres at the English Woods site for the same purposes: protecting and defining the neighborhood community.[34]

At the Winton Terrace site, which USHA head Nathan Straus called "one of the finest in this country," the CMHA not only built 750 units in groups of six to ten dwellings with separate entrances for each family, but also constructed a separate community building. It would house the project's offices and maintenance shops as well as its recreational and social facilities. Housing Authority members also planned to locate a small commercial center next to the community center which would provide space for four neighborhood businesses. Finally, the CMHA developed on the site's northeast corner recreational space which included a playing field and a wooded picnic area.[35]

The English Woods project, located in North Fairmount just west of the Hopple Street viaduct and built on a 105-acre plot of open plateau and hilly, wooded terrain, also offered neighborhood community to its working-class inhabitants.[36] Both vacant land projects, then, proposed to help remedy the city's low-cost housing problems in similar ways. First, the projects would expedite downtown slum clearance by providing dwellings outside the basin for those displaced by slum removal. Just as important, however, vacant land projects allowed the city's Housing Authority to build a better environment for less than the cost possible in the basin.[37]

Soon after Winton Terrace opened on June 9, 1941, members of the Junior League toured the project and agreed that local housing officials had indeed created a community setting. According to one club member, "Winton Terrace is very much like a small independent village, as it has an administration building where community meetings are held and the people choose their own council." [38]

While Winton Terrace and English Woods thus reflected the community emphasis of Cincinnati housing reformers, the controversy over those projects demonstrated some of the problems involved in that approach to public housing. The emphasis on low-density, large-scale community projects required large plots of land. Clearing and rebuilding in the center city proved very expensive and time-consuming, while building in outlying areas created other types of difficulties. For instance, the city's neediest housing group, blacks, were excluded from the first two vacant land projects because of race prejudice. Members of the CMHA, facing increased public housing opposition in

Cincinnati, did not want to give their enemies greater ammunition by locating black public housing projects near predominantly white areas. The vacant land policy proved to be just one of many CMHA policies which caused controversy in the black community. Indeed, the entire homogeneous community approach to low-cost housing adversely affected Cincinnati's black residents.

CHAPTER 9

Addressing the Black Housing Problem: Community and Racial Segregation, 1933–44

For segregation offers the group, and thereby the individuals who compose the group, a place and a role in the total organization of city life. Segregation limits development in certain directions, but releases it in others.

—Ernest W. Burgess, 1923

To stress environmental factors is to open new doors of opportunities and hope to colored Americans.

—Robert C. Weaver, 1938

From its beginning, the CMHA identified the black housing problem as an important issue. In its initial request for federal help in slum clearance and public housing, the CMHA proposed to rebuild a section of the West End slum area with three separate neighborhood units—one for blacks and two for whites. The CMHA proposal also requested funds to develop a vacant land community project to house blacks north of suburban Lockland. Although the PWA Housing Division approved part of the proposal for the West End, the CMHA constructed neither a separate West End unit nor the vacant land project for blacks. Nevertheless, by the time it completed Cincinnati's $21-million federally aided public housing program between 1933 and 1943, the CMHA allotted 48 percent of its dwellings to blacks (see table 9-A).[1]

Housing developments for blacks, like those for whites, attempted to counter the ill effects of slum conditions, which according to the CMHA, had detrimental effects upon both health and citizenship within the West End. As we have seen, to resolve this crisis reformers prescribed carefully planned housing developments which they believed would create a sense of local identity and a feeling of community. Once they destroyed the cultural barriers imposed by the slum, reformers thought that the manifestations of impersonal urban living—crime, delinquency, and other anti-social behavior—would be greatly reduced.[2]

The development of community oriented public housing seemed particularly important for blacks because the antipathy of whites blocked their opportunities to move into good neighborhoods. Of the 107 census tracts found within the city in 1930, only sixteen contained more than 500 blacks. The heaviest concentration of blacks remained in the West End. And of the 33,419 blacks found there, 90 percent resided in the area west of Plum Street and south of Liberty Street. Walnut Hills, located to the northeast of the basin, contained the second largest settlement of blacks (7,000). Smaller black settlements outside the basin existed in Madisonville, Avondale, Cumminsville-Northside, Camp Washington, Oakley, and Saylor Park (see map 9-A).[3]

Reformers, then, believed that public housing would permit poor but ambitious blacks to separate themselves from the demoralized people and the deteriorating physical conditions that gave slums their bad reputation. Freed from these distractions, blacks could experience the benefits of a community setting promoting good citizenship rather than slum settings which encouraged anomie and alienation.[4]

Despite their commitment to improving Cincinnati's black cultural setting, local reformers were not ready to open all the doors of opportunity for blacks. Fearful of white protest and community disorder, they refused to push for integrated housing at any level, including publicly built projects. Rather, they sought to create new black neighborhoods for poorly housed blacks. Yet this strategy fell short, since the CMHA would build housing projects for blacks only in already predominantly black residential areas. Nor would the CMHA locate black vacant land projects in less populated areas of the metropolis unless a sizable black population resided nearby. Other policies, too, like the slum clearance efforts and the relocation strategies of the CMHA, further perpetuated residential segregation in the city, thus confirming Arnold Hirsch's assessment that "local and federal authorities sustained rather than attacked, the status quo."[5]

The combination of increased black migration to the city in the teens and twenties, an enforced building code which eliminated many of the most affordable dwellings, and the unavailability of new dwellings for blacks created housing problems before the depression. As a result, the city's worst slums were occupied by blacks. With the Great Depression, black housing deteriorated even more. Local reformers recognized this and sought public housing for blacks in their initial application to the PWA. But when the PWA Housing Division cut its allocation to the CMHA, and the authority failed to secure land south of Lincoln Park Drive at a reasonable price, local housing officials decided that blacks would have to wait for their first West End slum clearance project. In addition, the Housing Division disapproved of the CMHA's

Table 9-A. Units, costs, and racial occupancy data, Cincinnati public housing projects, 1933–43.

	Laurel Homes	Laurel Homes Addition	Lincoln Court	Winton Terrace	English Woods	Valley Homes	Total
Total units	1,039	264	1,015	750	750	350	4,168
White units	667**		0	750	750	0	2,167
Black units	636**		1,015	0	0	350	2,001
Total cost	$6,615,607	$1,173,016	$5,738,293	$3,335,345	$3,752,368	$1,216,925	$21,831,554

**Number of units allocated in 1943. Originally 304 units were available for blacks.

Source: CMHA, *Tenth Annual Report 1943.*

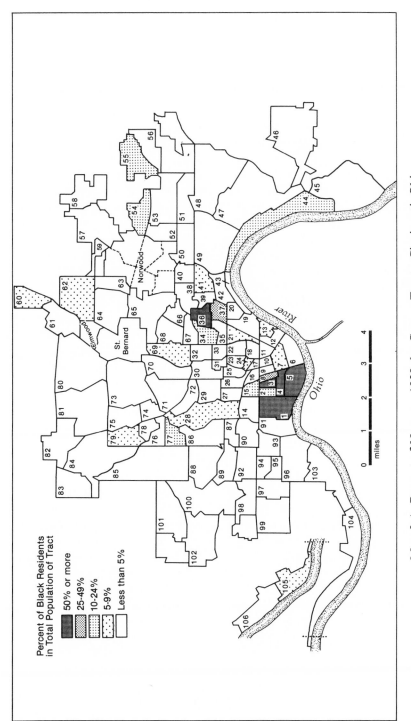

Map 9-A. Percent of Negroes, 1930, by Census Tracts, Cincinnati, Ohio

proposed vacant land project for black occupancy. Thus, when plans were completed, Cincinnati's first public housing project was scheduled for whites only.[6]

Although that decision was never officially announced, blacks feared the worst soon after the CMHA revealed that it did not intend to build in basin section F, an area earlier designated for black public housing. Not long after the Housing Division announced its $7-million housing project for sections J and K (see map 5-D), local blacks started questioning the CMHA over the proposed racial makeup of the project. The exchange between C. E. Dillard of the local branch of the NAACP and Stanley M. Rowe concerning the future occupancy of Laurel Homes typified the dialogue between blacks and housing officials over the issue. When Dillard asked the authority's specific intention, Rowe skirted the issue, noting that the buildings would be constructed as suitable dwellings for either white or black occupancy. He also claimed that the problem of tenancy was "largely a management problem" to be determined by the federal government "sometime later."[7]

Initially, local housing officials sought to postpone any formal announcement about the project's occupancy in the hope that they could obtain another PWA project for blacks, either the slum clearance or vacant land type, before Laurel Homes opened. They too feared that without publicly assisted housing the already intolerable living conditions of basin blacks would become worse. According to a survey of five basin tracts made in August 1933 by the Department of Public Welfare, 1,900 black families doubled up in dwellings with other families. An additional 1,200 families, according to the survey, lived in dwellings unfit for habitation.[8] Blacks, then, faced a severe housing shortage even before the demolition of the Laurel Homes site. After workers cleared that area, 769 black families comprising 61 percent of the site's occupants would be homeless. And since nearly 50 percent of those scheduled for displacement were on relief, relocation would be even more difficult. The CMHA, fearful of adverse publicity if the former Laurel Homes site occupants were not properly rehoused, met on October 26, 1934, with the Better Housing League and the Hamilton County director of public welfare to work out a suitable rehousing program. At that meeting the housing reformers decided to undertake a vacancy survey of the basin in hopes of finding adequate shelter for the dispossessed.[9] Toward this end, PWA District Manager Henry G. Chapman formally requested of FERA a works project covering the survey needs. Using grants from both the FERA and the WPA, local housing officials completed their inventory of available dwellings on August 2, 1935.[10]

The survey substantiated what local housing reformers had long suspected—there were few vacant tenements for blacks in the basin. It found only 674 dwellings in good or fair condition for the 769 black families to be displaced. With more than 400 of those families on relief, housing officials acknowledged that they would have problems moving the slum clearance site's residents.[11]

The County Welfare Department, charged with relocating relief families as well as paying their rent at the new location, had inadequate funds for the task and could offer only limited assistance. Because it never produced adequate rent money, landlords tended not to rent to relief families. No promise of better living conditions existed either, since all relief families fell well below the minimum income required to move into Laurel Homes.[12]

Despite the shortage of housing units for blacks and an inadequate relief system, local housing officials opened a field office at 526 Armory Avenue to help displaced tenants find new dwellings. The office furnished lists of vacant apartments, and gave special attention to routing the aged and the crippled to first-floor locations. Field office workers also attempted to relocate families of school-age children within the same school district. Families finding it particularly difficult to relocate in adequate housing were assisted by BHL visiting housekeepers, who helped in the search.[13]

The actual relocation process started on September 25, 1935, when officials first sent notices to tenants in the clearance site giving them one month to relocate. By February 20, 1936, all families had left the site.[14] According to the CMHA's report on relocation, slum site occupants needed neither coercion nor eviction to relocate. A follow-up study conducted by the visiting housekeepers of the Better Housing League reported that 75 percent of all displaced tenants relocated in accommodations as good or better than those they had been forced to vacate, including 228 black families who ended up in better housing after relocation. The housekeepers also discovered that 80 percent of the displaced persons relocated in their old school districts and another 10 percent moved to nearby neighborhoods.[15] Local housing officials admitted they had faced great difficulty in placing tenants housed on the Laurel Homes site, but proclaimed their relocation efforts a success.[16]

Local housing officials failed to emphasize that at least 102 black families were forced to relocate to substandard dwellings in need of extensive repair. Seventy-nine of those families suffered downward residential mobility, moving from housing rated good or fair by the building department into housing rated bad. Such statistics help explain why not all blacks viewed relocation with the same enthusiasm that white housing officials did. For instance, George W. B. Conrad wrote a scathing letter to President Roosevelt complaining that "no provision is being made for those who were forced to evacuate and those who may desire housing with modern conveniences." Such neglect, according to Conrad, bordered on criminality, and was "in every way morally and legally wrong and unjust."[17]

It is within this context that black leaders pleaded with CMHA officials to allow blacks into Laurel Homes. And when the CMHA responded that the

Housing Division of the PWA would ultimately determine the project's tenancy, local black leaders turned to the federal government. On December 10, 1935, Joshua M. Tadlock, chairman of the Negro Working Peoples Conference, inquired of PWA head Harold Ickes whether blacks would be housed in Laurel Homes. A. R. Clas, director of the Housing Division, answered his letter, replying that the federal government would be guided by the recommendations of the CMHA as to tenancy selection.[18] Other black leaders, such as Theodore M. Berry, head of the local branch of the NAACP, also questioned Washington about its plans and strongly urged housing allocations for blacks.[19]

Although the CMHA had decided to open up Laurel Homes for whites only, it continued to press Washington for additional housing. It lobbied hard for the vacant land project north of Lockland even after the Housing Division rejected the CMHA's initial application. The authority argued that the "great deal of racial feeling" in Cincinnati limited the sites in which it could build public housing for blacks. By locating the vacant land project near the black subdivisions which had appeared in the twenties, local officials hoped they could avoid the wrath of white neighbors and create at least some relocation housing for blacks from the basin. Something had to·be done, Bleecker Marquette warned, since "additional housing for Negroes is one of our pressing needs."[20]

Despite this admission, however, the CMHA still planned to open Laurel Homes as a housing project for whites only. Fearful of the response that such a decision might evoke from local blacks, the CMHA refused to publicize its plans despite pressure from various groups such as the Cincinnati Chapter of the NAACP, the Negro Working Peoples Conference, and the Negro Welfare Division of the Council of Social Agencies. Unhappy blacks from the Negro Welfare Division requested a formal hearing before the CMHA and forwarded a resolution to Washington requesting some black public housing. Not only did blacks continue to press for a decision on the Laurel Homes opening and black public housing in general, but they demanded some say in the selection process of tenants. For example, on September 15, 1936, a committee from the Negro Welfare Division met with George H. Wells and Bleecker Marquette of the CMHA and requested that a black be permitted to sit in an advisory capacity when the CMHA started choosing tenants for Laurel Homes.[21]

When the local authority failed to respond to the demands of the black community, frustrated blacks turned to elected officials for help. In the spring of 1937, local blacks sent a petition to President Franklin D. Roosevelt protesting the indifference shown them by local housing officials. In addition, they requested that the president intercede for them and order the local authority to admit blacks to the city's first public housing project.[22] Probably more important than their petition to Roosevelt, local blacks pressured city council to force a change in the CMHA's decision not to admit blacks to Laurel Homes.

Led by George W. B. Conrad, president of the Negro Housing Association, blacks protested at a May 19, 1937, meeting of council against the discriminatory and unjust treatment suffered at the hands of the CMHA. Conrad predicted the possibility of race riots if black housing conditions did not soon improve.[23] Council, however, appeared unimpressed and failed to act on the petition. Although council claimed it had no say in who should reside in Laurel Homes, local blacks disagreed, arguing that since council "had invested about $1 million in the project" it "should have something to say about the project."[24]

The combination of intense lobbying by Cincinnati blacks and its inability to secure a separate housing project for this vocal minority eventually convinced the CMHA to allow blacks admission into Laurel Homes. When he made the announcement on February 8, 1938, Stanley Rowe explained that the percentage of dwellings reserved for blacks would be in proportion to the ratio of blacks to whites eligible for admission to Laurel Homes.[25]

This decision hardly ended the controversy, however. Under the quota system, only 30 percent of the dwellings available in Laurel Homes were designated for blacks. And members of the CMHA apparently never considered housing blacks and whites in the same buildings. Instead, they set aside apartments A through F, located in the northernmost part of the project. Such a location for the 304 black families seemed rather curious because it lay far to the north of the supposed "natural" division between blacks and whites in the West End. However, these apartments were in the most isolated part of the project, a factor which probably explains their choice. Nor did the buildings designated for blacks contain any of the eighty-two five-room apartments included in the project, which effectively barred large black families from Laurel Homes.[26]

The stringent eligibility standards also served to limit the number of blacks admitted to Laurel Homes. Besides requiring good housekeeping standards and a high moral character, the CMHA checked the applicants' credit backgrounds and made sure they could pay the necessary rent. Furthermore, the CMHA refused to recognize common-law marriages and rented to married couples only.[27]

The allotment of limited public housing to blacks, then, merely changed the nature of controversy. Ad hoc groups such as the Negro Housing Association demanded that the CMHA allow more blacks into the project. Frustrated by its lack of influence on the CMHA, the association recommended that local officials appoint a black to serve on the CMHA. In addition, it requested that the CMHA hire a black assistant administrator "to provide a Negro point of view in public housing." Finally, the Negro Housing Association advised the

Division of Negro Welfare to pursue a more aggressive policy concerning public housing for blacks. Only with these changes did the Negro Housing Association believe that the CMHA might stop discriminating against blacks.[28]

The call for black representation in housing matters seemed justified, since blacks had been permitted little say in the low-cost housing program, despite the fact that the CMHA's housing policy clearly affected them. For instance, no black had ever served on the BHL's board of directors, a moving force behind the city's public housing movement. Although the league had black members, and employed black visiting housekeepers, neither of these groups strongly influenced BHL policy.

Prominent blacks, such as George W. B. Conrad, Dr. R. E. Beaman, and Boyd W. Overton, served on the board of directors of the Citizens' Committee on Slum Clearance and Low Cost Housing. That organization, however, primarily sought to mobilize public opinion for public housing and played a very small role in determining the nature and implementation of that policy in Cincinnati.[29]

Apparently the continued pressure of blacks for more participation in local public housing matters, along with the CMHA's desire to garner more support for its vacant land fight with council, led to some concessions. On October 31, 1938, the CMHA created the Negro Citizens' Advisory Committee, chaired by R. E. Clarke. The thirty-member committee provided blacks with their first chance to influence policy as it was being developed. About the same time, the CMHA employed Verna Greene, a black, to serve as management aid for Laurel Homes. These two developments suggest that Cincinnati blacks may have finally gained some influence in determining local housing policy.[30]

The impact of the new role of blacks should not be overestimated, however. According to one member of the Negro Advisory Committee, Oscar Grear, committee members faced the same type of resistance that other black groups had experienced from the CMHA—a preoccupation with quotas and fear of white antagonism to blacks in public housing. Both Marquette and Rowe argued that since whites made up nearly seven-eighths of Cincinnati's population, they should receive top priority in housing matters.[31] As long as the CMHA abided by such a philosophy blacks would find it nearly impossible to affect local housing policy.

Nevertheless, only after the formation of the Negro Citizens' Advisory Committee did the CMHA secure the USHA's approval for two black housing projects—one a slum clearance and the other a vacant land project.[32] The USHA approved a black slum clearance project for sites L and M, located south of Lincoln Park Drive in the West End (see map 6-A). Since its inception, the CMHA had planned clearance and public housing for that slum area.

When the CMHA altered its original decision to build its first public housing in areas E and L (see map 5-B) because of fiscal cutbacks and difficulty in securing the necessary land, it did not abandon this goal. Even as it oversaw the construction of Laurel Homes, the CMHA applied for monies to build a slum clearance project for blacks in areas E and L. After the passage of the Housing Act of 1937 which created the USHA, local housing officials submitted a proposal for a three-pronged attack on the city's housing problem, including both vacant land and slum clearance public housing for blacks. As we have seen, it found no adequate site for blacks, however, and built two projects for whites.[33]

Only after Cincinnati's black housing deteriorated to an all-time low did USHA head Nathan Straus waive the $1.50 per square foot slum land cost and grant the CMHA a $5,371,000 loan for black public housing in sections L and M of the basin.[34] Despite a tremendous influx of blacks into the West End since 1900, and a 22-percent increase in the black population between 1930 and 1940, observers discovered that the number of low-income housing units had declined by more than 5,000 between 1929 and 1937. Most of these units had been in the basin. Although builders erected 9,225 units during the same time, only 519 of these rented for $30 a month or less, the amount laborers could pay.[35] And even with the demolition of 5,582 low-rent housing units during these years, there remained over 40,000 substandard basin dwellings to help house the approximately 120,000 residents living there.[36] The resulting competition for housing left blacks on the short end. Racial segregation and price gouging limited the housing possibilities for blacks so much that the BHL reported in 1939 that of all the housing available for blacks, only 1.3 percent stood vacant. The normal vacancy rate was 5 percent.[37]

Such congestion made relocation for the 1939 slum clearance project even more difficult than earlier efforts. Although the project would eventually house 1,015 black families, it provided a net increase of only 38 additional black housing units, since prior to demolition, 977 black families, along with 302 white families, resided in the site area. Even worse, 410 of those black families depended on relief and another 184 required partial public assistance.[38]

The inadequacies of the city's relief program had not changed since 1936, when the CMHA relocated the Laurel Homes site tenants. Simply put, the City Welfare Department, which had taken over the relief duties in the city on October 15, 1937, when the County Welfare Department ran out of money, did not have enough funding to pay normal rents for families for which it accepted responsibility.[39] Not only was the Welfare Department's average rent payment of between $7 and $8 insufficient for many privately owned basin tenements, but it proved inadequate for publicly built housing too.[40]

Cincinnatians on relief not only received $4 less than Cleveland's maximum rate, but were required to pay $4 per month in rent money, even if they held no job. This policy resulted in a number of evictions.[41] The City Welfare Department's relief housing policy forced the poor into dilapidated buildings and crowded living conditions. Even more important for the CMHA, the miserly allocations made relocation even more difficult. Landlords refused to rent to relief families because the city's relief policy proved so stingy and unreliable. And finding affordable housing proved nearly impossible. In good times, the relocation of over 1,200 families would have been difficult, but during the depression it appeared nearly impossible.[42]

Placing white tenants, even those on relief, was not nearly as troublesome as relocating blacks, because there were approximately 1,900 vacancies for whites in the fourteen basin census tracks alone.[43] In contrast, a survey for black dwellings on the eve of the scheduled displacement found only 205 suitable vacancies for the 977 black families living on the site. Although this finding prompted some local officials to recommend the building of the new project in stages to prevent a massive housing shortage, the CMHA decided on another strategy to secure adequate housing for blacks.[44]

The CMHA concentrated on converting partially black neighborhoods into all black neighborhoods by persuading landlords currently renting to whites to rent to blacks. The relocation staff convinced landlords to switch by reminding them that blacks usually paid more than whites for equivalent housing. This exploitive plan apparently worked. Not only were most of the tenants moved relatively quickly, but a follow-up survey revealed that only 36 of the 1,346 families found after the move lived in worse conditions than they had at their old site. Moreover, 535 respondents claimed that they lived in better housing.[45]

Nonetheless, the problem of rehousing needy relief families persisted after most of the site's families relocated. On June 24, 1941, more than a month after the Cleveland Wrecking Company of Cincinnati started demolition of the future site of Lincoln Court, fifty-six families still remained on the site. Most of them were black and on relief. Sensitive to their problem, the CMHA made no effort to evict the families, the last of which finally moved on July 19, 1941.[46]

Not only did the CMHA successfully move over 1,300 families, but it claimed to have done so "without serious protest, either individual or organized, and with but a single eviction." Albert France, who along with Lois Jackson, Jeanne Biddle, Melvin Anderson, and Robert Wrenn, oversaw the effort, explained that their success stemmed from "an understanding of the 'West End'" and "common sense."[47]

Unfortunately for the CMHA, barriers other than tenant relocation impeded the completion of Cincinnati's first black slum clearance and public housing project. Defense preparations for World War II also complicated the local public housing project. This was not apparent at first, as both land acquisition and tenant relocation for Lincoln Court moved along more smoothly than for Laurel Homes. Because the CMHA rather than the federal government acquired the land, it could use the powers of condemnation authorized by the state housing law. Those powers allowed the local authority to assemble land for Lincoln Court in nearly half the time it had taken the federal government for Laurel Homes. Seventy-five condemnation suits facilitated land transfers and avoided lengthy title squabbles. Initiated on October 26, 1940, land acquisition was completed by May of 1941.[48]

During this same time, the CMHA advertised and awarded bids. On April 28, 1941, the CMHA signed contracts for the project's development totaling $3,392,834, including a single one for $2,293,750 to the M. J. Boyajohn Company of Columbus for general construction. Firms from New York, Cleveland, and Cincinnati also received contracts, for plumbing, heating, and electric work. A demolition crew from the Cleveland Wrecking Company began its work on the 400 buildings during the second week of May.[49]

Construction on the project, however, soon bogged down because of bad weather in the fall of 1941 and because of the shortage in building materials resulting from the nation's defense effort. Although Lincoln Court was supposed to be completed by September 1, 1942, wartime shortages delayed the project so that by December 15, 1941, the black housing project was six weeks behind schedule. To remedy some of the building delays caused by supply shortages, the CMHA obtained an A-4 blanket priority rating for its project from the War Productions Board. Although not a high priority rating such as the A-1 given to army or navy construction needs, A-4 seemed adequate to local housing authority members for obtaining needed Lincoln Court materials.[50]

The CMHA secured the A-4 rating only after making certain concessions to the War Productions Board, however. First, it agreed that all reasonable admission preference would be given to families of defense workers. Second, the CMHA agreed to permit defense workers with income ranges of up to $1,800 a year into the massive housing project, covering eighteen city blocks. Prior to wartime, the maximum income for admission was $1,550.[51]

Along with material shortages, another problem threatened the opening of Lincoln Court for the area's black families. In September 1942, housing officials and local blacks learned that the army might commandeer Lincoln Court for the billeting of white soldiers. Strong local opposition to the transfer probably helped influence the army to abandon the idea, but two months later it again eyed the project as a potential housing site, this time for black soldiers. Housing officials and blacks protested this possibility just as strongly as they had the earlier army proposition. Bleecker Marquette, acting for the CMHA, contacted the the newly created National Housing Agency and pleaded with it to forbid the army's threatened action because of the city's extreme housing shortage for blacks. At the same time, J. Harvey Kerns, executive secretary of the Community Chest Division of Negro Welfare, wrote to Henry Emmerich of the Federal Public Housing Administration (the replacement of the USHA), objecting to the army's contemplated action. The protests may again have helped the army decide against using the project, for on December 11, 1942, local blacks started moving into Lincoln Court.[52]

Many of the project's first tenants were not the basin's neediest blacks, but those fitting certain government criteria. According to the selection process, war workers who lived on the former site received first priority, and war workers living outside the site came next. Officials considered others only if vacancies remained after a thirty-day waiting period. As a result, although the CMHA dropped many of the credit and character checks used in screening prospective Laurel Homes tenants, new barriers appeared to thwart many of the basin's neediest from obtaining public housing in Lincoln Court.[53]

Except for its defense housing preference requirements, Lincoln Court resembled Laurel Homes in most other aspects. For example, Lincoln Court, like Laurel Homes, replaced congested housing and provided apartment units separated by open space, fresh air, and recreational space. Lincoln Court averaged 45.3 families per acre as opposed to 72 families per acre in the area before demolition. Furthermore, Lincoln Court was planned as a neighborhood community unit too. Toward this end, federal officials built the Lincoln Court Community Building on land donated by city council. Located at Gest and Linn Streets, the $396,000 community center included a gymnasium, an auditorium, and two swimming pools. In addition to the land, Cincinnati's council also shared in the cost of the outdoor swimming pool, the playground, and the center's landscaping. Completed on May 15, 1943, the center exemplified both federal and local government commitment toward providing a basis of neighborhood community. Accordingly, the $5,738,000 Lincoln Court project would provide more than mere shelter. The public housing project would furnish a community setting in which residents could experience the fullness of urban life within a smaller, cooperative neighborhood unit. The major difference between Laurel Homes and Lincoln Court was the all-black nature of the latter.[54]

Despite the construction of Lincoln Court, the housing shortage for blacks remained. WPA workers surveyed the number of housing vacancies in January of 1941, and found that only 1.2 percent of all livable dwellings available to blacks were unoccupied. By the summer of 1943, that vacancy rate fell to less than one-third of 1 percent. Had it not been for another black housing project completed for blacks in 1941, conditions might have been grimmer.[55]

Ever since its creation, the CMHA had attempted to develop low-cost housing for blacks in an unincorporated area north of the suburban town of Lockland. Only after the nation began rearmament and Congress passed new defense housing laws did the authority finally secure its long-sought project.

On July 27, 1940, the Wright Aeronautical Corporation announced its decision to locate a huge airplane engine factory in metropolitan Cincinnati. The federal government's decision to decentralize its source of airplane engines from the east and west coasts, along with an intensive lobbying effort by the local Chamber of Commerce, helped secure this economic plum. Funded by a $129-million loan from the Reconstruction Finance Corporation, the Wright Aeronautical Corporation's plant would become the largest employer in Hamilton County. As early as October 1941, the coordinator of defense housing predicted that the plant would employ more than 12,000 men and women, including 500 to 1,000 blacks.[56] The chamber predicted that the construction and operation of the plant would "carry general business activity to levels beyond even 1929," a pleasant prospect made even more satisfying by assurances from the company that the plant would continue to operate after the war.[57]

When the Wright Aeronautical Company announced nearly a month later that it would locate the plant on a 200-acre site north of Lockland near the old CMHA housing site, the CMHA acted quickly. Fearing that the airplane engine factory would draw more blacks to the area already experiencing deterioration and slum conditions, Bleecker Marquette and Stanley M. Rowe wired Washington and requested a $2-million black defense housing project near the plant.[58]

Local CMHA officials believed they now had a good chance of securing a vacant land project for blacks because Congress had recently authorized defense housing. On June 28, 1940, an amendment to the 1937 Housing Act permitted the USHA to build units for defense purposes. And later that same year Congress also passed the Lanham Act, which had an even greater impact on the Cincinnati metropolitan area. That act outlined a specific program for both publicly and privately built defense housing for temporary and permanent use. In fact, under Title I of the Lanham Act, the federal government undertook the largest public housing effort ever attempted in this country.[59]

Shortly after Congress approved the Lanham Act, local officials journeyed to Washington to confer with C. F. Palmer, defense housing coordinator. At that December meeting Palmer explained that only after Wright certified a need for housing near their plant would the federal works administrator and the housing coordinator act.[60]

Shortly after Wright did just that, Clark Foreman, assistant administrator for the Federal Works Agency, inspected the area around the plant and recommended a 350-unit housing project for blacks on the Medosch farm site recommended by the CMHA. During his June 28 visit, Foreman also explained that the FWA wanted the CMHA to act as its agent and construct the project. He also suggested that work should start immediately so that any further housing shortages might be arrested.[61] Formal approval came soon after the meeting in early July when Roosevelt authorized the 350-unit project and allocated $1,224,290 for the defense effort. On February 11, the CMHA formally agreed to build the defense housing project as the federal government's agent, thus becoming the first authority in the nation to do so.[62]

The CMHA assigned the responsibility of developing plans and negotiating contractors for the project to J. Stanley Raffety, manager of Laurel Homes. After specifications were drawn up, Raffety awarded the contract to Penker Associates, Cincinnati contractors, on a cost-plus-a-fixed-fee contract. Under this system, the Federal Works Agency paid the contractors a fixed fee and then furnished money for materials. This allowed the agency to build the project at the speed it desired because the more money it furnished for materials and labor, the quicker the project would be built.[63]

Work began on the project April 12, 1940, shortly after the government purchased the forty-six-acre Medosch farm site for $25,000. Builders completed the area's most rapidly constructed public housing project on October 23, 1941, four months after the Wright Aeronautical Corporation opened its nearby engine plant.[64] Called Valley Homes, the project consisted of three, four, and five-room apartments found in fifty-three two-story row houses. Although the foundation and first floors were concrete, the walls were wood frame with asbestos siding. According to the BHL, the contractors used the cheapest type of construction material for permanent housing available in the United States.[65]

Unfortunately for area blacks who desperately needed housing, Valley Homes' rent was not particularly cheap. And the CMHA, which managed as well as built the project for the FWA, admitted only defense workers into the project. Many blacks working at the Wright airplane engine plant found their 50 cents per hour income inadequate to pay the average $25 monthly rent at Valley Homes. Indeed, those who moved into Valley Homes paid almost $8 per month more than they had paid for their previous flats. This may help explain why Valley Homes filled up so slowly in its first years of existence. More than three months after it was completed, tenants occupied only 137 of the 350 dwelling units. Later, in May of 1942 after a slight rent reduction, the CMHA reported only a 63-percent occupancy rate, despite the severe housing shortage for local blacks.[66]

Both CMHA and FWA housing officials worried about the high vacancy rate of Valley Homes, since it had been constructed, in part, to alleviate the congestion blacks suffered in the West End.[67] Housing officials conceded that high rent discouraged occupancy, but cited other causes, too. BHL officials reported that Wright Company officials had discouraged its black employees from living at Valley Homes because it feared that black workers might easily

TABLE 9-B. Project rent and family income for 1942.

	Laurel Homes	Lincoln Court	Winton Terrace	English Woods	Valley Homes
Average monthly shelter rent[a]	$ 14.74	$ 14.94	$ 13.76	$ 13.30	$ 25.24
Average yearly shelter rent	$ 176.88	$179.28	$ 165.12	$ 159.60	$ 302.88
Average annual family income	$1,108.00	*	$1,778.00	$1,168.00	$1,512.74
Yearly rent as percentage of annual income	16.0%	*	9.3%[b]	13.7%	20.0%

*Unavailable data.

[a]Shelter rent does not include utilities, which were included in the quoted rent price for all projects except Valley Homes.

[b]Winton Terrace's percentage is lower than English Woods' because the former accepted over-income defense workers while English Woods did not.

Source: CMHA, *Ninth Annual Report 1942.*

organize. Another reason for the slow occupancy, according to the CMHA, was that blacks were reluctant to leave the familiar surroundings of the West End. Indeed, CMHA observers claimed that many blacks preferred to remain in the West End and wait for openings in Lincoln Court or Laurel Homes. Both these projects offered lower rents for their apartments than Valley Homes (see table 9-B). Also, those working in basin war industries were reluctant to move to Valley Homes because of its twelve-mile distance from their workplace (see table 9-C). Only after the summer of 1942 when additional work opportunities opened up for blacks at Wright did Valley Homes experience full occupancy.[68]

Despite the addition of new public housing units for the area's blacks between 1940 and 1942, the black housing shortage intensified. During this time nearly 1,680 public housing units had been either built or converted for black occupancy, in addition to the original 300 units at Laurel Homes.[69] Nevertheless, the housing shortage for blacks persisted (3,738 units in 1937), and even worsened, with the increase of black migrants during the war. By 1944, more than 30 percent of all doubled-up families were black, although blacks made up only 12 percent of the city's population. During that same year, the vacancy rate of habitable dwellings for blacks sank to .6 percent.[70]

Conditions deteriorated so rapidly that the city's Housing Bureau no longer vacated uninhabitable houses, and permitted the use of basements and attics

TABLE 9-C. Employers of heads of families at Valley Homes.

Wright Aeronautical Corporation	214
Cincinnati Milling Machine Company	63
Philip Carey Manufacturing Company	19
Sawbrook Steel Casting Company	18
Chemical Products Corporation	11
Lunkenheimer Company	5
Peerless Foundry Company	2
Cincinnati Foundry Company	2
Cincinnati Galvanizing Company	2
Buckeye Foundry Company	1
Chevrolet—Norwood	1
Chris Erhardt Foundry	1
E. I. DuPont Demours and Company	1
Heekin Can Company	1
King Mills Powder Works	1
W. S. Merrill Company	1
Williamson Heater Company	1
Total	344

Source: CMHA, *Ninth Annual Report 1942.*

for living purposes. The West End congestion spurred George Garties and Bleecker Marquette representing the CMHA to travel to Washington in 1943 to request funds for an additional white vacant land project so that Laurel Homes could be converted to an all-black project. Unsuccessful in this venture, they asked the War Manpower Commission to discourage further black migration to Cincinnati because of the housing shortage. When conditions failed to improve the next year, the BHL placed notices in selected Southern newspapers advising potential black in-migrants not to come to Cincinnati because of the housing shortage.[71]

In the midst of that black housing shortage, the CMHA's Laurel Homes white section suffered an unusually high vacancy rate. When Winton Terrace first opened its doors for whites in June of 1939, 136 white families transferred out of Laurel Homes to the new project. As late as May 1942, there remained about fifty vacant units in the white section of the Laurel Homes project. Meanwhile, many blacks languished on a waiting list for housing in their section of Laurel Homes. From this experience, the CMHA's leaders concluded that "there is definitely a tendency for white tenants to prefer other localities than the basin and not in such close proximity to colored sections."[72]

Local CMHA officials had worried about attracting whites to the biracial project from the beginning. As early as May 9, 1938, before Laurel Homes opened, housing officials requested the superintendent of schools to permit white families the privilege of sending their children to schools other than the crowded Washburn elementary school located in the project's immediate neighborhood. CMHA officials made such a request because they feared that whites would not want to send their children to the predominantly black school.[73] Eventually, the CMHA remedied this problem by securing permission from the federal government for the school board to erect temporary school buildings for project children (up to fifth grade) on the Laurel Homes grounds. Although the CMHA legitimately cited the crowded conditions at Washburn School as the reason for its request, J. R. Bassiger revealed another reason in his May 12, 1938, letter to Nathan Straus. Not only would the temporary school avoid further overcrowding Washburn School, Bassiger noted, but it "would remove one of the most serious objections that whites will have in moving into the area—the fact that their children would have to attend this school that was attended predominantly by colored children." [74]

Those temporary classrooms must not have been completely successful, since a March 21, 1939, examination of Laurel Homes' vacancy rate disclosed that most of the thirty-two vacant apartments were four and five-room units in the white section, suggesting that white families with several children might be avoiding Laurel Homes because of the large school-age population of blacks sharing educational facilities with the whites.[75] Despite the generally tight housing market for both whites and blacks, the white vacancy rate for Laurel Homes (including Laurel Homes Addition) continued to increase, compelling the CMHA to redivide the project between whites and blacks in 1942. As a result of this move, blacks received nearly 50 percent of all units in the 1,303-apartment project.[76]

In spite of the CMHA's addition to the black housing stock, congestion increased in the basin during the forties. According to the Cincinnati Police Department, the population of the basin's West End, which had been declining since 1900, actually increased by 10 percent between 1940 and 1943.[77] Not only did the ensuing congestion result in bad physical conditions for tenants, but it also resulted in rent increases. At a BHL executive meeting held in 1942, officials noted that since 1940 landlords had increased rents in the "colored West End" by approximately 20 percent. While rising costs caused some of that increase, the heavy demand for housing by black newcomers looking for work in the defense industry pushed rentals skyward too.[78] A federal mandate issued on November 1, 1942, halted further increases. It froze all local rents at their March 1, 1942, level. Nevertheless this proclamation did not produce new housing for blacks, and in fact may have discouraged conversion of single-family homes into multiunit dwellings.[79]

By the summer of 1943, black housing congestion intensified already strained race relations and led the Division of Negro Welfare's *Bulletin* to ask, "Will there be race riots in Cincinnati?" Although the *Bulletin* believed not, it warned that racial tensions were worsening. Unlike most contemporaries who blamed the racial tension on the large influx of black war workers into the area, the *Bulletin* proposed a different explanation. According to the paper, the influx of southern whites into the city caused the problem because these "hill people" were extremely prejudiced against blacks. Only after southern whites adjusted to Cincinnati patterns of behavior would the tensions ease up.[80]

Meanwhile, competition between whites and blacks for adequate housing brought racial tensions to a boiling point. In response to those tensions, local community leaders pressured Republican Mayor James Stewart to call a conference to discuss ways of easing the city's racial conflict. Participants at that October 7 meeting decided the city needed a permanent committee to promote "racial amity." Although the city's black leaders requested that this committee not be publicized as a "committee to ward off race riots," this, in fact, appeared to be the motive behind its formation.[81]

Council formally established a permanent race relations committee called the Mayor's Friendly Relations Committee on November 17, 1943. In a unanimous vote, Cincinnati's lawmakers authorized Stewart to appoint a committee "representing the various racial, industrial, religious and other groups, for the purposes of studying the problems connected with the promotion of harmony and tolerance and working out of our community problems and of acting as an advisory committee for their solutions." Stewart named Cincinnati School Superintendent Dr. C. V. Courte to head the new committee.[82]

That same month, local housing officials conferred with William K. Divers, regional director of the National Housing Agency, in an effort to secure more war housing. At that meeting, Divers refused the CMHA's request for war housing because of the city's inability to document the size of its inmigrant population. The Cincinnatians bitterly protested and claimed that black urban newcomers, fearful of the consequences, avoided any head count.[83]

The local quest for additional publicly subsidized housing did not end with that meeting, however. The following October, Marquette wrote to Frank Santry of the War Production Board and pleaded for housing assistance. In that letter Marquette observed that more than housing was involved. "Believe me," he warned, "I know that the racial situation is explosive and lack of decent housing is one of the two or three most important factors in the situation."[84]

Despite the critical black housing shortage, both the BHL and the CMHA continued their long-standing opposition to any temporary housing schemes that might relieve the suffering. Such buildings, the reformers warned, would eventually deteriorate into slums. That opposition hurt their quest for more wartime housing, since most publicly built projects after 1941 were temporary dwellings.[85]

Frustrated by their inability to obtain additional wartime public housing, local officials formed Norris Homes, Inc., on June 3, 1944, to build thirty individual dwellings for blacks north of Lockland. After securing priority ratings from the National Housing Agency, and with the help of an FHA loan, they began constructing the five-room brick houses on July 1, and finished them by the winter of 1945.[86] This project was one of several housing efforts by private companies to meet the black housing shortage. But only the eighty-house Lang Brothers project in a Lockland subdivision added more dwellings than the Norris effort. In all, private companies using public assistance built fewer than 150 new homes between 1941 and 1944, a meager effort which did little to improve the horrible housing conditions facing area blacks.[87] Neither public housing projects nor private housing endeavors sufficient to meet Cincinnati's black housing needs appeared during the war years.

Black community leaders responded in several ways to the failure of the better housing movement to substantially improve black living conditions. First, they increased their pressure for a black appointee on the policy-making CMHA board. To the credit of the CMHA, blacks held management roles in Cincinnati public housing throughout the forties. Verna Greene, a black, served as assistant manager for the Laurel Homes/Lincoln Court complex, and DeHart Hubbard, also black, managed Valley Homes. Nevertheless, as late as 1943, no blacks had ever served on the CMHA board.[88]

When Stanley M. Rowe announced his intention to resign from the CMHA in 1943, Arnold B. Walker, writing on behalf of the Division of Negro Welfare, requested Mayor James G. Stewart to appoint a "qualified Negro . . . to fill the vacancy."[89] Stewart ignored the appeal and selected his old law partner and fellow Republican, Ray Skirvin, to fill the post. Skirvin had been the city's most vocal public housing opponent and his appointment triggered an outburst of protest.[90] Both blacks and housing reformers denounced the appointment, which council narrowly approved only after the city's one black councilman, Jesse Locker, voted with his Republican colleagues.[91] Blacks finally secured representation on the CMHA the following year when the county commissioners appointed Dr. R. E. Clarke to fill the vacancy created by the sudden death of Fred Hock.[92]

Blacks not only pushed for improved representation in the city's most important housing agency but also questioned an important culprit in the local black housing shortage—the Cincinnati Real Estate Board. At an October 26, 1944, meeting, Douglas G. High, president of the Cincinnati Real Estate Board, along with fellow realtor Gordan Tarr, spoke to representatives of the black community about the realtors' policy toward blacks. High admitted that blacks suffered from inadequate housing and endorsed the rehabilitation of deteriorated dwelling units as the best strategy. However when asked if the board planned any such activities for Cincinnati blacks, High responded that realtors sympathized with blacks but had no plans to improve black housing. He further added that the Real Estate Board strongly supported residential segregation for blacks and whites.[93]

Such attitudes help explain why black housing in Cincinnati continued to decline during the forties. A survey of occupancy made by the Bureau of Census and published in August 1944 portrayed a gloomy picture. It both emphasized the scarcity of housing for blacks and documented the deteriorated nature of the existing housing stock. According to the survey, 82 percent of all black families in the West End resided in flats which failed to meet minimal housing standards.[94] Despite more than twenty years of housing reform, black housing seemed to be deteriorating. Although reformers believed they had developed a sound strategy for dealing with the the city's low-cost housing needs, they relied heavily on federal funding, so obstacles such as the war and unfavorable court decisions had interfered with their plans. As a result, they eagerly awaited the war's end and the return to "normalcy," when both blacks and whites could share in the benefits of large-scale community housing reform.

Through its public housing program of developing separate but equal facilities, the CMHA provided new housing opportunities and commmunity facilities for over 2,000 black families in the Cincinnati metropolitan area. But unlike earlier segregationalists, the CMHA apparently saw its housing projects not as barriers of permanent isolation, but as instruments for eventual assimilation. Certain slum cultural traits inhibited the upward mobility of blacks. Housing reform's goal was to eliminate the negative cultural traits by lifting blacks out of the disorganization of slums and into better neighborhood communities. Such a setting would result in a new civic-mindedness and a desire to become contributors to larger society.

Historian Arnold Hirsch uncovered the same type of response to the black housing problem in his examination of Chicago's Hyde Park urban renewal controversy. But he quickly dismissed what he called "the acculturation theory" as a simple ruse by community leaders to mask their racism. While both Chicago and Cincinnati community leaders, housers, and planners were racist, their racism needs to be examined. For a racism that argues black inferiority due to blacks' rural background and their need to be acculturated to a "completely industrialized civilization" calls for a different response than a racism emphasizing blacks' innate and unchanging biological inferiority. A community housing strategy makes sense for the former definition, while reservations make sense for the latter. At a time when blacks experienced neither opportunity nor integration, the former did not appear so terrible. Indeed, many blacks at the time, including New Deal Racial Advisor Robert

Weaver, argued that opportunity—particularly in regard to housing and employment—were the keys to black success.[95]

Of course this commitment to opportunity for blacks had its limits. Local housing reformers, aware that public housing evoked controversy and conflict, made no attempt to challenge the accepted residential patterns of the city. Integrated public housing might provoke disorder and fragmentation, something housers wished to avoid. And using the already controversial public housing program to push integration would probably kill the program in this southern-oriented city. As a result, black housing projects were placed in predominantly black areas and white projects in predominantly white areas. Because the CMHA built most of its black public housing in the West End, land and clearance costs reduced the amount of money available for the actual project.

In addition, the preoccupation of the CMHA with giving Cincinnatians their monies' worth limited the number of housing units allocated for blacks. A group's proportion of the eligible population, rather than need, determined the division of housing units among whites and blacks. Indeed, by accepting the established racial patterns in Cincinnati, and allocating public housing on the basis of group size rather than group need, reformers reinforced a status quo which clearly restricted black housing opportunity. Unwilling either to challenge the accepted social and economic bias against blacks, or to alter the political structure which supported it, white-led housing reform did little to fundamentally improve Cincinnati's black housing problem.[96]

PART IV

Abandoning the Neighborhood Community Approach

Both the 1940s and the 1950s proved significant decades for planning and public housing in Cincinnati and the nation. Nationally, the 1940s witnessed the culmination of the community development strategy in public housing with the passage of the Housing Act of 1949. Locally, Cincinnati's *Metropolitan Master Plan* of 1948 represented the maturation of the comprehensive metropolitan approach to community development planning. Both appeared at a time when war-induced problems directed much attention to the needs and problems of metropolitan America.

The 1950s, however, saw a radically different approach to both planning and public housing emerge. In many ways, that decade signaled the end of both public housing and planning as "reform" movements. For instance, the fortunes of public housing and the public housing movement rapidly deteriorated during the 1950s. The once vital and energetic national leadership of the public housing movement so quickly dissipated that as early as 1951 the *New Republic* published an article entitled "The Housing Movement in Retreat." It observed that the National Housing Conference, which had played such an important role in the development of public housing, no longer provided the necessary leadership or inspiration for the public housing movement. Nor did the National Association of Housing Officials, which the *New Republic* characterized as having "stodgy, cautious leadership." [1]

Traditional interpretations of this decline point to the impact of McCarthyism, the Korean War, and a strong and aggressive anti–public housing lobby. Others blame the experiences of public housing itself. [2] But only recently has the decline in enthusiasm been tied to changing assumptions in American social thought during the 1950s. [3] A clearer understanding of those changes should help explain the rapid decline of the community development strategy in public housing.

Sociologist Herbert J. Gans published an important essay in 1962 which clearly signaled changing assumptions about the impact of urban culture. "Urbanism and Suburban Ways of Life" challenged the ecological approach to urbanization popularized by the Chicago school of sociology between 1915 and 1950. It specifically questioned the validity of Louis Wirth's seminal essay "Urbanism as a Way of Life," written in 1938. That essay had proposed a theory of urbanism presenting the city as a "social entity." Wirth had argued that number, density, and heterogeneity were the keys to explaining the characteristics of urban life. Gans, however, countered and suggested that "economic condition, cultural characteristics, life-cycle stage and residential instability" explained "ways of life more satisfactory. . . ."[4]

Gans's article specifically questioned the supposed differences between city and suburb. It concluded that such differences were "often spurious or without much meaning for ways of life." Instead of being molded by place, the sociologist argued that people's choices, based on class and life-cycle stage, determined their behavior.[5]

Gans's questioning of the influence of place conflicted not only with the Chicago school of sociology, but also with assumptions that had been shared by planners and housers who embraced the community development strategy. For under Gans's view, neighborhoods or residential areas were "not necessarily . . . culturally distinctive."[6] Gans's writings were symptomatic of a broader set of assumptions about American society which professor Zane L. Miller has recently labeled "the revolt against culture." What he meant by that was "the tendency to no longer associate the culture of a group with a particular place and to attribute the characteristics of individuals to their membership in a particular group."[7] Individuals rather than groups now became identified as the basic elements in American society.

Under this new view, the community-building focus of public housing was discredited, and public housing lost its reform emphasis. Public housing now concentrated on providing shelter and services for the poor rather than on making better citizens through neighborhood community.

Coinciding with the changing focus of public housing was the decline of the type of comprehensive metropolitan planning characteristic of the 1940s. By the mid-1950s, the metropolitan planning embraced by Cincinnati reformers and business leaders gave way to a new emphasis on the need to revitalize the central business district. Creating an economically sound business district to compete with rival suburban districts now captured the attention of local planners and businessmen.

By the mid 1950s, then, individual desires replaced community needs as the focus of public housing. And planning both reflected a new concern with individuals and lost the comprehensive approach characteristic of the 1940s. Indeed, intense conflict between the urban periphery and the core developed in the 1950s and appeared symptomatic of the new preoccupation with promoting individual desires rather than improving the metropolitan whole.

CHAPTER 10

Clearing the Slums: From Community Services to Individual Desires, 1945–60

Cincinnati's Master Plan is going to remain a scrap of paper and its expressways imaginary lines in a futile map, unless Cincinnati can provide housing for the thousands of families that must be displaced by scheduled municipal improvements. That is the simple, unmistakable reason why action on housing—housing for lower income groups—must come first. Housing is truly the key to all our contemplated progress.

—*Cincinnati Enquirer*, May 3, 1949

Building . . . homes is a complicated hardboiled job requiring the best practical administrative and business talent available. But housing is also still a "cause," a great reform movement, which, in all its aspects, needs idealists, promoters, and experimenters—people with bold vision, independence, ingenuity, and a feeling for their fellowmen.

—*A Housing Program . . . for Now and Later*, 1948

On June 3, 1942, the Ohio State Supreme Court ruled that the state's housing authorities were not tax exempt. Despite the verdicts of twenty-three other state courts to the contrary, the Ohio justices concluded that authority-owned public housing projects constituted private rather than public activity and were therefore taxable. According to the 5–2 verdict, such projects gave an "unfair tax advantage" to a "selected few persons who are not paupers and who are not aged, infirm, or without means of support." [1] The court argued that the Ohio State Housing Authority Law never stipulated that housing built by the state's housing authorities was exclusively public property. Efforts to revise the law began almost immediately after the court's ruling. [2]

Only after Ohio legislators passed such a law would new public housing be built in Cincinnati, since the 1937 Housing Act stipulated that the local governmental unit needed to contribute to the project. Tax exemption fulfilled that requirement. Moreover, the court's ruling made the authority's bonds unmarketable, thus preventing it from raising the 10-percent capital necessary to initiate new public housing projects. In fact, the unfavorable decision forced the CMHA to breach its contract with the Federal Public Housing Authority on the CMHA's completed projects. Federal law mandated that Cincinnati provide annual subsidies for all completed public housing projects. Local officials had met this requirement through tax exemption but now were prohibited from such action. As a result, on April 1, 1943, the FPHA took title to Lincoln Court, Winton Terrace, and English Woods.[3] Meanwhile, opponents of public housing howled at the project's new tax-exempt status while local reformers worked feverishly to secure a new state tax law and resume the construction of public housing.[4]

The tax problem persisted until the spring of 1949, when Ohio lawmakers amended the Housing Authority Law to correct the defects cited by the Ohio Supreme Court. The amended law established public housing as a public activity but also required that local housing authorities pay 10 percent of their rental income to local governments in lieu of taxes. Not until June 1951, however, did the Ohio court pass favorably on public housing in Ohio under the revised legislation.[5]

Even if there had been no court ruling in 1942, it is doubtful that Cincinnati would have seen any additional slum clearance or public housing between 1942 and 1946, because of the way federal officials responded to the war-related housing crisis. During this time, the federal government concentrated on defense housing for war industry workers flooding the nation's cities. To ease congestion in Cincinnati, federal officials required the local authority to open up Cincinnati public housing to overincome defense workers. Furthermore, it forbade local authorities from evicting tenants even when their income exceeded wartime limits. The combination of these factors, and a federal policy which encouraged the private sector to supply most of the defense housing (through FHA insurance and construction material priorities), resulted in few new dwellings for the nation's working poor during this era.[6]

Despite the preoccupation with resolving the city's war-related housing problems, Cincinnati housing reformers did not lose sight of long-term, low-cost housing goals. Indeed, the forties were a productive time as reformers planned new strategies for clearing the slums and making the metropolis closer to their image of what a metropolitan community should be like. The plan could be implemented, however, only after reformers overcame the court's ruling and resolved the most pressing war-related housing crisis.

In 1940, the Brookings Institution of Washington estimated that Cincinnati needed approximately 3,500 new dwellings for the next five years to meet the deficiency in building accumulated between 1930 and 1940. But with the wartime rationing of building materials, this goal was never met. The impact of this housing shortage on the city's wage earner, particularly its black wage earner, was especially severe. And the war's end created further complications as returning servicemen joined the competition for the area's limited housing stock.[7]

A memorandum prepared by the BHL and the Citizens' Committee on Slum Clearance and Low Rent Housing (CCSC) for city council on November 20, 1945, suggests how serious local housing reformers perceived the anticipated crisis to be. After noting that the city had "a grave shortage of housing, greater than any that the city has experienced in decades," it concluded that "unless emergency measures are taken now, indications are that the situation is going to be completely out of hand by Spring of 1946." After observing that "overcrowding is at an unprecedented peak," the memo predicted that within months 40,000 veterans would be returning to the area to face housing shortages of between 3,000 and 6,000 units.[8]

In order to meet the impending crisis, the BHL and the CCSC offered a four-step program. First, they recommended that council create an official Emergency Housing Bureau to help place returning veterans and to persuade owners of large houses to share their accommodations. Along this line, housing officials proposed a plan to encourage the conversion of large homes into apartments. The memo also recommended that the local government petition the National Housing Agency to reestablish its wartime conversion plan so that the Home Owners Loan Corporation would lease and convert houses suitable for use by several families. Third, the housing organizations requested that the city manager call a conference of builders and labor to see how they could speed up local home building. Toward this end, the memo suggested that council should pressure Congress to enact a bill authorizing building material priorities for areas with veteran housing shortages. Finally, the joint BHL-CCSC communication advised council to obtain 420 demountable housing units from the Federal Housing Authority and make arrangements to place them on vacant land at Greenhills and in the area north of Lockland. The BHL and the CCSC apologized for their recommendation of temporary housing, describing it as "justifiable only as an extreme measure" to meet the present crisis. Almost as an afterthought, the memo suggested that the CMHA add 1,000 public housing units to its Winton Terrace property as soon as possible.[9]

Although city council failed to adopt all these recommendations, it did embrace several of them and implemented some programs of its own. Ten days after receiving the memo, on November 30, city council's law committee recommended immediate acquisition of 100 temporary housing units from the federal government. Aware that it would cost about $100,000, council nevertheless agreed with the committee about the need. In a further attempt to create more housing, the committee proposed relaxing city building and zoning codes to permit attic and basement apartments.[10]

About ten days later, the law committee ordered the city's policemen to watch for vacancies on their beats in an effort to facilitate the placement of veterans. More important, however, it advised Mayor James Stewart to follow the BHL-CCSC's memo suggestion that he appoint a special committee to facilitate building in the area. As a result, on January 21 Stewart formed the Mayor's Committee on Housing, and appointed John J. Rowe chairman.[11] Once established, the Mayor's Committee assisted in forming an Emergency Housing Bureau. Financed by funds from the War Chest, the bureau collected housing information and publicized the plight of needy veterans.[12]

Despite the proliferation of new committees and bureaus to help remedy the housing emergency, council's decision to secure temporary housing units from the federal government brought the most immediate relief to those needing housing. On December 19, 1945, council approved a motion by Vice Mayor Willis Gradison authorizing the city manager to apply for 200 housing units from the National Housing Agency. Council would provide $500,000 from a deferred maintenance fund to transport the units to Cincinnati.[13]

The moving expenses proved unnecessary, since Congress passed the Mead Amendment to the Lanham Act soon afterward. Under its terms the city obtained 620 temporary units which had been used as army barracks. And since the army paid moving expenses, the costs per unit decreased from $2,500 to $1,600. Major expenses now resulted from council's obligation to provide sites for the temporary units through rough grading and extending sewer lines, as well as other utilities.[14]

Council placed the temporary army barracks on public land, such as the Winton Terrace public housing site, which received 328 units. Other units were erected at Valley Homes, Laurel Park, Anderson Park, Johnson Park and near the Hamilton County Home.[15] Although the veterans' committee of the Cincinnati NAACP opposed segregating blacks as "contrary to all progressive thinking on the subject," the 20 percent of units allocated for blacks were indeed segregated from the white locations.[16]

These three, four, and five-room dwellings provided the only "new" low-cost housing available to the needy veteran at this time. The CMHA, which managed the units, admitted "distressed veterans only," defined as those either being evicted from their present homes or living in substandard dwellings.[17] Apparently quite a number of "distressed" veterans lived in Cincinnati: by August 6, 2,300 former soldiers had applied to live in the 630 apartment units renting for about $30 per month. Because of the demand, the CMHA formed a veterans committee to select eligible candidates not only on the basis of need, but also on the length of overseas service, disability, and other war-related factors.[18]

From the beginning this small but important low-cost housing effort ran into problems, particularly time delays and high costs. Nearly ten months after workers started preparing the sites, only 245 units were ready for occupancy. According to the *Enquirer*, the slow progress stemmed from the tardy flow of needed materials to the contractor, M. Shapiro and Sons of New York. Blame later shifted to the contractor, chosen by Washington, for not having enough plumbers to finish the job on time.[19]

Along with the temporary effort, local officials wished to promote massive and rapid permanent housing activity to alleviate the veterans' housing problem. Although both the CMHA and the BHL favored strong public housing programs to meet the shortage, the federal government's immediate postwar effort centered on encouraging private construction for families above the public housing income limits. To achieve this goal and secure scarce building materials, local officials and interested citizens met with Willis Winkler, representing Wilson W. Wyatt, the national housing expediter.[20]

President Harry S Truman named Wyatt, former mayor of Louisville, to the newly created post on January 26, 1946. Wyatt, charged with preparing programs to combat the veterans' housing problem, oversaw the Veterans' Emergency Housing program. It called for the erection of 2.7 million new nonfarm housing units by the end of 1947. To achieve this goal, Truman restricted all nonessential building projects. Only houses costing under $10,000 or apartments renting for less than $80 per month would be considered by the National Housing Agency. Other aspects of the program included subsidy payments to stimulate the rapid production of needed construction materials, and the authorization by Congress of a billion dollars in additional home mortgage loans covered by the FHA. This money allowed the FHA to restore its Title VI program for insuring mortgage loans up to 90 percent both for multiunit apartments and single-dwelling houses.[21]

Hoping to ready Cincinnati for the federal program, Mayor James Stewart called together a committee composed of labor leader Rollin Everett, architect Standish Meacham, lawyer Morse Johnson, black Councilman Jesse Locker, assistant BHL head, Ethel Ideson, CMHA Directors George Garties and Ramsey Findlater, and City Manager William R. Kellogg. They met on April 19, 1946, with Willis Winkler, representing the national housing expediter. Winkler emphasized the need for all of those involved in the house-building business to coordinate their efforts and work together to solve the local supply problem. Specifically, he urged the mayor to create still another emergency housing council, this one made up of representatives of the building industries, labor, veterans groups, housing officials and other civic groups. This committee would help the city prepare for better housing by collecting necessary data and by identifying worthwhile sites so that construction could begin as soon as possible.[22]

Shortly after the meeting, the mayor followed Winkler's suggestion and formed the Cincinnati Committee to Expedite Housing (CCEH). He named Joseph A. Noertker, a Cincinnati Street Railway Company electrical engineer, to head the organization's small steering committee. Other members included N. R. Whitney, an economist at Procter and Gamble; John Spilker, a realtor; Henry Bettman, an architect; and Frank Simpson, branch manager of Clark Controller Company. Under this leadership, the committee surveyed the city's housing needs, and investigated building obstacles such as construction bottlenecks, the insufficient skilled labor pool, and the hoarding of building materials by black markets. In addition, the committee's headquarters served as a "swap shop" where builders arranged to trade their surplus materials.[23]

Funded by city council, which granted it $6,000 for the rest of 1946 and $10,000 for 1947, the CCEH employed Charles H. Stamm as its executive secretary. Stamm produced a handsomely printed report on its activities in 1947 which observed that "the greatest obstacle in dealing intelligently with the housing problem was a lack of comprehensive and accurate statistical information for the Greater Cincinnati Metropolitan Area," the real unit of concern. That same report also called 1947 a "year of disappointment and frustration on the local building level" and noted the continued lack of new housing for low and moderate-income veterans. It particularly decried the plight of families just over the maximum income limits imposed for public housing.[24]

Notwithstanding the CCEH's observation, families traditionally eligible for public housing also suffered greatly. Not only were the majority of West End families crowded together in two-room flats without shower, toilet, or central heat, but war and postwar priorities gave them even less chance of moving into public housing than before.[25] In Lincoln Court and Winton Terrace, war workers with incomes above the amount permissible in normal times were not only admitted but given priority during wartime. And at the request of the War Manpower Commission on September 7, 1944, the CMHA agreed not to evict families exceeding even maximum wartime limits.[26] After the war, the CMHA gave veterans preference in filling vacancies within the projects and waived the eligibility requirement that they live in substandard housing. As a result, by the end of 1947, 1,006 overincome families (occupying 24.1 percent of all available local public housing units) resided in Cincinnati's public housing. Even after the CMHA started evicting overincome families the following May, 871 overincome families remained housed in the CMHA's projects as late as October 28, 1948.[27] Although these tenants paid higher rents

than the low-income families, thus paying for operating costs and debt service, they took needed housing from the area's poorer ill-housed wage
earners.

The war and postwar housing shortage emergencies, then, temporarily
halted the local low-cost housing reform program of slum clearance and
neighborhoodlike public housing projects. Indeed, the city's housing stock
deteriorated as housing codes were relaxed and migrant wartime workers,
seeking cheap shelter, crowded into an already congested housing market.
Despite the wartime housing emergency and the general distraction of wartime activities, local housing officials were not content to deal with only the
immediate problems, but undertook to plan for low-cost housing needs in
postwar Cincinnati. For instance, in May of 1942, the CMHA informed a
council-appointed committee of Alfred Bettman, Willis Gradison, and City
Manager Clarence O. Sherrill that it planned a six-year postwar public housing program to produce 3,600 units at a cost of $19,800,000.[28]

This proposal was based on the *Real Property Survey* of Cincinnati and
urbanized Hamilton County made under the auspices of the City and Regional
Planning Commissioners with partial funding from the federal government.
The local sponsors of the survey, the Cincinnati City Council, the county
commissioners, and the Cincinnati Board of Education, provided $15,000 for
the project, which started on September 28, 1939.[29] Completed on July 1,
1940, the survey disclosed that nearly 66,100 dwellings, most of them in the
basin, were either physically substandard or overcrowded. It further confirmed the trend toward a stagnant and nonexpanding urban core that local
reformers had identified in the thirties. Indeed, the analysis noted that the city
was losing population to its suburbs and suggested that the only way to check
the "outward flow" was "by physical redevelopment of existing, blighted
neighborhoods."[30]

With a clearer picture of Cincinnati's housing needs, the CMHA developed
a six-year plan which would provide 600 public housing units for each of
those years. In preparation for the building, CMHA members worked closely
with the City Planning Commission over site selection. Later, when the Federal Public Housing Authority requested applications for postwar housing
needs, the CMHA revised its estimates downward and requested a 2,850-unit
allocation for after the war.[31]

The *Real Property Survey* encouraged others besides the CMHA to act.
The final survey report recommended that the city manager should appoint an
advisory committee representing housing-related interests to study its findings
and "to develop and report back to council an adequate program looking
toward the solution of the problems of shifting population and economic deca-
dence apparent from the findings of the survey."[32] As a result, another committee soon appeared.[33]

Even before the *Real Property Survey*, some Cincinnatians like Bleecker Marquette and Alfred Bettman had noticed how the new urban realities of core deterioration and rapid suburbanization made the city plan of 1925 somewhat dated. During the mid-thirties, Bettman, who chaired the City Planning Commission, pushed that body to upgrade its plan to deal not only with the present problems but also future needs.[34] As interest in the problem of decaying city cores increased in Cincinnati and the rest of the nation during the thirties, Bettman launched an unsuccessful campaign to secure more money from council so that the Planning Commission could revise the 1925 plan.[35]

Frustrated by his inability to obtain needed money from city council, which since 1941 had been controlled by a 5–4 Republican majority, Bettman, a Democrat in national politics and a Charter member locally, developed a different strategy to bring metropolitan planning to Cincinnati. With the help of his friend Stanley Rowe, Bettman started piecing together a citizens' committee of business leaders and industrialists to pressure council for planning funds. He also sent to council's finance committee a strongly worded letter, dated June 21, 1943. It requested $25,000 seed money for initiating a new, comprehensive master plan for metropolitan Cincinnati. And after an August 2 public hearing before the Planning Commission, Bettman's efforts at encouraging a new planning movement seemed to gain momentum.[36]

Even more important than the public hearing, Bettman gained the confidence of several prestigious Cincinnatians, who pledged their support to planning. The help and initiative of R. R. Deupree, president of Procter and Gamble; and Frederick Geier, president of the Cincinnati Milling Machine Company, proved particularly useful in attracting both leadership and financial support from the business community.[37]

These business leaders organized a formal committee under Bettman's guidance—the Citizens' Planning Association (CPA)—at a meeting held at Deupree's home on December 21, 1943. They chose Stanley M. Rowe, who had recently retired as chairman of the CMHA, to preside over the new association. Neil McElroy, John J. Hurst, Charles F. Cellarius, W. Howard Cox, and Milton H. Schmidt were also elected officers to serve along with R. R. Deupree, Walter Draper, Charles W. Dupuis, John J. Emery, and Frederick V. Geier on the executive committee, the real controlling force behind the organization.[38]

At the meeting, Rowe recommended that the committee embrace four objectives. Most important, it should urge council to fund the making of a new master plan for metropolitan Cincinnati. Second, it should see that the work on the plan be properly organized. Third, it should make sure that the best people were employed for developing the plan. Finally, Rowe urged that the committee keep close tabs on the plan to make sure the best solutions were reached for Greater Cincinnati.[39]

The Cincinnati case, then, fully contradicts the Chicago experience with postwar planning and redevelopment as described by historian Arnold Hirsch. According to Hirsch's view, Chicago's efforts in these areas were initiated and controlled by downtown interests concerned solely with preserving the vitality of the central business district. The Cincinnati movement for planning and redevelopment originated from the efforts of Alfred Bettman, planning enthusiast, who had little to gain from downtown revitalization. The Cincinnati planner, who played a leading role in the debate over a national redevelopment law, firmly believed in comprehensive planning and treatment for the whole metropolitan area and argued that "no rebuilding which . . . will produce the desired social and economic welfare can be accomplished unless we start with the conception that we are dealing with all types of appropriate uses in accordance with good city planning." [40] Bettman and his businessmen supporters then promoted a document focusing on the metropolis and not merely downtown Cincinnati. Indeed, central business district redevelopment did not become a major issue in Cincinnati until the late 1950s.

City council apparently agreed with the metropolitan strategy, for on February 16, 1944, it granted the CPA's request and appropriated $100,000 to the Planning Commission for the new master plan. With the money, the commission organized a special Division of City and Metropolitan Planning. After an intensive national search, the city hired Sherwood L. Reeder, a public administrator, to supervise the Master Planning Division. It also employed as consultants Ladislas Segoe, the Cincinnati planner who had helped formulate the 1925 plan, and Tracy Augur, another prominent planner associated with the Tennessee Valley Authority. Work began on the Cincinnati plan in June 1944. [41]

The master plan, completed in October 1947 and issued in 1948, called for, among other things, massive slum clearance and residential development, nonresidential redevelopment on the riverfront and in part of the West End, and a new urban expressway system, the first portion of which would go through the West End. All of these projects would displace low-income people, especially blacks, and thus increase the need for low-income relocation housing—a need expected to be met in part with public housing. The master plan also endorsed the homogeneous neighborhood community and racial residential segregation principles on which planning, housing officials, and housing reformers had operated since the 1920s. [42]

As Zane L. Miller has pointed out, the plan of 1948 defined a circular metropolitan area consisting of Hamilton County, Ohio, and Kenton and Campbell Counties in Kentucky and emphasized the redevelopment of the existing structure within this area rather than the creation of a new form. The plan described the metropolitan area as a "mature" metropolitan community with modest prospects for economic and population growth—but one within which the popularity of the automobile would encourage a continuing drift outward. The plan also divided the metropolitan landscape into two systems, one for "living" (residential) and one for "making a living" (industrial area, major transportation trunkline routes, and the central business district).[43]

The residential strategy of the plan of 1948 defined three arenas of activity: neighborhood, community, and the metropolis. This vision and strategy rested on the conviction that "when a city expands beyond a certain size it reaches the point of diminishing returns in terms of the advantages which a city, as a social community, should provide for its inhabitants." To gain maximum advantages, and to secure a sense of community at both metropolitan and submetropolitan levels, the plan proposed to organize Cincinnati's metropolitan residential areas into "communities" of about 20,000 to 40,000 people, not self-governed but "self-contained in respect to the everyday life of their inhabitants except for such facilities and services as will continue to be located in or supplied by Cincinnati as the central city, and by institutions serving the Metropolitan Area."

The conception of the metropolitan residential areas as a cluster of medium-sized "cities," some inside and some outside the jurisdiction of the area's major municipality (Cincinnati), and like "real" small cities in every way except governmentally, seemed to offer several advantages according to the master plan and one of the plan's special studies entitled *Communities*. This volume sketched a history of Cincinnati as the growth of neighborhoods around the original settlement, the annexation of a number of them to Cincinnati, their retention of "identities," and the grouping of some of them into "communities" by virtue of the Cincinnati area's hill and valley topography. This process the study deemed "most fortunate" because it tended "to preserve as the city grew, some of the better qualities of small town life, such as the spirit of neighborliness and the sense of attachment to a locality— qualities so easily lost in the full flood of urban expansion." Specifically, asserted the study, people in "smaller cities . . . participate to a greater extent in community activities; a larger percentage goes to the polls; a higher proportion contribute to the Community Chest; more are interested in public affairs." And "here in the Cincinnati Area, to a greater degree than in most large cities, residents enjoy the economic and cultural advantages of a metropolis while living in residential localities small enough to satisfy the urge for intimacy in home surroundings and/or a social life in scale with the average family."[44]

Unfortunately, however, history had not adequately completed the task of community building, and the plan proposed "to strengthen the present rudimentary neighborhood composition of the Metropolitan Area . . . to form an organized 'cluster' of communities, each further divided into neighborhoods." The boundaries of each community should encompass 20,000 to

40,000 people on 1,000 to 2,000 acres and be drawn with reference to "separators," such as topographic features, industrial belts, railroads, large parks, greenbelts, cemeteries, institutions, and projected expressways; and each community would be connected to the expressways by community thoroughfares, and by expressways or intercommunity thoroughfares to the central business district and the larger metropolitan community of work, entertainment, education, and social and cultural activities.[45]

The plan cited four internal elements critical to the viability of the new communities: school, business, civic, and balanced housing facilities. That is, each community should be served by a high school, or at least by two junior high schools. Each should possess a "community business district, a secondary business district in relation to the Metropolitan Area as a whole, but the chief center of commercial activities as far as the community is concerned." Each should contain near its business district a community civic center composed of a branch library, a recreation center, a health center, a branch post office, and, in some cases, appropriate semipublic buildings. In addition, each community should possess both single-family homes and apartments of various density levels so as to accommodate "young couples, . . . growing families and . . . elderly persons," therefore eliminating the necessity for a family "to move away from friends, neighbors, churches and other associations as it arrives at various stages of the life cycle." And while the plan expected future single-family home construction to predominate outside the central city and apartments inside, thereby dividing the metropolis spatially into homeowners and renters, the distinction made little difference to the planners, who thought of both locales simply as sites for communities, small towns exhibiting the social and civic characteristics ascribed to such small towns by the planners.[46]

The 1948 plan's communities scheme, with its emphasis on accommodating the family life cycle, presented all communities as equal and in many respects identical, but also provided a way of permitting and accommodating racial, ethnic, and class heterogeneity within a community without talking in those terms about diversity—a classic example of a pluralistic taxonomic system that harmonized heterogeneity with homogeneity and that accepted racial residential segregation as normal and something to be preserved. The mechanism for doing this was the notion of neighborhood, for in forming each community the planners tried to group "traditional" and therefore segregated neighborhoods on the basis of spatial contiguity without specific reference to their class, ethnic, or racial profiles.

According to the master plan, an ideal neighborhood would contain 400 to 800 acres and a population of 4,000 to 8,000 and would be connected to its community and the metropolis by thoroughfare and expressway systems and bounded, but not entered, by major traffic streets. Each neighborhood, moreover, would have all the attributes of a community except a civic center. Each neighborhood, that is, would have an elementary school with a children's playground as well as additional playgrounds where necessary, one of several "neighborhood" shopping centers, and "sometimes" additional "local" shopping centers consisting of a few stores. And each neighborhood would have some mix of single-family homes and apartments, depending on its proximity to the metropolitan central business district, the symbolic and functional center and central cohesive element of the metropolis.[47]

The plan of 1948 recognized, of course, that it had to apply its ideal neighborhood and community treatment to a real city, not an abstraction. To adjust the ideal to reality, it returned to a historical analysis, one that pictured the metropolis roughly as a concentric circle of older and newer neighborhoods, with the older neighborhoods at the core, the middle-aged in the next ring, and the new ones toward the periphery. In this connection the plan also analyzed the life cycle of a neighborhood. Together these analyses depicted a declining core, with its poor and black residents gradually moving from old residential neighborhoods falling to nonresidential uses into declining residential neighborhoods nearby. The plan thus depicted a filter-down process of urban growth by which blacks and the poor spread from the oldest and worst neighborhoods into adjacent and declining neighborhoods.[48]

The plan quite specifically elaborated the stages in this process. "Each neighborhood," it said, "has a distinct 'life-cycle,' and the urban area . . . consists . . . of a vast patchwork of neighborhoods which had their origins at different points in time." Each had a period of growth, shortly after the initial subdivision, then a period of stability "during which the neighborhood tends to retain its original character." Then comes "decline . . . the sale of homes rises again, with changes in the type of population coming into the neighborhood . . . a shift from owner to tenant occupancy, accelerated perhaps by the conversion into smaller apartments of larger homes," changing land-use patterns, heavier traffic, more institutions, and the incursion of industry or heavy commercial uses.[49]

Then comes the nadir, exemplified by the basin. In the oldest, and hence the most centrally located neighborhoods, not only will the deterioration and obsolescence of the housing have proceeded to a marked degree, with exceptionally high vacancy, a high percentage of tenant occupancy, and very low rents, but the pattern of land use may also have changed radically from its original character into what is familiarly known as slums and blighted areas, or, in this report, "deteriorated areas." The best examples in Cincinnati of this situation— neighborhoods that have already reached, or are approaching the end of their life cycle—are found, of course, in the Basin area. Here neighborhoods that were in their time among the finest in the city, have become through force of circumstance ripe for the most complete redevelopment.[50]

The master plan then classified Cincinnati's neighborhoods by their age groups and by the housing conditions in each age group as a preface to the prescription of treatments for each category. This analysis produced five categories and recommendations for handling each. Deteriorated areas received the most drastic care: "complete clearance and a fresh start through redevelopment for either private or public use, in accordance with the master plan." Those areas verging on deterioration but not yet slums (blighted) were scheduled for "neighborhood conservation and rehabilitation," which meant demolition of the worst structures and/or areas, reduction of heterogeneity in land-use patterns and of residential overcrowding, repair and modernization of dwelling units, and the introduction of playgrounds and schools. Middle-aged neighborhoods fell into the "conservation" rubric, a program to be carried out for the most part by owner occupants through organized neighborhood effort with Planning Commission staff assistance to induce property owners to modernize buildings and adhere to the master plan, and to help arrange financing. Newer neighborhoods would require only "protection" through adequate zoning and careful planning. The last category was called "preparation for new growth," applying to "neighborhoods which are just beginning to develop," and involved an assessment of the character of future development and the arrangement and ordering of the parts of the neighborhood and community structure to meet the size and nature of these youngest of urban places.[51]

Thus the residential strategy of the 1948 master plan aimed to perpetuate and perfect past patterns of urban growth and the familiar form and structure of the metropolitan area, including its social and racial geography and the filter-down process that facilitated residential racial segregation, a process the plan described specifically. It predicted and encouraged rapid population growth "in the major peripheral communities" of the metropolitan areas and modest increases or decreases "in the built-up portions of the urban area lying generally between the basin and the peripheral communities." In the "older neighborhoods" of the basin, the plan projected a 50-percent population decrease by 1970, "assuming adequate redevelopment," and a 27-percent decrease without it. Other "middle-aged sections" within the city of Cincinnati—namely, in predominantly white Avondale, St. Bernard, Clifton, Cumminsville, Norwood, and Walnut Hills—could expect to maintain their levels of population but would experience a population change nevertheless. That change, the planners predicted, "will be in the composition and character of the population and in the types of residential structures, rather than in . . . size." In short, poor white and black inhabitants of the basin would move out to the next band of neighborhoods on the north and east with the implementation of the master plan of 1948, which sought to preserve rather than to create a new urban form, structure, or social and racial geography.[52]

In this sense a "conservative" document, the master plan of 1948 nonetheless proposed drastic solutions to the problems of the metropolitan area, including residential and nonresidential redevelopment schemes and expressway construction through deteriorated areas that would require the relocation of thousands of poor families, most of them black. The plan called specifically for federal subsidies to relocate these families in appropriate neighborhoods and communities, such as the three major existing black enclaves: the West End, Walnut Hills, and the recently (1946) incorporated village of Lincoln Heights, which encompassed the black subdivisions north of Lockland.[53]

Local housing reformers supported the master plan because it spoke the same language they were used to—community and a comprehensive approach. The plan advocated many of the same causes that housing reformers did—elimination of slums and the promotion of community in salvageable neighborhoods. Just as the housing reformers conceived of their projects as more than simply the sum of residential dwelling places, the planners recognized that the metropolis was more than the sum of its people and economic functions.

Postulating that their public housing projects were related to the greater whole of the metropolis and that their success depended, in part, on their location, the area's public housing activists apparently agreed with Bettman, who observed that "the study of the redevelopment of any area, if it is to be intelligent requires the comprehensive planning study of other parts of the city." Furthermore, Bettman asserted, "One cannot know how much area to devote to housing, for instance, and where those districts should be without knowing a good deal about how much area shall go to business, industry, educational community activity, recreation, streets, etc., etc., and etc."[54]

Although much of this sounded like a rehash of justifications for the city plan of 1925, major differences existed between the two documents. Not only did the 1948 plan spend much more time discussing the peripheral areas of Greater Cincinnati, but it recognized the urban core as a different type of problem than in 1925. The 1925 plan pictured a growing and dynamic urban system and offered more of a plan for that growth and development. The 1948 plan portrayed a partially stagnant urban system, recognizing that only through outside help would the blighted core be revitalized. Indeed, the call for complete redevelopment of certain portions of the city most distinguished that plan from the plan of 1925.

Toward this end, local housing officials and reformers fully expected to use federal subsidies for both residential and nonresidential redevelopment. Indeed, Alfred Bettman in the 1940s participated in writing and introducing the necessary state and federal laws, both of which passed in 1949. The federal legislation provided loans and capital grants covering up to two-thirds of slum clearance costs and permitted the sale and lease of the cleared land at a price below its market value. The state law required city councils to certify the existence of feasible plans for the temporary relocation of families displaced by clearance.[55]

From the beginning of postwar redevelopment plans, officials identified relocation housing as a major obstacle to be hurdled before actual work could begin. And with the passage of the 1949 Housing Act, which provided not only public housing but an urban redevelopment program, the city proposed massive slum clearance in the West End for both residential and industrial redevelopment, a strategy called for in the 1948 plan. Later, the city also turned to rehabilitation and conservation for blighted areas lying outside the basin area, once again a recommendation found in the master plan of 1948. Rehabilitation and conservation seemed particularly attractive to Cincinnatians because, as we will see, the city suffered from insufficient relocation housing.[56]

Even if no war-related shortage had existed, rehousing thousands of low-income tenants displaced by the proposed highway system and redevelopment program would have proved difficult. With the shortage it seemed nearly impossible without a massive construction program.[57] Yet until the city found a solution, redevelopment would be delayed. Chamber of Commerce President Morris Edwards summarized the situation succinctly when he observed that "we can't tear down the homes that must make way for improvement until we provide other homes for these people."[58]

This problem stymied several public works projects (such as the Sixth Street viaduct), even before the 1949 redevelopment laws.[59] Rollin H. Everett, local labor leader and city councilman, urged council on April 7, 1948, to build housing for those displaced by public projects. Everett feared that the inability of local officials to relocate the 3,705 families scheduled for displacement due to the city's highway construction and other projects would delay the public works proposals and interfere with the labor force's employment opportunities. As a result, he introduced in council on August 31, 1948, a resolution proposing that the city government contribute $1 million of its councilmanic bonds as a capital grant to the Housing Authority for construction of 125 dwellings.[60]

The CMHA agreed to construct and manage the proposed relocation housing if the city accepted responsibility for deciding such matters as the type of housing, the method of financing, and the location, since authority members wanted to avoid these controversial questions.[61] The city agreed to these terms and appointed still another special emergency housing committee to work out the details of how best to spend the $1 million for housing. Joseph B. Hall, president of the Kroger Company, headed the new committee.[62]

That committee investigated a number of possible relocation strategies, including the use of trailers, old streetcars, and prefab steel homes. It also looked into building more permanent relocation housing and finally settled on that course. In its final report the committee explained that public housing could be erected to house temporarily people displaced by highway construction and other public works, giving them time to find more permanent quarters. As a result of this study, in 1950 council appropriated $175,000 for such a project on Irving Street near the zoo on the edge of Avondale, a neighborhood then undergoing racial transition from white to black. Construction began in April 1951 and produced sixty-six units renting at approximately $50 per month, a relatively high figure because this was not a federally subsidized project but one designed to earn a return on the initial investment and pay debt service on the forty-year, 3-percent bonds sold by the CMHA to finance the undertaking. The project opened with all black tenants.[63]

Recognizing that the Irving Street project did not meet the pressing need for relocation housing for the poor whites and blacks expected to be displaced by the initial West End expressway project, council made other attempts to help. On February 2, 1949, it approved a program to provide local incentives for the construction of rental housing for low and moderate-income families. Council agreed to pay up to 90 percent of the costs of land improvement for new rental housing, provided that developers agreed to hold rents down to $35 per month for two-room apartments and $50 per month for three-room dwellings. Council also appropriated $500,000 to help pay the costs of sidewalks, streets, water lines, and sewer connections for such units.[64]

Council's efforts at replacement housing paled in comparison to efforts by the private sector with the creation of the Cincinnati Community Development Company (CCDC). Formed on April 21, 1948, it sought "to aid in community growth and development by helping to alleviate shortages of housing that from time to time exist."[65] The organization resulted from the initiative of Mayor Albert Cash, who believed that private housing projects would have to supply most of the relocation housing. As a result, he called selected community leaders to his office on February 6, 1948, for a discussion of how to house the displaced, the city's "biggest problem." They decided to form a large-scale housing company. Cash oversaw a subscription campaign which netted over $500,000 for the new company. On April 22, 1948, it formally incorporated as the Cincinnati Community Development Company. Investors included a diversified group of commercial and industrial corporations, as well as many civic-minded individuals.[66] Those shareholders elected Earle J. Wheeler, a building contractor, company president and hired Lawrence H. Tucker, former city manager of Greenhills, to manage the CCDC.[67]

Under their leadership, the CCDC decided to build a large-scale apartment project on a twenty-six-acre tract of land between Bond Hill and Roselawn, south of Seymour Avenue and west of Reading Road. The CCDC believed that it could construct a 208-unit project with rentals between $60 and $80 per month by securing mortgage insurance from the FHA.[68] The CCDC never actually built its project, called Glen Meadows, but sold its land, plans, and contractual commitments to the Western and Southern Life Insurance Company in the spring of 1950. By May of that same year, Western and Southern broke ground for the Glen Meadows complex.[69]

Although this marked an important start in relocation housing, it was only a start. Indeed, Charles Stamm, head of the Urban Redevelopment Division warned that "the present slum areas are overcrowded to such an extent that redevelopment of these areas is impossible without first providing large numbers of additional dwelling units to provide a vacancy reserve into which the slum occupants can be moved during the period in which their present homes are torn down and new ones built back on the same site."[70] In order to build its highways and redevelop its slums, he concluded, "the city must adopt a positive, definitive policy on housing and must activate that policy as quickly as possible."[71]

Stamm recommended a four-part relocation housing policy. First, the city should establish a relocation center. Second, it should promote new housing by private enterprise, especially for those whose incomes were just above public housing maximum income limits. Third, Cincinnati needed more temporary shelter on the Irving Street plan. Finally, more public housing was absolutely necessary, particularly after the City Planning Commission chose a twenty-block area in the West End as its first redevelopment site.[72]

On February 3, 1950, the Housing and Home Finance Administration earmarked $3,742,830 for Cincinnati redevelopment in an area planners identified as Laurel-3 and Richmond-1 (see map 10-A). The area, which would be cleared for redevelopment by private enterprise, had appeared on the Planning Commission's 1933 agenda for action. Now it was inhabited by 1,600 families, most of them black and poor.[73] For instance, 42.9 percent of the primary wage earners in the R-1 area earned below $2,000 per year while more than 80 percent of the R-1 residents earned below $3,000 per year. As a result, these families could only afford apartments renting under $50 per month. Very few such units were vacant.[74] And even if they had been, Stamm told council that "the great majority of people living in the project area are colored, and are certain to be discriminated against in their efforts to relocate in other parts of the city."[75]

Still, Stamm remained optimistic about meeting the need to relocate blacks. Using a market survey done by the Cincinnati Bureau of Research, Stamm claimed that some 4,000 to 5,000 of the city's blacks could afford to pay $50 or more per month for housing. If these blacks could be provided new housing, then their vacated dwellings might provide much of the needed space for the displaced. Local builders assured Stamm that they could, in fact, build rental housing for blacks in the $40 to $70 per month range and prefab-

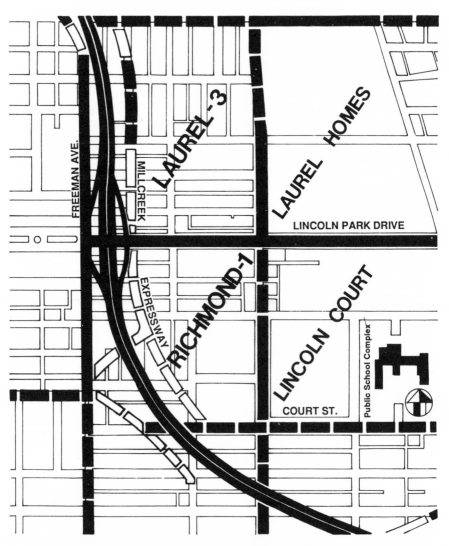

Map 10-A. Urban Redevelopment Sites, Laurel-3, Richmond-1

ricated homes for purchase between $9,000 and $10,000. Stamm conceded that finding sites would be difficult because housing for blacks would stir "considerable opposition from the surrounding neighborhoods." But he added that, if necessary, outside builders could be obtained who would "not be subject to the pressure which would be placed on the local builder." [76]

Persuaded that the black relocation housing problem could be handled, council initiated the West End redevelopment housing scheme by placing a $2.35-million urban redevelopment bond issue on the ballot for November 1951. At the same time, black Charterite Councilman Theodore Berry secured the passage of a redevelopment policy asserting that no families would be displaced from a site unless suitable housing existed for them elsewhere. It also stipulated that displaced families should receive first preference in redevelopment projects and that developers using cleared land could not practice racial discrimination in their projects. But the bond issue failed, defeated by 61 percent of those voting in one project site and by 58 percent of those voting in the other site. The BHL ascribed the West End's rejection of the bond issue to the vagueness of relocation plans. [77]

Indeed, private efforts at providing relocation housing for the poor and the black floundered during this period. After selling its Glen Meadows land and plans, the CCDC attempted to build housing for blacks. As expected, the company faced difficulties in finding adequate low-density sites. One report observed that building for blacks "automatically removed from consideration" about seventy sites. [78] Nevertheless, the CCDC found two small tracts in Woodlawn and Lincoln Heights, and built thirty-three prefabricated single-family houses. But sales in the Chester Road Development and the Lindale Subdivision moved slowly, resulting in the termination of the CCDC's black housing efforts, since little demand seemed evident among blacks for the $9,000 and $10,000 houses in these sites. [79]

Although the city gained nearly 3,000 new rental units by September of 1952, including the Warner-Kanter Company's 910-unit Stratford Manor and the Jonathan Woodner Company's 1,170-unit Swifton Village, private industry failed to provide adequately for those scheduled for relocation, blacks and the poor. [80] Only the defeated bond issues, and the postponement in starting the city's expressway system, scheduled for 1952, saved the city from a major relocation housing mess. The first stage of highway construction, which would have displaced about 3,000 families, did not commence until 1955 principally because of the inability of Elmwood Place and St. Bernard, separate municipalities, to agree on the location, design, and financing of their parts in the expressway system. [81]

These postponements bought time for both public and private housing developers who planned to build relocation housing, which despite the claims of city council, simply did not exist. This was particularly true of low-cost housing for families earning under $2,000. None of the efforts at privately sponsored relocation efforts included this group because it was assumed that the CMHA could take care of it. Indeed, public housing in the 1950s became a primary vehicle for relocation housing. And the city's relocation strategy for the pending urban redevelopment program acknowledged that the bulk of displaced persons would be black, that those blacks who could afford private-sector housing would find it in all-black neighborhoods or in neighborhoods undergoing racial transition from white to black, and that the CMHA would take care of the rest.[82] However, that agency, dependent on favorable court rulings and facing increased opposition from the local real-estate lobby, did not complete its first postwar public housing project until 1954.

Part of the delay stemmed from the tenuous legal status of public housing in Ohio. Although the Ohio General Assembly in 1949 passed a revised housing authority law which seemed to meet the court's earlier objections, no Ohio housing authority attempted to build public housing until the state supreme court ruled on the law's constitutionality. And its decision on June 20, 1951, left some doubt about the future of public housing in the state, since five of the seven court justices declared the law unconstitutional. According to the Ohio constitution, however, six votes invalidated a law. While the court thus upheld the new state housing authority law in practice, the CMHA feared its ability to secure federal grants or to market bonds because the law so narrowly missed being voided. Its fears were allayed on October 12, when the Public Housing Administration agreed to allow the local authority to participate in the 1949 Housing Act.[83]

The CMHA, however, ran into new barriers and opposition when it attempted to modify its previous strategy of building massive, self-contained public housing communities in favor of the construction of housing projects that would use existing neighborhood and community facilities, a policy dovetailing neatly with the 1948 master plan's goal of dividing all the metropolitan area's residential sector into neighborhoods and communities. Earlier large-scale developments were now criticized for isolating tenants from the larger community, rather than providing a positive community experience. Although some proponents of public housing argued that the 160 CMHA-owned acres immediately north of Winton Terrace were the logical site for a "little city" of public housing, like "a little Greenhills with schools, stores and recreation," Ramsey Findlater, director of the CMHA, opposed making the Winton Terrace area "an island in the community." Others agreed and predicted that public housing tenants in such a project "would withdraw from community activities" and lose "their constructive values as individuals." Less than a year later, a representative of the Citizens' Committee on Slum Clearance opposed large-scale, self-contained projects for another reason. "Such a plan," he observed, was "based on the point of view that low income families are undesirable and should be segregated from the rest of the community to avoid contamination."[84]

By the fifties, then, the strategy of segregating low-income families in supervised, self-contained neighborhood community projects for social/cultural experiences deemed necessary for a productive life gave way to a new strategy emphasizing the tenants' right to participate in the larger community from the start, by living in smaller projects in established neighborhoods.[85]

Implementation of this new strategy proved difficult for several reasons. First, appropriate building sites' were hard to find. The CMHA limited its possibilities by deciding to build only in areas where the "topography or other characteristics would preclude development by private builders but where costs of grading, sewers, water mains and street paving would not be immeasurably excessive."[86] In addition, the CMHA announced that it would not build public housing on redevelopment sites, for they seemed more appropriate for private sector construction.[87]

Even after the CMHA found sites fitting these criteria, local public housing continued to face severe problems. Most of the city's neighborhoods simply did not want "projects" located near them. For instance, the authority's first postwar attempt at public housing ran into strong resistance from the Northside–South Cumminsville–College Hill–Mt. Airy Home Owners Association, an organization specifically founded to fight contemplated public housing on that side of town.[88] This group formed after the CMHA announced in April 1952 that it intended to build a 340-unit project on a 35.8-acre site formerly used for dairy farming.

Neighbors of the Kirby Road public housing site (just north of Frederick Avenue) vehemently protested on finding out the CMHA's intentions.[89] Realtor John Bullock, organizer of the resistance, secured 1,000 signatures on a petition which charged that public housing would increase crime and delinquency while decreasing property values in surrounding neighborhoods. Housing officials, however, believed that since blacks would be admitted to the project, the racial issue most rallied neighborhood opposition. According to one report, those passing petitions had asked homeowners, "Do you want Niggers in your backyard?"[90]

Although the petition drive failed to sway the CMHA, the Home Owners Association lawyer, Gordon Scherer, secured a temporary injunction restraining immediate building on the site. And during the delay, the CMHA's option to buy the land expired and the parcel was sold to another developer. The CMHA still could have obtained the land through eminent domain proceedings, but decided against this, perhaps because of the controversy, or perhaps because the new developer, S. A. Ruebel and Company, planned to build moderately priced homes.[91]

Soon after the Kirby site controversy, the local real-estate board mounted a citywide challenge to public housing in Cincinnati. In July 1952, the realtors initiated a petition campaign to mandate a public referendum on public housing in the upcoming election. If passed, the referendum would require voter approval of all new public housing projects before council could contract with the CMHA to provide local services. Furthermore, the proposed amendment to the city charter forbade council to accept payments in lieu of taxes from the CMHA at less than the full taxed value of the project. This clause alone would prevent additional public housing in the city.[92]

Other organizations, such as the Home Builders Association and the Home Savings and Loan Companies, joined the campaign for the charter amendment. Despite claims by Cincinnati public housing proponents that the local fight against public housing was part of a new strategy by the National Association of Real Estate Boards to defeat subsidized low-cost housing, Oscar E. Bauman, chairman of the Committee to Amend the City Charter for Public Housing, argued that "this petition is a grass roots movement confined entirely to Cincinnati." He continued that "when the Metropolitan Housing Authority began scattering the slums throughout the city by selecting sites on vacant land, . . . representatives of home owning groups, building and others, were of the opinion that public housing should be put to a vote of the people for determination."[93]

The petitioners succeeded in placing their referendum on the November ballot. In a vitriolic campaign, proponents of the referendum charged that public housing was expensive, wasteful, and robbed local builders of opportunities and the city of valuable tax dollars. Others saw the amendment as a way to combat increasing encroachment of the federal government into local affairs. For example, A. R. Tenhundfeld, president of the Greater Cincinnati Savings and Loan Exchange, favored the amendment because "it is time we retained home rule instead of bureaucratic rule dictated from Washington."[94]

Opponents of the amendment, such as the powerful Citizens Development Committee (formerly the Citizens Planning Association), campaigned against the charter amendment because they believed it would prevent the construction of needed relocation housing and thus delay the construction of Millcreek Expressway and redevelopment in the West End. Other groups, including the Citizens' Committee on Slum Clearance, and the three municipal newspapers, also opposed the amendments for similar reasons. Their efforts proved fruitful when on November 6, 1952, Cincinnatians defeated the referendum by more than 35,000 votes, 113,671 to 76,025.[95]

Only after the referendum's failure did the CMHA actually begin building public housing again. It erected its first project in an isolated and depressed area near Beekman Street, not far from the Mill Creek Valley railroad yards in Cincinnati. Actually, the CMHA planned two projects for the area, Millvale North, a 336-unit effort, and Millvale South, a 280-unit project. However in the spring of 1953, just before construction started, the CMHA's Kirby site nemesis, John Bullock, obtained a temporary injunction to prevent the CMHA from taking some land he owned at the Millvale project site.[96] Since the CMHA feared the suit might not be settled until the fall of 1953, it developed Millvale North without the disputed land. An early and favorable court decision allowed the CMHA to add the forty units Bullock's suit had delayed, so that Millvale North opened by the spring of 1954. The CMHA finished Millvale South the following year and dedicated that 280-unit project on December 2, 1955.[97]

Additional housing sites proved harder to come by, delaying the erection of additional public housing. For instance, the CMHA never found an appropriate alternative site for the cancelled Kirby Road project. Unable to locate another acceptable site on which to build a 340-unit project, the CMHA decided to build two 170-unit projects, one at the 13.7-acre Red Bank–Corsia Road site, and another on 11.6 acres situated near Camargo Road, both rural slums just east of the city. However neighborhood resistance and legal technicalities prevented the CMHA from starting either project. The CMHA also failed to acquire a Madisonville site planned for black housing. Because of its inability to find suitable new sites for public housing, the CMHA was forced after 1955 to add the remaining allocated dwellings to its old project sites, an idea it had strongly resisted.[98]

Nor did private builders, assisted by Section 221 of the National Housing Act, have any better luck finding sites for their developments. The Section 221 program, created by the Housing Act of 1954, provided a type of mortgage insurance designed to promote the construction of dwelling units for low and middle-income families displaced by the government's slum clearance and highway building programs. Although plenty of vacant land existed, particularly on the outskirts of Cincinnati, opposition developed almost immediately once plans for Section 221 housing became public. For example, one builder found a site for a 200-unit project in an unincorporated but developed area known as Delhi Hills, west of the city. However, after neighbors found out that the builder planned Section 221 housing, opposition stirred. For Cincinnatians identified Section 221 housing with relocation housing, and relocation with black housing, something that the Delhi residents wanted to avoid. No Section 221 housing was ever built in Delhi. This scenario was repeated throughout the metropolitan area. A builder from Dayton planned to build a 250-unit Section 221 project in Sharonville, a pleasant industrial community thirteen miles northeast of central Cincinnati. At the Regional Planning Commission hearings, necessary to change zoning for the site from industrial to residential, Sharonville suburbanites protested that a mass housing project for low-income families would crowd their schools, congest their traffic, and lower property values. Less publicized, but nevertheless just as important, was their commitment to keep Sharonville white.[99] Unable to secure new housing once they were displaced, blacks started flooding into nearby neighborhoods, resulting in a rapid transition of many inner-city areas from white to black. And increased building on the city's periphery for whites encouraged the tendency for whites to move out.

The largest of these suburban projects was built with a specific eye toward providing more room in the corporate city by encouraging white flight to the suburbs. In 1951 the Public Housing Administration announced its intention to sell 3,400 acres of land originally assembled for Greenhills, the federal greenbelt project of the mid-1930s. After pressure from Charles Stamm, assistant to the city manager in charge of urban redevelopment, the federal government agreed to sell the entire tract intact. Consequently, the Cincinnati Community Development Company purchased the land for $1,250,000 on September 22, 1952. The housing company hoped to attract a capable developer who would build middle-class community housing on the largest tract of land for residential housing ever assembled in the metropolitan area. The CCDC succeeded in arousing the interests of Robert Gerholz of Flint, Michigan, and Richard J. Seltzer of Philadelphia. These two tentatively committed themselves to develop a 10,000-home model community. They, in turn, procured the services of Cincinnati's nationally prominent planner, Ladislas Segoe, to draw up plans for the project. Before work began on this community project, Gerholz and Seltzer pulled out of the venture for a variety of reasons, including their doubt of its economic feasibility.[100]

In their stead, the CCDC secured the services of the Warner-Kanter Company of Birmingham, Alabama. That company proceeded to construct the new community of Forest Park in 1955, thus encouraging the outward movement of Cincinnati whites. Other developers joined this trend and found no difficulty in building middle-class suburban developments for white Cincinnatians. Meanwhile Cincinnati blacks moved into slightly rundown neighborhoods, creating new tensions and adjustments, and encouraging even more white flight.[101]

Neighborhood community, which in the thirties had been hailed as the salvation of the metropolis by creating a new commitment to civic consciousness and metropolitan loyalty, now helped fragment the metropolis between white and black, poor and rich, city and suburb. Public housing no longer served as a training ground for the upwardly mobile, but as a receptacle for society's refuse. Although the language of community neighborhood remained a part of public housing in the 1950s, the meaning of that language changed drastically.[102]

Moreover, by the fifties, housing reform failed to attract the vibrant leadership of an earlier era. Leaders of that movement in the first half of the century had believed that territorial-based communities were basic units of society and could mold individual behavior. Housing activists in the fifties replaced that vision with one that stressed the individual over the community and downplayed the life-shaping impact of neighborhood community. This shift coincided with a changing conception of the metropolis from a social system made up of natural but differentiated social and cultural parts to a more mechanistic view which emphasized the artificiality of the metropolis and envisioned the individual as the real and fundamental unit of society.[103] As a result, good low-cost housing in the fifties provided basic services to individuals, such as shelter, health care, and even recreation.[104] Housing officials, however, no longer emphasized community as a molder of group behavior in the way that they had during the era of large-scale community neighborhood developments.

This shift took place about the time Congress passed the Housing Act of 1954, a law which reflected the older comprehensive emphasis of the metropolitan/community mode of thought. Just as the 1948 Cincinnati plan called for the rehabilitation and conservation of neighborhoods throughout the city, rather than merely clearance and redevelopment of selected slum areas, the 1954 bill made provisions for a similar strategy.[105]

Soon after President Eisenhower signed the new housing bill, Cincinnati initiated a renewal program of rehabilitation and conservation in the Avondale-Corryville section of the city near the University of Cincinnati. But because the Housing Act of 1954's appearance coincided with the redefinition of planning and housing priorities, it is best remembered in that city for allowing civic leaders to undertake a massive redevelopment of Cincinnati's core area, i.e. the central business district, riverfront, and lower West End. Revitalizing the urban core through developing industrial parks, constructing sports stadiums, and modernizing the central business district replaced the emphasis on low-cost housing as the central issue in the 1950s and 1960s. Indeed, comprehensive planning for the central business district, rather than for the metropolitan area, characterized this era.[106]

Although downtown deterioration had been underway since at least the 1930s, only in 1955 did the City Planning Commission decide to examine business district decay as a discrete problem. That year it initiated such a study, and published the city's first central business district plan in 1957 and 1958. The two-volume document, developed to make the central business district "a better place to do business," focused on traffic circulation, land use, and building groups. It called for the implementation of a circulation system plan to improve the accessibility of the central business district; recommended a special zoning ordinance; requested that a committee be formed to improve the district's physical appearance; and called for the formation of a Public Buildings Group in downtown Cincinnati.[107]

The findings of the City Planning Commission's study served as a focal point for a growing discourse in Cincinnati about the needs of the central business district. Old planning groups such as the Citizens' Development Committee joined with the more recently created Central Business District Advisory Board to discuss how congestion, inadequate parking facilities, and a deteriorating physical setting threatened the central business district's future.[108]

Several years later the Cincinnati Planning Commission issued the "Central Business District and Riverfront Report," which also confronted the problem of decay. That somber report observed how "the efforts of both private and public enterprises [had] failed to attract new investment in the core in sufficient quantity." It called for urban renewal not only to reverse the trends of blight and decay, but to provide new opportunities for public and private enterprise to work together to improve the center of the city.[109] By 1961, local officials and downtown interests had made a firm commitment to downtown redevelopment.

Even the Avondale-Corryville neighborhood renewal project took a tone different from earlier community housing programs. The public and private community housing programs of the 1920s, 1930s, and 1940s had been planned by experts to encourage the economic and social health of the entire metropolitan community. But new neighborhood renewal efforts suggested that neighborhoods should be shaped to meet the desires of their residents. D. Reid Ross, executive secretary of the BHL, echoed this sentiment when he observed that urban renewal aimed to develop "neighborhood environments in line with specific needs of the residents of the particular neighborhoods to be renewed." The city's workable program, a plan of action to meet the problems of slums, blight, and community development generally, repeated the same theme and required citizen participation in the planning process. Because of this program, required to secure federal urban renewal monies, "the occupants of any neighborhood chosen for a specific renewal project" were for the first time in the city's history "to participate in carrying out the renewal of their immediate environment."[110] Moreover, it was after 1955 that the city's community council movement appeared, due to the efforts of City Planning Director Herb Stevens. He promoted the establishment of a community council in Avondale to help neighborhood residents cope with the changing racial composition expected in their community as a result of the highway and renewal projects. Stevens's efforts, based on assumptions that planning ought to be with rather than merely for city residents, marks an important shift in the Cincinnati planning establishment's approach.[111] A similar emphasis appeared in approaches to central business district renewal. Planners asked businessmen what they wanted for their district. In all cases, the desires and needs of those citizens associated with areas affected by urban renewal gained new importance.[112]

The 1950s, then, saw the breakdown of the metropolitan/community mode of thought. Metropolitan planning and housing reform lost out to a more parochial focus emphasizing the health and vitality of the city's core. The vision of an organic metropolis stressing cooperation gave way to metropolis as battleground for the contest between city and suburb over the region's wealth and population. And low-cost housing, once seen as a tool for true social change, now merely served as a receptacle for the displaced—a vehicle that allowed Cincinnati to improve the efficiency and appearance of its urban core, so that that core could retain its dominance in the metropolitan area.

Of course too much can be made of the low-cost housing and planning movements under the old vision. Reformers never successfully resolved the low-cost housing problem as they had conceptualized it. They failed to address the tension between the centralizing tendencies of their vision (i.e., creating a more unified metropolis through making better citizens) and the fragmenting reality of their projects (often island communities sharing nothing in common with nearby neighborhoods.) Nor had they ever really solved the black housing problem. For their definition of good community discouraged integration and played a major role in creating the "second ghetto." The persistence of inadequate black housing also shows the limitations of a movement dominated by white professionals and businessmen and suggests how powerless this group was in some circumstances to affect change as they perceived the need.

Moreover, the community development strategy's unwillingness to address the issue of the very poor proved unfortunate. In many cases, housing reformers and planners prescribed remedies for the city which actually hurt the poor by eliminating the only housing they could afford. The constant shifting of this population also precipitated new slum areas, the very thing these community reformers sought to prevent. Moreover, the neglect of the neediest made public housing vulnerable to the charges of the real-estate lobby that public housing undercut the private-housing market by focusing on the worthy poor. Thus, at the very time public housing started providing shelter for the neediest, it faced strong objections from opponents made during the years that good housing emphasized citizen-building for the salvageable rather than adequate shelter for the destitute.

Indeed a major problem with the community development strategy was its dependence on federal money at a time when dependence made its programs vulnerable to the uproar surrounding the new federal-urban relationship. Furthermore, Congress never seemed fully committed to the reformers' vision. And barriers within the American federal system sometimes impeded successful implementation of the programs.

Despite the serious shortcomings which complicated housing programs under the new vision of the 1950s, the community development strategy, with its emphasis on a cooperative approach to neighborhood and metropolitan problems, reminds us that there are ways of addressing and responding to metropolitan problems other than today's highly fragmented and adversarial approach. Finally, it suggests the importance that problem definition plays in our response to the needs of our urban areas. These lessons seem important, since today's metropolis also faces a set of housing and planning problems which need prompt and decisive action.

Notes

Introduction

1. *Housing Act of 1949, Statutes at Large*, vol. 63, sec. 2, p. 413 (1949).

2. This is in contrast to the recent literature, which has emphasized conflict between housers and planners. For the best presentation of this view, see Peter Marcuse, "Housing in Early City Planning," *Journal of Urban History* 6 (February 1980): 153–76. Also see Donald A. Krueckeberg, "Between the Housers and the Planners: the Recollections of Coleman Woodbury," in *The American Planner: Biographies and Recollections*, ed. Donald A. Krueckeberg (New York: Methuen, 1983), pp. 341–45; Marc A. Weiss, "The Origins and Legacy of Urban Renewal," in *Urban and Regional Planning in an Age of Austerity*, ed. Pierre Clavel et al. (New York: Pergamon Press, 1980), pp. 63–65.

3. Roderick D. McKenzie, *The Metropolitan Community* (New York: McGraw Hill Book Co., 1933), p. 293.

4. The clearest and most engaging interpretation of early housing reform as racist belongs to Thomas Philpott, *The Slum and the Ghetto: Neighborhood Deterioration and Middle-Class Reform, Chicago, 1880–1930* (New York: Oxford University Press, 1978). For another example of conventional literature which stresses the dual themes of central business district preservation and racism in its history of housing reform, see Arnold R. Hirsch, *Making the Second Ghetto: Race and Housing in Chicago, 1940–1960* (Cambridge: Cambridge University Press, 1983). Also see Roy Lubove, *Twentieth Century Pittsburgh: Government, Business and Environmental Change* (New York: John Wiley and Sons, 1969); Christopher Silver, *Twentieth-Century Richmond: Planning, Politics, and Race* (Knoxville: University of Tennessee, 1984); Weiss, "The Origins and Legacy of Urban Renewal," pp. 53–80.

5. U.S. Department of the Interior, Census Office, *Statistics of the United States in 1860*, p. lviii; U.S. Department of Commerce, Bureau of the Census, *Fourteenth Census of the United States, 1920: Population*, 3: 799–800; Zane L. Miller, "Cincinnati Germans and the Invention of an Ethnic Group," *Queen City Heritage* 42 (Fall 1984): 13–22.

6. Robert W. DeForest and Lawrence Veiller, eds., *The Tenement House Problem Including the Report of the New York State Tenement House Commission of 1900*, 2 vols. (New York: Macmillan Co., 1903), 1: 144; U.S. Department of Commerce, Bureau of the Census, *Sixteenth Census of the United States, 1940*, 2: 125–27.

7. "Cincinnati Completes Master-Plan Project," *American City*, June 1949, p. 149.

8. "A New Experiment in Town Planning to Fit the Motor Age," *New York Times*, August 24, 1924.

9. *Cincinnati Enquirer*, May 18, 1954.

10. John Ihlder, Bleecker Marquette and Charlottee Rumbold, "Definitions and Causes," appendix 6, in *Slums, Large Scale Housing and Decentralization*, ed. John M. Gries and James Ford (Washington: President's Conference on Home Building and Home Ownership, 1932), 3: 41–45; Eugenie Ladner Birch, "Edith Elmer Wood and the Genesis of Liberal Housing Thought, 1910–1942," (Ph.D. diss., Columbia University, 1975), p. 204.

11. Wolfgang G. Roeseler, "Reflections on Segoe," *Planning* 46 (November 1980): 5.

12. Lawrence C. Gerckens, "Bettman of Cincinnati," in *The American Planner*, pp. 128–45; *Cincinnati Times-Star*, January 22, 1945; Laurence C. Gerckens, "Glancing Back," *Planning* 46 (October 1980): 23–24; Daniel Schaffer, *Garden Cities for America: The Radburn Experience* (Philadelphia: Temple University Press, 1982), p. 73.

13. *Cincinnati Times-Star*, January 22, 1945.

14. Gerckens, "Bettman of Cincinnati," p. 133–35.

15. Arthur C. Comey, ed., *City and Regional Planning Papers by Alfred Bettman*, with a foreword by John Lord O'Brian (Cambridge, Mass.: Harvard University Press, 1946), pp. iv–xix; Mark I. Gelfand, *A Nation of Cities: The Federal Government and Urban America, 1933–1965* (New York: Oxford University Press, 1975), pp. 127–31, 140–42; Gerckens, "Bettman of Cincinnati," pp. 142–43.

16. Gerckens, "Bettman of Cincinnati," p. 145.

17. Interview, Ladislas Segoe, November 30, 1979; "The Recollections of Ladislas Segoe," edited by Donald A. Krueckeberg from an interview conducted by Sydney H. Williams, in *The American Planner*, pp. 301–5, 315.

18. "The Recollections of Ladislas Segoe," p. 302; "Segoe on Cincinnati," *Planning* 46 (October 1980): 24.

19. Urbanism Committee, *Our Cities: Their Role in the National Economy* (Washington: Government Printing Office, 1937), p. v; Gelfand, *Nation of Cities*, pp. 87, 117.

20. Ralph A. Straetz, *PR Politics in Cincinnati* (New York: New York University Press, 1958), pp. 82–87; Geneva A. Seybold, "Dykstra of Cincinnati," *Survey Graphic*, April 1937, p. 204. Also see "The Cincinnati Miracle Seen through Boston Eyes," *American City*, January 1928, p. 381.

Part I

1. Henry D. Shapiro, "The Place of Culture and the Problem of Identity," in *Appalachia and America: Autonomy and Regional Dependence*, ed. Allen Batteau (Lexington: University of Kentucky Press, 1983), p. 112.

2. Paul Boyer, *Urban Masses and Moral Order in America, 1820–1920* (Cambridge, Mass.: Harvard University Press, 1978), p. 224.

3. M. Christine Boyer has recently emphasized how late nineteenth-century reformers desired to discipline and regulate the urban masses. Toward this end, much attention was given to the social impact of the environment. M. Christine Boyer, *Dreaming the Rational City: The Myth of American City Planning* (Cambridge, Mass.: MIT Press, 1983), pp. 1–59. Also see Philpott, *The Slum and the Ghetto*, pp. 3–109.

4. See for example, Carroll D. Wright, *The Slums of Baltimore, Chicago, New York and Philadelphia: Seventh Special Report of the Commissioner of Labor* (Washington: Government Printing Office, 1894); DeForest and Veiller, eds., *The Tenement House Problem*.

5. Robert H. Bremner, *From the Depths: The Discovery of Poverty in the United States* (New York: New York University Press, 1956), pp. 140–63.

6. Ernest W. Burgess, ed., *The Urban Community* (Chicago: University of Chicago Press, 1926), preface.

7. Late nineteenth-century Americans placed high value on good home life and believed that it offered the key to self-improvement. Gwendolyn Wright, *Building the Dream: A Social History of Housing in America* (New York: Pantheon Books, 1981), pp. 91–134.

8. DeForest and Veiller, eds., *The Tenement House Problem*, 1: 11. For more on Veiller see Roy Lubove, *The Progressives and the Slums: Tenement House Reform in New York City, 1890–1917* (Pittsburgh: University of Pittsburgh Press, 1962), pp. 117–84.

Chapter 1

1. Bremner, *From the Depths*, pp. 3–15; Alan I Marcus, "In Sickness and in Health: The Marriage of the Municipal Corporation to the Public Interest and the Problem of Public Health, 1820–1870. The Case of Cincinnati" (Ph.D. diss., University of Cincinnati, 1979), pp. 189–91.

2. *Sixteenth Annual Report of the Cincinnati Relief Union* (Cincinnati: Times Stean Book and Job Office, 1865), pp. 5, 9.

3. *Eighteenth Annual Report of the Cincinnati Relief Union* (Cincinnati: Times Stean Book and Job Office, 1867), p. 25.

4. U.S. Department of the Interior, Census Office, *U.S. Ninth Census, 1870*, vol. 1, *Statistics of the Population of the United States*, p. 598.

5. Cincinnati, "Thirteenth Annual Report of the Health Department . . . for the Year Ending December 31, 1879," *Annual Reports of the City Departments of the City of Cincinnati for the Year Ending December 31, 1879* (Cincinnati: F.O. Carnahan and Co., 1880), p. 550. The report defined tenements as "all dwellings occupied by more

than two families . . . hotels and large Boarding houses excluded." U.S. Department of the Interior, Census Office, *U.S. Tenth Census, 1880*, vol. 17, *Report on the Social Statistics of Cities*, pt. 2, *The Southern and Western States*, p. 344.

6. Lubove, *Progressives and the Slums*, p. 31; Philpott, *The Slum and the Ghetto*, p. 7–12. Chicago tenements in the nineteenth century were often frame dwellings of one or two stories which looked to the casual observer like single-family, working-class housing.

7. C. M. Hubbard, "The Tenement House Problem in Cincinnati," *Proceedings of the National Conference of Charities and Correction* (Atlanta, 1903), pp. 352–54.

8. Dudley W. Rhodes, *Creed and Greed* (Cincinnati: n.p., 1879), pp. 124–25.

9. Cincinnati, "Annual Report of the Board of Administration . . . for the Year Ending December 31, 1897," *Annual Reports of the City Departments of the City of Cincinnati . . . for the Year Ending December 31, 1897* (Cincinnati: Commercial Gazette Job Print, 1898), p. 1530.

10. Zane L. Miller, *Boss Cox's Cincinnati: Urban Politics in the Progressive Era* (New York: Oxford University Press, 1968), pp. 18, 6; *Houses or Homes: The First Report of the Cincinnati Better Housing League* (Cincinnati, 1919), pp. 10–11.

11. U.S. Department of the Interior, Census Office, *U.S. Eleventh Census, 1890, Vital Statistics, Cities of 100,000 Population and Upward*, pp. 182–97; Miller, *Boss Cox's Cincinnati*, p. 13.

12. Cincinnati, "Housing Department Report for 1913," *Annual Reports of the Officers, Boards, and Departments of the City of Cincinnati for 1913* (Cincinnati, 1914), p. 592.

13. Marcus, "In Sickness and in Health," p. 189; C. R. Hebble, "Housing Reform in 1869," *Survey*, February 10, 1917, p. 559.

14. Cincinnati, "Eighth Annual Report of the Board of Health . . . for the Year Ending December 31, 1874," *Annual Reports of the City Departments . . . for the Year Ending December 31, 1874* (Cincinnati: Cincinnati Times Stean Job Printing Establishment, 1875), p. 432; Hebble, "Housing Reform in 1869," p. 559; James Ford, *Slums and Housing*, 2 vols. (Cambridge, Mass.: Harvard University Press, 1936), 1: 154–55.

15. Ohio, *An Act to Regulate the Construction of Buildings within Any City of the First Class . . . , Statutes (1888)*, 85: 34–53.

16. A similar component approach to the city can be found in the commission form of government popular at the turn of the century. The commission charters usually provided for a mayor-president plus commissioners of discrete departments such as finance and revenue, waterworks and sewage, streets and public property, and fire and police. These semiautonomous departments often focused on their specific functions rather than the city as a whole. See Bradley Robert Rice, *Progressive Cities: The Commission Government Movement in America, 1901–1920* (Austin: University of Texas Press, 1977). For more on the component approach to the turn-of-the-century city, see Miller, *Boss Cox's Cincinnati*, p. 117; and David Handlin, *The American Home: Architecture and Society, 1815–1915* (Boston: Little, Brown, and Co., 1979), p. 142; Dana Francis White, "The Self-Conscious City: A Survey and Bibliographical Summary of Periodical Literature on American Urban Themes: 1865–1900" (Ph.D. diss., George Washington University, 1969).

17. Robert H. Wiebe discusses the late nineteenth-century concern with the poor in *The Search for Order, 1877–1920* (New York: Hill and Wang, 1967), pp. 76–110. See also Marcuse, "Housing in Early City Planning," p. 168; Zane L. Miller nicely lays out the late nineteenth-century tensions between the circle (his term for the inner city), the zone of emergence, and the hilltop "suburban" residents. Miller, *Boss Cox's Cincinnati*, pp. 3–56. A strong contemporary statement about the threat of the poor can be found in Jacob A. Riis, *The Battle with the Slum* (New York: Macmillan, 1902).

18. Miller, *Boss Cox's Cincinnati*, pp. 117–18.

19. James Albert Green, *History of the Associated Charities of Cincinnati, 1879–1937* (n.p., n.d.), p. 11; Associated Charities of Cincinnati, *Twelfth Annual Report, 1891–1892* (Cincinnati, n.d.), p. 7.

20. Ohio Bureau of Labor, "Tenement Houses in Cincinnati," *Eighteenth Annual Report of the Bureau of Labor Statistics . . . 1894* (Norwalk, Ohio: Laning Printing Co., 1895), p. 72; Wright, *The Slums of Baltimore, Chicago, New York and Philadelphia*, pp. 13–19.

21. Ohio Bureau of Labor, "Tenement Houses in Cincinnati," pp. 72–73.

22. Ibid., p. 73.

23. Ibid., pp. 74–75.

24. Constitution and By Laws, United Jewish Charities of Cincinnati, Minutes, June 4, 1896, United Jewish Charities of Cincinnati (UJC) Papers, American Jewish Archives, Hebrew Union College–Jewish Institute of Religion; United Jewish Social Agencies File, ibid.; United Jewish Charities of Cincinnati, Minutes, Board of Governors, August 13, 1896, p. 86, ibid. Cincinnati, a stronghold of American Reform Judaism, exhibited little of the prejudice toward its German Jews that might be expected at that time. According to Zane Miller, by 1900 Jews had been fully accepted in the Chamber of Commerce and other commercial civic and fraternal organizations. Moreover, Miller argued that Cincinnati Jews participated in local politics—"more so, perhaps, than the German Jews of any other American city—but not as a self-conscious ethnic bloc." Miller, *Boss Cox's Cincinnati*, pp. 129–30. Two German Jews, Julius Fleischman (1900–1905) and Frederick Spiegel (1914–15) served the Republican machine first controlled by Cox and later by Rudolph Hynicka. During the 1920s, however, Charter reform Mayor Murray Seasongood, a German Jew, played a major role in crushing the Republican organization. Melvin G. Holli and Peter d'A. Jones, eds., *Biographical Dictionary of American Mayors, 1820–1980* (Westport, Conn.: Greenwood Press, 1981), pp. 119–20, 340, 323–24.

25. *Cincinnati Enquirer*, August 16, 1898, p. 12; *General Ordinances of the City of Cincinnati, 1887–1905* (Cincinnati: Commercial Gazette Job Printing Co., 1905), Ordinance 218, pp. 53ff; *Charities Bulletin* 1 (October 1901): 5.

26. Constitution and By Laws, United Jewish Charities of Cincinnati, Minutes, June 4, 1896, UJC Papers.

27. *Charities Bulletin* 3 (October 1903): 4.

28. *Eighteenth Annual Report of the Cincinnati Relief Union*, p. 25.

29. Associated Charities of Cincinnati, *Twelfth Annual Report, 1891–1892* (Cincinnati, n.d.), p. 7; Minutes, Central Board of Asssociated Charities, May 24, 1895, Associated Charities/Family Services Files, Cincinnati Historical Society (CHS);

Cincinnati Tribune, October 11, 1895, p. 8; *Cincinnati Enquirer*, October 11, 1895, p. 8.

30. Barbara L. Musselman, "The Quest for Collective Improvement: Cincinnati Workers, 1893–1920," (Ph.D. diss., University of Cincinnati, 1975), p. 199.

31. *Charities Bulletin* 1 (October 1901): 5; Associated Charities of Cincinnati, *Twenty-Second Annual Report, 1901–2* (Cincinnati, 1902), pp. 8–9.

32. Philpott, *The Slum and the Ghetto*, pp. 204–5.

33. *Charities Bulletin* 2 (July 1902): 10.

34. *Charities Bulletin* 3 (February 1903): 8; Associated Charities of Cincinnati, *Twenty-Third Annual Report, 1902–3* (Cincinnati, 1903), p. 10.

35. Cincinnati, "Report of the Health Officer," *Annual Reports of the City Departments . . . for the Year Ending December 31, 1903* (Cincinnati: Commercial Gazette Job Rooms Print, 1903), p. 827.

36. *Charities Bulletin* 1 (October 1901): 8.

37. Miller, *Boss Cox's Cincinnati*, p. 179; *Citizens' Bulletin*, August 6, 1903; *Cincinnati Commercial Tribune*, March 6, 1903.

38. *Citizens' Bulletin*, Aug. 1, 1903, p. 2; *Cincinnati Commercial Tribune*, March 6, 1903. The Monday Evening Club was formed from the Business Men's Benevolent Advisory Committee and included professional social workers, clergymen, educators, and public-minded citizens. Julie Ann Mooney, "Private Welfare and the Cincinnati Community Chest, 1915–1956," (M.A. thesis, University of Cincinnati, 1966), p. 35.

39. *Charities Bulletin* 3 (October 1903): 4.

40. "City Club Tenement Report," *Citizens' Bulletin* (March 2, 1907), p. 4; *Midsummer Bulletin* (Associated Charities), July 1905, p. 5; Associated Charities, *Twenty-Fourth Annual Report, 1903–4* (Cincinnati 1904), p. 6.

41. *Charities' Review* 9 (May 1909); ibid., (January 1909), p. 12.

42. Cincinnati, *Building Code, Codification of Ordinances of the City of Cincinnati, 1911* (Cincinnati: City of Cincinnati, 1911), pp. 219–24. The code defined a tenement as "a house or building or portion thereof which is rented, leased, let or hired out to be occupied, or is occupied as the home or residence of three or more families living independently of each other and doing their cooking upon the premises, but having a common right in the hallways, stairways, yards, waterclosets or some of them" (p. 140).

43. *Williams' Cincinnati Directory, June 1917* (Cincinnati: Williams' Directory Co., 1917), p. 7.

Chapter 2

1. Minutes, Board of Trustees of Associated Charities, March 7, 1910, Associated Charities/Family Service Papers, CHS.

2. *Citizens' Bulletin*, April 16, 1910, p. 1.

3. The Bureau of Municipal Research was created in 1909 by the business community to apply the new standards of political science and business efficiency to local government. Miller, *Boss Cox's Cincinnati*, p. 158; *The Cincinnati Bureau of Research: Its First Year's Work* (Cincinnati, 1910), pp. 19–20; *Report of Cincinnati*

Bureau of Municipal Research for the Two Years Ending June 30, 1913 (Cincinnati, 1913), pp. 19–20. For more on the Bureau of Municipal Research movement see Martin J. Schiesl, *The Politics of Efficiency: Municipal Administration and Reform in America, 1800–1920* (Berkeley: University of California Press, 1977), pp. 122–23.

4. Miller, *Boss Cox's Cincinnati*, pp. 200–22.

5. City of Cincinnati, *Annual Reports of the Officers, Boards and Departments of the City of Cincinnati for 1912*, p. 183.

6. *Testimony Taken before the Housing and Welfare Committee of the Chamber of Commerce, Cincinnati, Ohio*, 1914, CHS, pp. 90–91; *Report of the Bureau of Municipal Research for the Two Years Ending June 30, 1913*, p. 12; Cincinnati, *Annual Reports of the Officers and Departments of the City of Cincinnati for 1914*, p. 9. This new tenement house arrangement lasted only until August 17, 1914, when the city council returned the Tenement House Department to the Building Department, despite the protests of housing reformers. One reason for the move, according to John R. Holmes, director of public safety, was that under the independent department, the social welfare people were too much in control. Holmes claimed that the chief tenement house inspector, John R. Richards, recognized them and not the safety director as his supervisor. What this really seemed to be was an attempt by the so-called political machine to regain some of its power at the reformers' expense. Cincinnati, "Building Department Report of the Tenement House Work for the Year 1914." Cincinnati Better Housing League Papers (CBHL Papers), CHS; John R. Holmes to Lawrence Veiller, June 5, 1914, CBHL Papers, CHS.

7. George Daniel Smith, "History of the Anti-Tuberculosis League of Cincinnati, Ohio, from 1907 to 1950" (M.A. thesis, University of Cincinnati, 1951), p. 38; *Fourth Annual Report of the Cincinnati Anti-Tuberculosis League, 1910* (Cincinnati, n.d.), p. 38.

8. *Cincinnati Times-Star*, February 1, 1907; Smith, "History of Anti-Tuberculosis League," pp. 38–40.

9. *Sixth Annual Report of the Cincinnati Anti-Tuberculosis League, 1912* (Cincinnati, n.d.), p. 10.

10. Ibid.; *Fourth Annual Report of the Cincinnati Anti-Tuberculosis League, 1910*, p. 8; *Fifth Annual Report of the Anti-Tuberculosis League, 1911* (Cincinnati, n.d.), p. 21.

11. Speaking at the meeting were Dr. Samuel Iglaver, president of the Anti-Tuberculosis League; Dr. H. Kennan Dunham, medical director of the Branch Hospital; Judge Benton Oppenheimer; Professor William H. Parker of the University of Cincinnati; and Robert E. Todd, temporary chief tenement house inspector. *Sixth Annual Report of the Cincinnati Anti-Tuberculosis League, 1912*, p. 11.

12. Ibid., p. 12.

13. "Twenty-Seventh Annual Report of the Commissioner of Buildings," *Annual Reports of Officers, Boards and Departments of City of Cincinnati for 1913*, p. 330.

14. *Cincinnati Commercial Tribune*, December 6, 1912; *Cincinnati Enquirer*, December 7, 1912.

15. Despite Hitchens's speech, and the editorial support of the city's labor newspaper, the *Chronicle*, labor seemed to play a minor role in the local movement. Instead, the city's more prosperous citizens, who feared the social and civic conse-

quences of unsanitary and immoral housing conditions, led the better housing crusade. For a similar situation in Chicago see Philpott, *The Slum and the Ghetto*, pp. 89–110.

16. *Cincinnati Enquirer*, December 7, 1912.

17. *Sixty-Fifth Annual Report of the Cincinnati Chamber of Commerce, and Merchants' Exchange for the Year Ending December 31, 1913* (Cincinnati: Robert T. Morris Printing Co., 1915), p. 47.

18. Andrea Tuttle Kornbluh, *Lighting the Way . . . The Woman's City Club of Cincinnati, 1915–1965* (Cincinnati: Woman's City Club, 1986), pp. iii–v, 1.

19. Unlike the earlier Woman's Club founded in 1894, which had been composed exclusively of the city's wealthier women, the Woman's City Club made a commitment to recruit a large and diverse membership. Members of differing religious and ethnic backgrounds were welcomed as were those of various ages and marital status. Only black women were excluded. Kornbluh, *Lighting the Way*, pp. 3–6.

20. Minutes, Housing Committee of the Woman's City Club, December 9, 1915, Woman's City Club (WCC) Papers, CHS; ibid., June 6, 1916; Lawrence Veiller to Setty S. Kuhn, March 3, 1916, WCC Papers, CHS.

21. Lawrence Veiller, "A Program of Housing Reform," *Proceedings of the National Conference of Housing* (New York, 1911), p. 4.

22. Men and women differed over who should run the organization. When Max Senior suggested that the housing organization be made up of a board of ten men who had contributed to the association, Annette Mann objected. She argued that the city's boosters and its social workers might have an entirely different viewpoint about the nature and goals of the housing association. Minutes, Housing Committee of the Woman's City Club, June 13, 1916, WCC Papers, CHS; ibid., June 6, 1916; Minutes, BHL Board of Directors, July 10, 1916, BHL Papers, Urban Studies Collection, Archival Collection of the University of Cincinnati (UC).

23. Minutes, BHL Board of Directors, July 10, 1916, BHL Papers, UC. Shortly after the United States entered World War I, Bradstreet left the league to join the armed services. He was replaced by Frank E. Burleson.

24. Minutes, BHL Board of Directors, November 14, 1916, BHL Papers, UC. The league's first board of directors consisted of businessmen, professionals, and their wives. Members included W. A. Julian, president of Julian and Kokenge Shoe Manufacturing Co.; Max Senior, lawyer and philanthropist; Tylor Field, vice president of Ferro Concrete Construction Co.; Fred A. Geier, machine tool industrialist; Max Hirsch, president of the Star Distillery Co.; Myers Y. Cooper, a realtor and builder; George D. Crabbs, president of the Philip Carey Manufacturing Co.; Walter A. Draper, president of the Cincinnati Traction Co.; Walter S. Schmidt, realtor; Frank P. Goodman, high-school teacher; Rev. Joseph Reiner, professor at St. Xavier College; A. O. Elzner, architect; Courtenay Dinwiddie, superintendent of the Cincinnati Anti-Tuberculosis League; Alfred Bettman, lawyer; Louise Pollak, wife of a wealthy industrialist; Mrs. Charles Rockhill, married to a prominent physician; and James Wilson, labor's sole representative and head of the Pattern Makers League of North America.

25. *Houses or Homes*, p. 4.

26. Ibid., p. 15.

27. Ibid.

28. Ibid., p. 16; Minutes, BHL Board of Directors, February 14, 1918, BHL Pa-

pers, UC; ibid., January 15, 1918. Bleecker Marquette, *Health, Housing and Other Things* (Cincinnati: n.p., 1972), p. 45.

29. *Houses or Homes*, p. 16. Marquette, *Health, Housing and Other Things*, p. 43.

30. Alfred Bettman to Lawrence Veiller, July 26, 1917, CBHL Papers, CHS; Letter of Solicitation from W. A. Julian, M. W. Mack, A. O. Elzner, Alfred Bettman, and Edward P. Moulinier, July 28, 1917, CBHL Papers, CHS.

31. Minutes, BHL Board of Directors, October 12, 1917, BHL Papers, UC; *Cincinnati Social Service Directory, 1918–1919* (Cincinnati: Council of Social Agencies, n.d.), pp. 20–22.

32. Minutes, Special Meeting of the BHL Board of Directors, June 7, 1918. Bleecker Marquette, "A History of the Better Housing League," n.d. (typescript) BHL Papers, UC. Marquette became the Public Health Federation's (PHF) secretary in 1920. The joint appointment to the BHL and the PHF probably made it possible to keep the much sought-after Marquette in Cincinnati. Under the arrangement each organization paid half of Marquette's $5,000 annual salary. Minutes, BHL Board of Directors, October 26, 1920, BHL Papers, UC.

33. *Houses or Homes*, p. 23.

34. Marquette, *Health, Housing and Other Things*, p. 50.

35. *Houses or Homes*, p. 23; *Housing Progress in Cincinnati: Report of the Cincinnati Better Housing League* (Cincinnati, 1921), pp. 27–28. The Cincinnati case suggests that Peter Marcuse might have overstated his thesis about the divorce of the housing and planning movements. Marcuse, "Housing in Early City Planning," pp. 153–76.

36. *Houses or Homes*, p. 25.

37. *Housing Progress in Cincinnati*, p. 28.

38. Bleecker Marquette to Alfred Bettman, September 27, 1919, CBHL Papers, CHS; *Housing Progress in Cincinnati*, pp. 7–9.

39. *Cincinnati Enquirer*, December 19, 1914; Harris Ginberg to W. R. Clark, September 13, 1921, Model Homes Company Files, CHS.

40. Jacob G. Schmidlapp, *Low Priced Housing for Wage Earners* (New York: National Housing Association, 1916), pp. 1–8; Schmidlapp, "Housing Reform," paper read before the City Club, November 6, 1915, Jacob G. Schmidlapp Papers, Urban Studies Collection, Archival Collection of the University of Cincinnati. Schmidlapp also adapted the economic philosophy of Sternberg's model dwelling activity as his own. Sternberg's plan called for housing units to rent at 10 percent over the gross building costs with 3 percent set aside for taxes, 2 percent for upkeep, and 5 percent for profit, hence "Philanthropy and Five Percent." Schmidlapp, "Housing Reform," November 6, 1915.

41. *Cincinnati Enquirer*, May 4, 1912; Herbert F. Koch, "The Housing Problem and Housing Reform," unpublished report, 1915, CHS, pp. 53–54; Schmidlapp, *Low Priced Housing*, pp. 9–10; Schmidlapp, "Housing Reform," November 6, 1915.

42. Louis A. Cornish to Jacob G. Schmidlapp, March 21, 1916, Schmidlapp Papers, UC; Schmidlapp, "Housing Reform," November 6, 1915.

43. *Cincinnati Enquirer*, December 12, 1912. Of the ninety-six apartment units Schmidlapp built between 1911 and 1915, only sixteen were rented to blacks. Harris Ginberg to W. R. Clark, September 13, 1921, Model Homes Co. Files, CHS.

44. *Cincinnati Times-Star*, May 27, 1913; *Annual Report of the Chamber of Commerce and Merchants Exchange for . . . 1914* (Cincinnati, 1915), p. 41.

45. Articles of Incorporation of the Cincinnati Model Homes Company, January 30, 1914; Model Homes Co. Files, CHS; Cincinnati Model Homes Company, Special Investigation, December 31, 1919, Model Homes Co. Files, CHS.

46. Schmidlapp, *Low Priced Housing*, pp. 1–8; Schmidlapp, untitled speech, November 6, 1919, Schmidlapp Papers, UC; Schmidlapp, "Housing Reform," November 6, 1915. The efforts of the Emergency Fleet and U.S. Housing Corporations during World War I were also manifestations of this new focus on community planning. U.S. Department of Labor, *Report of the United States Housing Corporation*, 2 vols. (Washington: Government Printing Office, 1919). Also see Roy Lubove, "Homes and 'A Few Well Placed Fruit Trees': An Object Lesson in Federal Housing," *Social Research* 77 (Winter 1960): 469–89.

47. Schmidlapp, untitled speech, November 6, 1919.

48. *Houses or Homes*, p. 3.

Part II

1. Robert Park, "The City: Suggestions for the Investigation of Human Behavior in the Urban Environment," in *Classic Essays on the Culture of Cities*, ed. Richard Sennett (New York: Appleton-Century-Crofts, 1969), pp. 91–95.

2. Marcuse, "Housing in Early City Planning," pp. 153–76.

3. Schaffer, *Garden Cities for America*, pp. 49–77; Roy Lubove, *Community Planning in the 1920s: The Contributions of the Regional Planning Association of America* (Pittsburgh: University of Pittsburgh Press, 1963), pp. 31–105. Although addressing regional issues from a different perspective than the RPAA, the *Regional Plan of New York and Its Environs* also shared a concern about neighborhood and regional matters. See Lubove, *Community Planning in the 1920s*, pp. 114–27.

4. Lubove, *Community Planning in the 1920s*, pp. 49–66.

Chapter 3

1. The Cincinnati Chamber of Commerce appeared to be particularly active in the movement for comprehensive planning. As early as 1912 it established a committee on civic center and city planning, and that committee became a leading proponent of planning after 1914. H. C. Mathes chaired the committee, which included Alfred Bettman, Max Hirsch, Jacob Vogel, Rudolph Wurlitzer, Nicholas G. Pounsford, James N. Gamble, and W. M. Dunbar. In addition to the committee's activities, the chamber sent architect Frederick Garber to Europe so he could study city planning activity there, particularly in Vienna. *Sixty-Fifth Annual Report of the Cincinnati Chamber of Commerce . . . 1913*, p. 46; *Sixty-Sixth Annual Report of the Chamber of Commerce . . . 1914*, p. 44. Other organizations interested in planning included the Men's City Club and the Architects' Association. Minutes, City Planning Committee of the Woman's City Club, April 7, 1916, WCC Papers, CHS.

2. There had been earlier attempts at planning in Cincinnati, such as the Kessler Park Plan of 1907, as well as legislation restricting wooden buildings and cemeteries

in the early nineteenth century. But these had been specific efforts to remedy specific problems and attempted no comprehensive coordination of all the city's important physical elements. See George E. Kessler et al., *A Park System for the City of Cincinnati* (Cincinnati, 1907). An act to prohibit the erection of wooden buildings in some places was passed on October 31, 1827. A later but similar ordinance passed on September 10, 1856. City of Cincinnati, *The General Ordinances and Resolutions of the City of Cincinnati in Force April, 1887* (Cincinnati: Robert Clarke and Co., 1887), ch. 4, pt. 2, p. 128.

The modern planning movement, like the modern tenement movement, was a late nineteenth-century response to the perceived chaos of urban America. An early aspect of city planning was the city beautiful movement, an attempt to promote a new civic consciousness by the provision and orderly arrangement of parks, streets, and civic centers. But according to David Handlin, "Reformers before 1910 had no concept of how the physical environment of a city functioned and, therefore, how it could be controlled and shaped to produce a desired end." This changed shortly thereafter, Handlin observed, "when a new generation realized this deficiency and in a few short years started to formulate a discipline of city planning." David P. Handlin, "Housing and City Planning in the United States, 1910–1945," *Transactions of the Martin Centre* 1 (1976): 317–19; Handlin, *The American Home*, pp. 142–60. See also Paul Boyer, *Urban Masses*, pp. 275ff.; and Mel Scott, *American City Planning since 1890* (Berkeley: University of California Press, 1971), pp. 1–182; M. Christine Boyer, *Dreaming the Rational City*, pp. 1–56.

3. Minutes, City Planning Committee of the Woman's City Club, April 14, 1915, WCC Papers, CHS; "Annual Report," City Planning Committee of the Woman's City Club, April 28, 1917 (typescript), WCC, CHS.

4. Gerckens, "Bettman of Cincinnati," pp. 121–24.

5. Alfred Bettman, "City Planning," September 22, 1922, p. 2, Citizens' Development Committee Papers (CDC), CHS.

6. *Cincinnati Enquirer*, February 26, 1918; *Cincinnati Commercial Tribune*, January 17, 1920, Woman's City Club Scrapbook, WCC Papers, CHS.

7. Bettman, "City Planning," p. 2; George B. Ford, "The Cincinnati Plan Is Now Law," *Proceedings of the American Society of Civil Engineers* 52 (October 26, 1926): 1636–38; State of Ohio, *Legislative Acts Passed . . . by the Eightieth General Assembly* 105 (1915): 456–57.

In Cincinnati, historical landmarks meant sites commemorating important social events such as the first settlement of Losantiville or the house of the city's first surgeon. Cincinnati City Planning Commission, *The Official City Plan of Cincinnati, Ohio* (Cincinnati: City Planning Commission, 1925), p. 214.

8. For example, on January 5, 1922, the commission turned down an application of Piper and Piper for a permit to erect a grocery store at 2643 Observatory Road because local residents wanted to keep that road purely residential. Minutes, City Planning Commission, January 5, 1922, City Planning Commission Office, Cincinnati City Hall. See also Bettman, "City Planning," pp. 1–4.

9. Bettman, "City Planning," p. 3; "History of Planning Commission" in City Planning Minute Book, 1921, City Planning Commission Office, Cincinnati City Hall. The Cincinnati interest in zoning, seen as a critical part of planning, was not unique.

As of September 1921, forty-eight cities and towns had adopted zoning ordinances. Two years later, 218 municipalities had zoning laws. Scott, *American City Planning since 1890*, p. 160; see also Gordon Whitnall, "History of Zoning," *Annals of American Political and Social Science* 155, pt. 2 (May 1931): 1–14.

10. Alfred Bettman, untitled paper, June 17, 1925, p. 4. CDC Papers, CHS; Technical Advisory Corporation, "Report of Preliminary City Planning Survey and Program for a City Plan of Cincinnati, Ohio," New York City, March 1922, Alfred Bettman Papers, Urban Studies Collection, Archival Collection, UC (mimeographed).

11. Technical Advisory Corporation, "Report of Preliminary City Planning," pp. 22, 7.

12. Lent D. Upson, ed., *The Government of Cincinnati and Hamilton County* (Cincinnati, n.p., 1924), p. 399.

13. *Official City Plan*, p. 54.

14. Bettman, "City Planning," p. 1; Alfred Bettman, "The City Planning Situation of Cincinnati," *Cincinnati Commercial Tribune*, January 17, 1920, Woman's City Club Scrapbook, WCC files.

15. *Official City Plan*, p. 50.

16. "Report of the Public Health Federation" in *Statement of Evidence Submitted on Pending Zoning Ordinance to City Council of Cincinnati, on the 24th day of January, 1924*, United City Planning Committee of Cincinnati (Cincinnati: Jos. Berning Printing Co., 1924), p. 25.

17. Ibid., p. 24.

18. "Relation of Zoning to Housing: Report of the Committee on Zoning Ordinance of the Better Housing League," in *Statement of Evidence*, p. 31. M. Christine Boyer discusses the "selling" of zoning in *Dreaming the Rational City*, pp. 153–58.

19. "Statement by Bleecker Marquette," in *Statement of Evidence*, p. 35.

20. Ibid., p. 37.

21. Ibid., p. 32.

22. *Official City Plan*, p. 26; Whitnall, "History of Zoning," p. 11.

23. *Official City Plan*, appendix B, "Building Zone Ordinance," pp. 362–63.

24. Cincinnati's population increased 11.6 percent between 1900 and 1910 while it grew 10.4 percent the following decade. The 1900 population was 325,902 compared with the 1920 population of 401,247. Columbus, Dayton, and Toledo each experienced growth at least three and one-half times as great as Cincinnati. Other Ohio cities, such as Youngstown, Canton, and Akron, were growing even more rapidly during these decades. *Official City Plan*, p. 7.

25. Myron Downs to Alfred Bettman, August 7, 1934, Bettman Papers, U.C.; *Official City Plan*, pp. 31–32.

26. *Official City Plan*, p. 51.

27. Cincinnati Chamber of Commerce, "Cincinnati Industrial Survey, 1925" (New York: Technical Advisory Corporation, 1925), vol. 2, sec. 9, p. 2 (mimeographed).

28. *Official City Plan*, p. 51.

29. Ibid., pp. 32, 51.

30. The BHL remained very interested in and supportive of city planning throughout the early twenties. See the Minutes, BHL Board of Directors, October 10, 1922, and November 13, 1923, BHL Papers, UC. Also see "Relation of Zoning to Housing:

Report of the Committee on Zoning Ordinance of the Better Housing League," in *Statement of Evidence*, pp. 35–37.

31. Bleecker Marquette, "What is the Better Housing League?" Cincinnati, 1933, p. 1 (mimeographed).

32. *Official City Plan*, pp. 7, 24. Other Cincinnati reformers besides the local housing and planning people advanced the idea that the metropolitan region should be recognized as a basic unit of society. See for instance, Upson, ed., *The Government of Cincinnati*. This report, sponsored by the City Survey Committee of the Republican Executive and Advisory Committee, was prepared by Lent D. Upson of the Detroit Bureau of Governmental Research. For more on this report, as well as other aspects of Cincinnati metropolitanism during the twenties, see Judith Spraul-Schmidt, "Local Government and the Urban Community: Cincinnati and Hamilton County, 1924–1934" (seminar paper, University of Cincinnati, 1977). For another view of American metropolitanism see Jon Teaford, *City and Suburb: The Political Fragmentation of Metropolitan America, 1850–1970* (Baltimore: Johns Hopkins University Press, 1974), pp. 82–122.

33. *Official City Plan*, p. 250. Although the Census Bureau started compiling data for metropolitan districts in 1910, it was not until the 1930 census that the concept warranted special attention . See Kenneth Fox, *Better City Government: Innovation in American Urban Politics, 1850–1937* (Philadelphia: Temple University Press, 1977), pp. 141, 201; U.S. Department of Commerce, Bureau of the Census, *Fifteenth Census of the United States, 1930: Metropolitan Districts: Population and Area*, pp. 5–7.

34. "Cincinnati Industrial Survey, 1925," vol. 7, pp. 21–23.

35. *Official City Plan*, p. 250.

36. *Official City Plan*, pp. 244–45. The Ohio State Conference on City Planning, founded in 1919, was made up of city planning commissioners, city engineers, civic association members and interested citizens from almost every Ohio municipality. According to Alfred Bettman, president of the conference, the city planning organization was "engaged in promoting the cause of orderly and intelligent arrangement of public utilities." He also noted that the conference was interested in pushing state legislation which would "enable Ohio urban communities to be built up in an orderly and healthful way." Toward this end, the conference successfully lobbied for the 1923 county and regional planning bill. Alfred Bettman to Hon. Vic Donahey, Gov. of Ohio, April 5, 1932, Bettman Papers, UC.

37. For a particularly lucid example of the emerging metropolitan consciousness of the twenties and early thirties see McKenzie, *The Metropolitan Community*, a volume from the President's Research Committee on Social Trends. This book discusses the modern regional community in functional terms and notes that "modern social life is so closely integrated as a whole that no change can occur in any of its places without affecting other places in some measure" (p. 49).

38. *Cincinnati Enquirer*, April 23, 1922; "Mariemont: A Satellite Town in the Making," *Survey* (March 15, 1923): 777.

39. John Nolen, "Town Planning for Mariemont," in *Mariemont: The New Town. "A National Examplar,"* [ed. Charles J. Livingood], p. 37.

40. Ibid.; "Mariemont: A Satellite Town in the Making," p. 778.

41. [Livingood], *Mariemont: The New Town*, p. 25.

42. "Bifocal" was the term used by Harlan Paul Douglass to describe the fragmented worlds of work and home which suburban dwellers experienced. See Harlan Paul Douglass, *The Suburban Trend* (New York: Century, 1925), pp. 215–20.

43. [Livingood], *Mariemont: The New Town*, p. 25; "Mariemont: A Satellite Town in the Making," p. 778. The more famous City Housing Corporation, builder of Sunnyside and Radburn, appeared to have the same goals. According to Clarence Stein, the purpose of the CHC was "to create a setting in which democratic community might grow." Clarence Stein, *Towards New Towns for America* (Liverpool, England: University of Liverpool, 1951), p. 34.

44. [Livingood], *Mariemont: The New Town*, pp. 9, 5, back cover.

45. Prospectus of the Mariemont Company as quoted in the *Cincinnati Enquirer*, April 23, 1922.

46. [Livingood], *Mariemont: The New Town*, p. 5.

47. Julian A. Pollak to C. J. Livingood, April 24, 1922, CBHL Files, CHS.

48. *New York Times*, August 24, 1924. To compare Mariemont with another garden city of the twenties, see Schaffer, *Garden Cities for America*, pp. 135–209.

49. Clarence Arthur Perry, "The Neighborhood Unit," in *Neighborhood and Its Environs*, vol. 7 (New York: Regional Plan of New York and Its Environs, 1929). For more on Perry and on the neighborhood emphasis of the 1920s see Howard Gillette, Jr., "The Evolution of Neighborhood Planning: From the Progressive Era to the 1949 Housing Act," *Journal of Urban History* 9 (August 1983): 421–30. Also see Lubove, *Community Planning in the 1920s*; Lubove, "Community Planning Approaches to City Building," *Social Work* 10 (April 1965): 56–63.

50. Patricia Mooney Melvin, "'A Cluster of Interlacing Communities:' The Cincinnati Social Unit Plan and Neighborhood Organization, 1900–1920," in *Community Organizations for Urban Social Change: A Historical Perspective*, ed. Robert Fisher and Peter Romanofsky (Westport, Conn.: Greenwood Press, 1981), pp. 59–88.

51. Perry, "The Neighborhood Unit," p. 34.

52. Ibid., pp. 34–39.

53. Ibid., p. 129.

54. John M. Gries and James Ford, eds., *Housing Objectives and Progress*, vol. 11 (Washington: President's Conference on Home Building and Home Ownership, 1932), pp. xii, xvii; Clarence S. Stein, "The President's Housing Conference—A Challenging Opportunity," *American City*, November 1930, pp. 141–43.

55. Gries and Ford, eds., *Housing Objectives and Progress*, p. xvii. For the dangers of heterogeneity see Harvey Warren Zorbaugh, *Gold Coast and Slum: A Sociological Study of Chicago's Near North Side* (Chicago: University of Chicago Press, 1929), pp. 260–74. The concern with homogeneity also helps explain the policies of the Home Owners Loan Corporation and the Federal Housing Administration, both created during the Great Depression to help middle-class home owners (or potential home owners). The HOLC, which refinanced home mortgages on a long-term basis, developed a rating system for neighborhoods which undervalued neighborhoods that were dense, mixed, or aging. To receive a top rating, the neighborhood had to be homogeneous. The FHA, which insured mortgages, also showed preference to homogeneous neighborhoods. See Kenneth T. Jackson, "Race, Ethnicity, and Real Es-

tate Appraisal: The Home Owners Loan Corporation and the Federal Housing Administration," *Journal of Urban History* 6 (August 1980): 419–52.

56. Gries and Ford, eds., *Slums, Large Scale Housing and Decentralization*, p. 97; John M. Gries and James Ford, eds., *Housing and the Community—Home Repair and Remodeling*, vol. 8 (Washington: President's Conference on Home Building and Home Ownership, 1932), p. 87.

57. John M. Gries and James Ford, eds., *Planning for Residential Districts,* vol. 1 (Washington: President's Conference on Home Building and Home Ownership, 1932), p. 7.

58. Alfred Bettman, "How to Lay Out Regions for Planning," *Planning Problems of Town, City and Region* (Baltimore: Norman Remington Co., 1925), p. 293.

59. Gries and Ford, eds., *Housing and the Community—Home Repair and Remodeling*, p. 101.

60. [Livingood], *Mariemont: The New Town*, p. 15.

61. Ibid., p. 39.

62. Minutes, BHL Board of Directors, November 13, 1923, BHL papers, UC; Bleecker Marquette, "Cincinnati's Garden Village Nears Completion," *Nation's Health* 7 (May 1925): 324. By 1926, minimum rents had increased to $45 a month for a four-room apartment. *Mariemont Messenger*, October 15, 1926.

63. Minutes, BHL Board of Directors, January 9, 1923, BHL Papers, UC; *Mariemont Messenger*, August 20, 1926. According to one article, new houses were originally to sell for between $4,000 and $25,000. Robert T. Small, "Wealthy Widow Plans Model City," *Providence Journal*, n.d., clipping in Mariemont Scrapbook, CHS.

64. In 1925 the Mariemont Company announced that it was erecting in Mariemont "some three hundred homes for those least able to build for themselves, that is, the average wage earner, to be rented at a rate based upon cost." [Livingood], *Mariemont: The New Town*, inside back cover. BHL, *The Housing Situation Today: Report of the BHL* (Cincinnati, 1925), p. 5.

65. BHL, *Ten Years of Housing Work in Cincinnati* (Cincinnati, 1928), p. 20. The eight subdivisions north of Lockland were established by both Cincinnatians and out-of-towners. The Haley-Livingston Company of Chicago created the Cincinnati Industrial Subdivision, the Washington Heights Subdivision and the Oak Park Subdivision. Cincinnatian C. W. Steele established Grandview Heights. Other local entrepreneurs included Daniel Laurence, who established Lincoln Heights Subdivision; J. I. Estes, who developed Lincoln Heights Annex; Albert Armstrong, who established Woodlawn Terrace Subdivision; and Dora and Edward Rempe, who developed the Valley View Subdivision. BHL, "New County Housing Subdivisions," November 1928, pp. 1–2, Stanley Rowe Office Files, Mariemont. Also see Henry Louis Taylor, Jr., "The Building of a Black Industrial Suburb: The Lincoln Heights, Ohio Story" (Ph.D. diss., State University of New York at Buffalo, 1979), pp. 165–217.

66. BHL, "New County Housing Subdivisions," pp. 1–5; Minutes, BHL Board of Directors, April 19, 1928, BHL Papers, UC. It is ironic that at a time when housing reformers pushed community development they totally overlooked the spirit of cooperation and neighborhood community that had developed in the so-called Lockland slums. As historian James Borchert has clearly pointed out, middle-class bias and perceptions of community blinded housing reformers from seeing the growing sense

of community in the black suburban "slums." James Borchert, *Alley Life in Washington: Family, Community, Religion, and Folklife in the City, 1850–1970* (Urbana: University of Illinois Press), pp. 100–142.

67. BHL, "New County Housing Subdivisions," pp. 1–5.

68. Minutes, Board of Incorporators of the Better Housing League of Cincinnati and Hamilton County, Inc., May 16, 1929, BHL Papers, UC. A year earlier the league had explained why it had broadened its vision from the tenement districts. It reported that "as far back as 1918, we realized that the original objective as stated in our constitution—namely, to improve conditions in the tenement house district—was altogether too circumscribed." As a result, "since 1918, the BHL has applied itself to the task of not only improving bad existing conditions but to the great and more important task of safeguarding the future." BHL, *Ten Years of Housing Work in Cincinnati*, p. 13.

69. Woman's City Club, Housing Committee Report, ca. 1929, WCC files, CHS.

70. UCPC, untitled report, January 28, 1928, p. 3, Bettman Papers, UC; *Cincinnati Times-Star*, February 19, 1929.

71. George M. Melville, "Regional Planning Assures Livable Cities of the Future," *Cincinnatian*, March 1929, p. 5.

72. Minutes, Regional Planning Commission Organization Meeting, March 21, 1929, Regional Planning Commission Minutes, Ohio Network Collection, Archival Collection, UC; Minutes, First Meeting to Organize the Regional Planning Commission, February 6, 1929, Regional Planning Commission Minutes, UC.

73. Minutes, Regional Planning Commission, June 27, 1929, UC; Minutes, Regional Planning Organization Meeting, March 21, 1929, UC.

74. See "Regional and County Planning Law of April 17, 1923, An Act" in *Official City Plan*, pp. 244–45. Only municipalities with city planning commissions could participate, although adjoining counties were also permitted through the county commissioners to join the body. See ibid., sec. 4366–13; Minutes, Regional Planning Commission, April 11, 1929, UC.

Chapter 4

1. James M. Laux, "The One Great Name in Valves: A History of the Lunkenheimer Company," *Queen City Heritage* 41 (Spring 1983): 25–29.

2. Guido A. Dobbert, *The Disintegration of an Immigrant Community: The German Americans, 1870–1920* (New York: Arno Press, 1980), pp. 431–32. Don Heinrich Tolzmann, "The Survival of an Ethnic Community: The Cincinnati Germans, 1918 through 1932" (Ph.D. diss., University of Cincinnati, 1983), pp. 47, 217.

3. Olivier Zunz, *The Changing Face of Inequality: Urbanization, Development, and Immigrants in Detroit, 1880–1920* (Chicago: University of Chicago Press, 1982), pp. 199–284.

4. *The Cincinnati Metropolitan Master Plan* (Cincinnati: City Planning Commission, 1948), p. 79.

5. See for example William E. Leuchtenburg, *The Perils of Prosperity, 1914–1932* (Chicago: University of Chicago Press, 1958); Frederick Lewis Allen, *Only Yesterday* (New York: Bantam Books, 1946); John D. Hicks, *Republican Ascendency, 1921–1933* (New York: Harper Torchbooks, 1960).

6. Bleecker Marquette, "Are We Losing the Battle for Better Homes?" in *Proceedings of the National Conference of Social Work for 1923* (Chicago: University of Chicago Press, 1923), p. 344.

7. Minutes, Board of Directors of the BHL, November 13, 1923, BHL Papers, UC. The league estimated that the city suffered a shortage of between 4,000 and 5,000 homes. Ibid., January 9, 1923; "Lights and Shadows," April 21, 1924 (typescript), BHL Papers, UC. For a discussion of the impact that the city's financial problems had on local housing betterment efforts see William C. Folsom, comment, *Proceedings of the National Housing Conference, 1916* (Providence, R.I.: 1916), pp. 519–21.

8. Chamber of Commerce, "Cincinnati Industrial Survey," 1925, vol. 2, p. 20.

9. Gerckens, "Bettman of Cincinnati," pp. 130–31.

10. Chamber of Commerce, "Cincinnati Industrial Survey," 1925, vol. 1, pp. 11–12; William A. Baughin, "Murray Seasongood: Twentieth Century Urban Reformer," 2 vols. (Ph.D. diss., University of Cincinnati, 1972), 2: 585–607.

11. For more on Charterite rhetoric and the early history of the City Charter Committee see Charles P. Taft, *City Management: The Cincinnati Experiment* (New York: Farrar and Rinehart, 1933).

12. Minutes, BHL Board of Directors, October 4, 1917, BHL Papers, UC; Minutes, Budget Committee of the BHL, January 23, 1923, BHL Papers, UC. The salaries of the visiting housekeepers ranged from $900 to $1,080 per year. Minutes, Committee on Salaries of the BHL, December 18, 1922, BHL Papers, UC. For more on the Community Chest see *The First Twenty Years, 1915–1935: The Community Chest of Cincinnati and Hamilton County* (Cincinnati: Board of Directors of the Community Chest, 1935).

13. Minutes, Committee on Salaries of the BHL, December 18, 1922, BHL Papers, UC; BHL Board of Directors, December 9, 1924, BHL Papers, UC.

14. BHL, *Ten Years of Housing Work in Cincinnati,* p. 11.

15. *Cincinnati Union*, April 5, 1919; April 23, 1919.

16. BHL, *Housing in Cincinnati: Yesterday, Today and Tomorrow* (Cincinnati, 1929), p. 7; *Cincinnati Post*, December 12, 1912; Minutes, BHL Board of Directors, June 23, 1930, BHL Papers, UC.

17. *BHL Housing Progress in Cincinnati: Second Report of the Cincinnati Better Housing League* (Cincinnati, 1921), p. 10.

18. Ibid., pp. 22–23; Minutes, Conference on Negro Migrants, January 7, 1925, BHL Papers, UC.

19. U.S. Department of Commerce, Bureau of the Census, *Thirteenth Census of the United States, 1910: Population*, 3: 427; *Fourteenth Census of the United States, 1920: Population*, 3: 799–800.

20. U.S. Department of the Interior, Census Office, *Twelfth Census of the United States, 1900: Population*, pt. 1, p. 672; *Thirteenth Census of the United States, 1910: Population*, 3: 427; *Fifteenth Census of the United States, 1930: Population*, vol. 3, pt. 2, p. 491. During this same time, Cincinnati's foreign-born population declined from 17.8 percent in 1900 to 7.8 percent in 1930, giving Cincinnati proportionally the smallest foreign-born population of any comparable northern industrial city. See Baughin, "Murray Seasongood," 1: 238.

21. For example, workers demolished fourteen tenement buildings housing 107 families in the lower West End in 1922 and replaced them with a new Parcel Post

Building. The Housing Bureau also contributed to the shortage by tearing down 772 tenements between 1917 and 1926 because of code violations. BHL report, untitled, 1922, CBHL Papers, CHS; BHL, *Ten Years of Housing Work in Cincinnati*, p. 10. The Cincinnati Real Estate Board's policy mandating that "no agent shall rent or sell property to colored in an established white section or neighborhood" further complicated the housing problem. Quoted in the *Cincinnati Union*, May 14, 1921.

22. BHL, *Housing Situation Today: Report of the BHL*, p. 2; Minutes, BHL Executive Committee, November 13, 1923, BHL Papers, UC.

23. BHL, "Do You Live in a House?" pamphlet (Cincinnati, December 1922); "Housing Progress," *Report of the BHL*, Cincinnati, 1922, p. 9 (typescript).

24. BHL, "Do You Live in a House?"; Minutes, BHL Board of Directors, October 10, 1922, BHL Papers, UC.

25. Minutes, Special Committee on the Negro Housing Problem, February 4, 1924, BHL Papers, UC.

26. "Lights and Shadows," BHL Papers, UC; Bleecker Marquette, "A Discouraging Situation in Cincinnati," *Housing Betterment: A Journal of Housing Advance*, February 1925, p. 98.

27. "Lights and Shadows," BHL Papers, UC; Minutes, BHL Board of Directors, December 9, 1924, p. 5, BHL Papers, UC; Special Committee on the Negro Housing Problem, February 4, 1924, BHL Papers, UC.

28. Minutes, Special Committee on the Negro Housing Problem, February 4, 1924, BHL Papers, UC.

29. *Cincinnati Enquirer*, December 19, 1919.

30. Marquette, "A Discouraging Situation," p. 99; Inflation victimized the Model Homes Company in another way, too. In 1926, the tax duplicate of Model Homes more than doubled ($400,000 to $900,000) when tax assessors reappraised its property. Minutes, BHL Board of Directors, April 27, 1926, BHL Papers, UC. The increase in taxes had the expected effect on rents. One Model Homes apartment's rent increased from $11.50 per month in 1925 to $16.73 per month in 1927. Charles S. Johnson, ed., *Negro Housing: Report of the Committee on Negro Housing and Home Ownership* (Washington, D.C.: Government Printing Office, 1932), p. 244.

31. Minutes, BHL Board of Directors, October 7, 1924, BHL Papers, UC.

32. Harris Ginberg, "Interesting Facts about Model Homes and Their Tenants," *Housing* 20 (March 1931): 70.

33. Minutes, Special Committee on the Negro Housing Problem, February 4, 1924, BHL Papers, UC.

34. Minutes, BHL Board of Directors, October 7, 1924, BHL Papers, UC.

35. Bleecker Marquette, "Progress in Cincinnati," *Housing Betterment: A Journal of Housing Advance*, February 1927, pp. 98–100; Marquette, "History of the Better Housing League," *The West End Problem: First Annual Report of the Shoemaker Health and Welfare Center* (Cincinnati: n.p., 1927), pp. 10–12; *Housing in Cincinnati: Annual Report of the CBHL* (Cincinnati, 1928), p. 5.

36. *West End Problem*, p. 7.

37. Ibid.

38. Marquette, "Progress in Cincinnati," p. 98.

39. *Housing, Forward or Backward? Better Housing League Annual Report for 1930* (Cincinnati, 1930), p. 4.

40. Although the housing shortage had eased in the basin by 1928, conditions had not changed enough to placate reformers. *Housing in Cincinnati: Annual Report of the CBHL* (Cincinnati, 1928), p. 4.

41. BHL, *Housing in Cincinnati. Yesterday, Today and To-Morrow* (Cincinnati, 1929), p. 7.

42. *Housing, Forward or Backward?*, p. 4.

43. BHL, *Housing Situation Today*, p. 5.

44. Philpott, *The Slum and the Ghetto*, p. 209.

45. Bleecker Marquette, speech given at the Woman's City Club, quoted in the *Cincinnati Times-Star*, January 30, 1929, clipping from Woman's City Club Scrapbook, WCC files, CHS.

46. Ibid.

47. Ibid.

Chapter 5

1. *Official City Plan*, p. 51.

2. Ibid., p. 6.

3. Ibid., pp. 31–32.

4. Marquette, *Housing in Cincinnati*, p. 16.

5. Cincinnati Board of Health, *Cincinnati's Health*, 2 (November 15, 1929): 10.

6. *Webster's International Dictionary of the English Language . . . revised and enlarged under the supervision of Noah Porter* (Springfield, Mass.: G. and C. Merriam and Co., 1891), p. 1357.

7. Manuel C. Elmer, "Social Service for the Slum: What Constitutes a Slum," in Gries and Ford, eds., *Slums, Large Scale Housing and Decentralization*, pp. 32–33; James Ford, *Slums and Housing*, 1: 5, 72.

8. Marquette, *Housing in Cincinnati*, p. 16; Interview, Stanley M. Rowe, December 6, 1979.

9. Minutes, Veiller Meeting, November 25, 1929, BHL Papers, UC. Under Ohio law, cities were permitted to undertake excess condemnation, that is the taking of more private property than is strictly needed for public use.

10. "Cincinnati Cited by Woods, Prepared for Unemployment," *Business Week*, November 12, 1930, pp. 18–19; "Employment in Cincinnati, 1936," *Monthly Labor Review* 43 (October 1936): 873–75.

11. *Emergency Relief and Reconstruction Act, Statutes at Large*, vol. 47, sec. 201(a), p. 711 (1932); Nathaniel S. Keith, *Politics and the Housing Crisis since 1930* (New York: Universe Books, 1973), pp. 21–22. The National Public Housing Conference created in 1931 by Edith Elmer Wood, Mary Kingsbury Simkhovitch, and Helen Alfred is usually credited for persuading Sen. Robert F. Wagner to include the limited dividend provision in the bill. J. Joseph Huthmacher, *Senator Robert F. Wagner and the Rise of Urban Liberalism* (New York: Atheneum, 1971), p. 206.

12. *Emergency Relief and Construction Act, Statutes at Large*, vol. 47, sec. 201(a), p. 711 (1932): Ernest M. Fisher, "Housing Legislation and Housing Policy in the U.S.," *Michigan Law Review* 31 (January 1933): 322.

13. Before 1932, only three state housing agencies existed in this country, in New York, Massachusetts, and California. Dorothy Schaffter, *State Housing Agencies*

(New York: Columbia University Press, 1942), pp. 376, 5; Bleecker Marquette, "The History of Housing in Ohio," paper presented at the Conference of Ohio Housing Authorities, Youngstown, Ohio, June 9, 1939, BHL Papers, UC; Edmond H. Hoben, "The Activities of Official State and Regional Agencies," *Housing Officials' Yearbook for 1936*, p. 57.

14. Schaffter, *State Housing Agencies*, pp. 377–80. The law authorized the governor to appoint four members. Three others were to be state department heads. Cincinnatian Clyde P. Johnson, an executive of the Western and Southern Insurance Company, sat on the first board. Hoben, "Activities of Official State and Regional Agencies," p. 57.

15. *Cincinnati Times-Star*, October 7, 1932; *Cincinnati Post*, January 17, 1933.

16. In 1933, when the County's Public Welfare Department surveyed families of the basin, 44.8 percent claimed that they chose their place of residence because of its closeness to work, while another 24.4 percent claimed that low rents attracted them to the basin. Hamilton County Department of Public Welfare, *A Survey of Housing Conditions in the Basin of the City of Cincinnati* (Cincinnati, 1933), p. 1.

17. *Report on Vital and Social Statistics in the United States at the Eleventh Census*, pt. 2, *Vital Statistics, Cities of 100,000 Population* (1896), p. 366; James A. Quinn, Earle Eubank, and Lois E. Elliot, *Population Characteristics by Census Tracts, Cincinnati, Ohio, 1930 and 1935* (Columbus: Bureau of Business Research, Ohio State University, 1940), p. 8.

18. *An Act. To encourage industrial recovery, to foster fair competition, and to provide for the construction of certain useful public works, and for other purposes*, *Statutes at Large*, vol. 48, sec. 202(d), p. 201 (1933); ibid., sec. 203(a), p. 202 (1933). Mary Kingsbury Simkhovitch and Father John O'Grady of the National Conference of Catholic Charities are credited with inserting the housing provision in the National Recovery Act. Huthmacher, *Senator Robert Wagner*, p. 206; Gelfand, *A Nation of Cities*, pp. 60–61.

19. Cincinnati Housing Corporation, Application for a PWA Loan for Slum Clearance and Low Cost Housing, August 16, 1933, Public Housing Administration Records, Record Group 196, National Archives (NA), Washington, D.C. To compare Field's project with other limited dividend efforts see Mark B. Lapping, "The Emergence of Federal Public Housing: Atlanta's Techwood Project," *American Journal of Economics and Sociology* 32 (1973): 379–85; Eric J. Sandeen, "The Design of Public Housing in the New Deal: Oskar Stonorov and the Carl Mackley Homes," *American Quarterly* 37 (Winter 1985): 645–67.

20. Ladislas Segoe, "Low Cost Housing and Slum Clearance Project, Cincinnati, Ohio," proposal for the Cincinnati Housing Corporation (July 1933), pp. 7–8. Ladislas Segoe Papers, Department of Manuscripts and University Archives, Cornell University Libraries, Ithaca, New York.

21. Cincinnati Housing Corporation, Application for a PWA Loan for Slum Clearance and Low Cost Housing, August 16, 1933, PHA, RG 196, NA; Memorandum, "Cincinnati Housing Projects before the Federal Government," September 20, 1933, Alfred Bettman Papers, UC.

22. The project proposal was first presented to Washington officials on July 27, 1933, by Tylor Field and Ladislas Segoe. But the Cincinnati Housing Corporation did not make the formal application until August 16, 1933. Memorandum, "Slum Clear-

ance Projects in Cincinnati," July 27, 1933, PHA, RG 196, NA; Cincinnati Housing Corporation, Application for a PWA Loan for Slum Clearance and Low Cost Housing, August 16, 1933, PHA, RG 196, NA; Telegram, Tylor Field to Robert Kohn, July 31, 1933, PHA, RG 196, NA; Cincinnati Housing Corporation, Application for a PWA Loan, November 1, 1933, PHA, RG 196, NA.

23. Memorandum, "Slum Clearance Projects in Cincinnati," July 27, 1933, PHA, RG 196, NA.

24. Downs, who worked for one of the nation's leading planners, Harland Bartholomew, before coming to Cincinnati, served as city planning engineer and secretary of the City Planning Commission from 1928 to 1951. According to Stanley Rowe, Downs was a very capable engineer who "loved to antagonize people." Rowe, Interview, December 6, 1979.

25. Myron D. Downs, Memorandum on Proposal by Tylor Field of Proposed Rehousing, September 11, 1933, Bettman Papers, UC.

26. Alfred Bettman to Myron D. Downs, September 18, 1933, Bettman Papers, UC.

27. One of the few PWA limited dividend projects to get built, the Carl Mackley Homes of Philadelphia also embraced the community development strategy characteristic of the Ferro project. Not only did that project provide dwelling space, but it was laid out in a way that "encouraged tenants to use the common space of the complex to associate with one another in formal and informal ways." Its designer, Oskar Stonorov, echoed the sentiments of Mariemont's designers when he observed that "housing projects must be more than sanitarily constructed and equipped dwellings. They must be sources of community happiness. The ideal community," he continued, "should nurture and educate, as well as provide shelter for its inhabitants." Sandeen, "Design of Public Housing," pp. 647, 667.

28. Average rental in the census tract for which the project was planned was $19.11 per month. Clifford M. Stegner, "The Menace of the City" (typescript), in the possession of Stanley M. Rowe. City Housing Corporation, Application for PWA Loan, August 16, 1933, PHA, RG 196, NA; ibid., November 1, 1933.

29. Standish Meacham, Application for a PWA Limited Dividend Loan for Slum Clearance and Low Cost Housing, September 6, 1933, PHA, RG 196, NA; Robert D. Kohn to Rapp and Meacham, March 30, 1934, PHA, RG 196, NA.

30. Prospectus. Lane Gardens Corporation, September 26, 1933, PHA, RG 196, NA; Memorandum, Col. Henry Waite to Robert Kohn, October 11, 1933, PHA, RG 196, NA. "Cincinnati Public Housing Projects before the Federal Government, September 20, 1933, Bettman Papers, UC; Rudolph Tietig to Harold D. Hynds, October 25, 1933, PHA, RG 196, UC.

31. *Cincinnati Enquirer*, October 24, 1933.

32. Rudolph Tietig to Robert D. Kohn, September 22, 1933, PHA, RG 196, NA; Resolution of the Special Board for Public Works, February 9, 1934, PHA, RG 196, NA.

33. Bleecker Marquette, *Annual Report of the BHL for 1933* (Cincinnati, 1933), p. 1. Of the 500 applications submitted to the PWA for limited dividend housing, seven were built. Timothy L. McDonnell, *The Wagner Housing Act: A Case Study of the Legislative Process* (Chicago: Loyola University Press, 1957), p. 39.

34. Christopher Silver, who found the same planning emphasis in his study of Rich-

mond, called it the "suburban orientation of city planning." Silver, *Twentieth-Century Richmond*, p. 106.

35. C. A. Dykstra, "Report of the City Manager," *City Bulletin* (January 16, 1934), p. 4387. Earlier, the City Planning Commission had pictured the basin as the future home of industry and business, but now planners included low-cost housing projects for the area. *Official City Plan*, pp. 51, 31–32.

36. Bleecker Marquette to Alfred Bettman, June 20, 1933, Bettman Papers, UC; Bleecker Marquette, Memorandum of Suggestions for Congested Area Study, January 18, 1933, Bettman Papers, UC.

37. Earle Edward Eubank, "A New Census Map for Cincinnati," *American Sociological Society Publication* 24 (1930): 156–58. The Chamber of Commerce and the University of Cincinnati's Department of Sociology led the movement for the establishment of local census tracts. A committee of seven, appointed from the City Manager's Office, the City Planning Commission, the Chamber of Commerce, the Community Chest, the Bell Telephone Company and the Department of Sociology (UC), drew up the map. Earle Eubank led the movement and B. H. Kroger made the initial financial contribution. Stegner, "The Menace of the City," p. 4.

Census tracts were first used in 1910 by eight cities. By 1930, seventeen cities collected data by census tracts. Quinn et al., *Cincinnati Population Characteristics by Census Tracts*, p. 2.

38. Marquette, Memorandum of Suggestions for Conjested Area Study, January 18, 1933, Bettman Papers, UC.

39. Bettman to Marquette, February 1, 1933, Bettman Papers, UC; *Cincinnati Enquirer*, August 10, 1933; Myron Downs, "The Cincinnati Slum Clearance Survey," *Proceedings of the Ohio State Planning Conference* (Columbus, 1933), p. 17.

40. Hamilton County Department of Public Welfare, *A Survey of Housing Conditions*, p. 1; *Cincinnati Enquirer*, August 10, 1933.

41. Hamilton County Department of Public Welfare, *A Survey of Housing Conditions*, schedule nos. 3, 5, 14.

42. Elizabeth Longan, "The Work of Municipal and Metropolitan Housing Agencies," *Housing Officials' Yearbook*, 1939, p. 69.

43. Cincinnati City Planning Commission, "Cincinnati Basin District Plan," Cincinnati, 1933, in CMHA, "Proposal of Public Housing Project, 1933," Stanley M. Rowe Papers, CHS.

44. Segoe, "Low Cost Housing and Slum Clearance Project. Cincinnati, Ohio," (July 1933), pp. 4–6, Segoe Papers, Cornell Univ.; [Livingood], *Mariemont: The New Town*, p. 21.

45. *Cincinnati Post*, April 7, 1934.

46. Cincinnati Department of Buildings, "Classification of Residential Buildings," Cincinnati, 1934, in CMHA "Proposal for Supplementary Housing Project for Cincinnati and Hamilton County," Cincinnati, 1936; Bleecker Marquette, Memorandum on Census Tract 5 as a site for housing redevelopment, May 14, 1935, Rowe Papers, CHS; Cincinnati, *Municipal Activities, 1933* (Cincinnati, 1933), p. 48.

47. It agreed with an earlier site survey made by Segoe. Ladislas Segoe, "Low-Cost Housing and Slum Clearance Project, Cincinnati, Ohio" (July 1930), Segoe Papers, Cornell University; Memorandum, CMHA to Col. Horatio B. Hackett, Selection

of the West End Site, September 18, 1934, PHA, RG 196, NA. This memo observed that the city's eastern basin section south of Mount Adams was too hilly and claimed that an area between Eastern Avenue and the Ohio River was not large enough to warrant consideration "for a development of the kind now under consideration."

48. A "blighted area" referred to urban space which had become "an economic liability to the community and . . . lost its power to change to a condition that is economically sound." Blight, then, referred more to physical and economic conditions while "slum" referred more to the social-cultural state of an area. Blight became a problem only after the twenties when the new vision of slow, uneven growth was embraced. Gries and Ford, eds., *Slums, Large Scale Housing and Decentralization*, appendix 7.

49. "Public Housing in Cincinnati: Chronological Developments," p. 1, Rowe Papers, CHS.

50. Memorandum of the Meeting Called by Mrs. Lehman in the Interest of Housing, July 20, 1933, Bettman Papers, UC.

51. Frederick W. Garber, Charles F. Cellarius, and Stanley Matthews to the City Planning Commission, October 5, 1933, Bettman Papers, UC.

52. Schaffter, *State Housing Agencies*, p. 382.

53. Eminent domain is "the power to take property for public use by the state, municipalities, and private persons or corporations authorized to exercise functions of public character. The Constitution limits the power to taking for public purposes and prohibits the exercise of the power without just compensation to the owners of the property which is to be taken." *Black's Law Dictionary*, 5th ed., (St. Paul, Minn.: West Publishing Co., 1979), p. 47. *Ohio State H.B. 19, A Pamphlet of the Law*, in CMHA Proposal of Public Housing Project, 1933, Rowe Papers, CHS; Schaffter, *State Housing Agencies*, pp. 381–83.

54. Schaffter, *State Housing Agencies*, pp. 381–83; Telegram, Bleecker Marquette to Robert D. Kohn, August 23, 1933, PHA, RG 196, NA.

55. Minutes, Citizens' Committee on Low Cost Housing, October 31, 1933, BHL Papers, UC.

56. Ibid.; ibid., November 20, 1933; *Cincinnati Enquirer*, November 23, 1933.

57. Bleecker Marquette, "Address to Citizens' Committee on Low Cost Housing," March 21, 1934, BHL Papers, UC; Minutes, CMHA, December 9, 1933, CMHA Files, CMHA Office.

58. Bleecker Marquette to Robert D. Kohn, December 9, 1933, Bettman Papers, UC; Minutes, CMHA, December 9, 1933, CMHA Files. Recollecting about that board later in his life, Rowe remembered Setty Kuhn as the most idealistic of the group and believed that she always placed the tenant's welfare first. Urban and Spilker, according to Rowe, were not very committed but usually were willing to go along with what the other three wanted. Interview, Rowe, December 6, 1979.

59. Rowe, who later played an active role in the 1940s planning movement, appears symptomatic of the civic-business leadership involved in both the housing and planning movements. After graduating from Yale in 1912, Rowe returned to Cincinnati and entered business. Some time later, Rowe was approached by fellow Yale alum Lawson Reed, then president of the BHL board of trustees, about serving on the board. Rowe accepted, for as he explained in later reminiscences, he had been taught at Yale

to "do his part." Later on, when Marquette found it difficult to find competent people for the CMHA, he persuaded Rowe to serve on that body too. Rowe's involvement, then, appeared motivated not by selfish gain but by a real commitment to civic responsibility. Interview, Rowe, December 6, 1979.

60. Minutes, CMHA, December 9, 1933, CMHA Files; ibid., December 11, 1933; "Progress by Local and State Agencies," *Housing Officials' Yearbook for 1938*, p. 100.

61. Minutes, CMHA, December 11, 1933, CMHA Files; ibid., December 14, 1933; CMHA, "Proposal of Public Housing Project, 1933," CMHA Files; CMHA, "Proposal of Public Housing in Cincinnati, 1933," Rowe Papers, CHS.

62. Marquette, "Address to Citizens' Committee," p. 3.

63. Ibid., p. 5.

64. CMHA, "Proposal of Public Housing Project, 1933," Rowe Papers, CHS.

65. *Cincinnati Enquirer*, December 30, 1933; *Report of the CMHA for . . . 1934* (Cincinnati, 1934), p. 2; Marquette, "Address to Citizens' Committee," BHL Papers, UC; "Public Housing in Cincinnati: Chronological Developments," p. 2, Rowe Papers, CHS.

66. *Cincinnati Enquirer*, February 16, 1934.

67. Minutes, CMHA, April 17, 1934, CMHA Files; "Public Housing in Cincinnati: Chronological Developments," p. 2, Rowe Papers, CHS.

68. "Public Housing in Cincinnati: Chronological Developments," p. 2, Rowe Papers, CHS; Minutes, CMHA, March 13, 1934, CMHA Files; ibid., April 17, 1934.

69. Minutes, Executive Committee of the Citizens' Committee on Low Cost Housing, June 13, 1934, BHL Papers, UC; Minutes, CMHA, October 9, 1934, CMHA Files; *Report of the CMHA . . . 1934*, p. 2.

Part III

1. Charles Abrams, *The Future of Housing* (New York: Harper and Brothers, 1946), pp. 249–58; Gelfand, *A Nation of Cities*, pp. 61–62. Eugene J. Meehan has argued that local housing authorities have never been allowed "substantial participation." Eugene J. Meehan, *The Quality of Federal Policymaking: Programmed Failure in Public Housing* (Columbia: University of Missouri Press, 1979).

2. The CMHA readily cooperated with the Housing Division of the PWA because that agency, like the CMHA, viewed the housing problem as one of inadequate community, demanding demolition of slums and the construction of neighborhood communities. Indeed, the rhetoric of the PWA sounded similar to that of local reformers on this matter. For example, when federal housing officials toured the country during the Housing Division's first year of existence to explain its program, it emphasized the community aspects. According to one PWA official, "Housing should not be regarded as an aggregation of houses but as complete neighborhoods, planned at one time and carried out to the mutual benefit of every neighbor." Quoted in Michael W. Straus and Talbot Wegg, *Housing Comes of Age* (New York: Oxford University Press, 1938), pp. 35–36. See also Gillette, "The Evolution of Neighborhood Planning," pp. 421–44; Roy Lubove, "New Cities for Old: The Urban Reconstruction Program of the 1930's," *Social Sciences* 53 (November 1962): 203–13; Elizabeth Wood, untitled, in *Housing*

Form and Public Policy in the United States, ed. Cynthia Jara (New York: Praeger, 1980), pp. 61–67; Boyer, *Dreaming the Rational City*, pp. 233–67; John F. Bauman, *Public Housing, Race, and Renewal: Urban Planning in Philadelphia, 1920–1974* (Philadelphia: Temple University Press, 1987), pp. 22–39.

3. According to an in-house history, "The Housing Division required representative and enthusiastic sponsorship in each city where a project was under consideration. Unless such sponsorship was apparent, the Division did not feel justified in pushing its activities there." It went on to observe that "sentiment did not originate in Washington. It was generated in progressive cities like New York, Atlanta, Cincinnati, Cleveland, Milwaukee, Indianapolis and Chicago (to name only a few), whose studies antedated the Housing Division itself." *Urban Housing: The Story of the PWA Housing Division: 1933–1936* [Bulletin No. 2] (Washington, D.C.: n.p., 1936), p. 37.

4. Charles Abrams, "Housing Policy—1937 to 1967," in *Shaping an Urban Future: Essays in Memory of Catherine Bauer Wurster*, ed. Bernard Frieden and William Nash, Jr., (Cambridge, Mass.: MIT Press, 1969). See also Gelfand, *A Nation of Cities*, pp. 60–61.

5. Although Marc A. Weiss has found a clear distinction between the goals of downtown businessmen and public housers during the 1930s, no such distinction appeared in Cincinnati. Weiss, "Origins and Legacy of Urban Renewal," pp. 55–88.

6. For instance, Timothy L. McDonnell argued in *The Wagner Housing Act* that "the movement was not a mass movement, a so-called grassroots movement. Despite the fact that shortage of dwelling units was a local problem, and that the slums were under local jurisdiction and were the source of many legal problems both economic and social," he concludes, "it was necessary for the Federal Government, which was primarily interested in public works to relieve unemployment, to get some action with regard to housing legislation" (p. 42).

7. For more on the distinction between urban professionals and politicians see Barry D. Karl, *Charles E. Merriam and the Study of Politics* (Chicago: University of Chicago Press, 1974), pp. 226–59. The Cincinnati case seems to confirm the recent observation by Peter Marcuse that the story of public housing is far more complicated than the one portraying "conflict between progressive reformers and selfish real estate interests." However it doesn't seem to confirm his contention that it was the ill housed themselves who produced the immediate commitment to public housing. Unlike New York, Cincinnati experienced no riots during the depression and exhibited neither the radical left-wing political movements of New York City, nor militant tenant associations. In Cincinnati, the concern about the slum dwellers by the middle and upper classes, rather than the actual actions of the slum dwellers, resulted in action. Peter Marcuse, "The Beginnings of Public Housing in New York," *Journal of Urban History* 12 (August 1986): 355, 376–77.

Chapter 6

1. According to the PWA Housing Division, it took approximately twenty-one months from initiation to completion for public housing: three months for initiation and approval; four months for optioning, clearing and purchase; two months to advertise bids and let contracts; and twelve months for construction. The Cincinnati expe-

rience differed greatly from this rather optimistic schedule. *Urban Housing: The Story of the PWA Housing Division*, p. 38. "Cincinnati Metropolitan Housing Authority Program and Development—Laurel Homes," Stanley M. Rowe Office Files, Mariemont Office; *Cincinnati Enquirer*, February 15, 1935; August 6, 1938.

2. *Report of the CMHA . . . 1937* (Cincinnati, 1938); Straus and Wegg, *Housing Comes of Age*, pp. 88–90.

3. Straus and Wegg, *Housing Comes of Age*, pp. 122–23. The tension between immediate relief goals and the public housing program continued after the president signed the Emergency Relief Appropriations Act, which allocated $450 million for public housing. By September 15, Roosevelt decided to reallocate all but $100 million of this money to the FERA, an agency better equipped for speedy relief. Twenty-four projects, including Laurel Homes, were built with Emergency Relief money; twenty-seven had been built with National Industrial Recovery Act funding. Ibid.

4. Minutes, CMHA, January 3, 1934, CMHA Files.

5. "Cincinnati Metropolitan Housing Authority Program and Developments— Laurel Homes," Rowe Files.

6. Minutes, CMHA, April 17, 1934, CMHA Files; ibid., October 9, 1934; *Cincinnati Enquirer*, January 11, 1935. Citizens made enough complaints about Edgemon's appraisals that the Housing Division felt obligated to investigate them. After its examination, the division concluded that the appraisals were "extremely conservative and in many instances very definitely low." Memorandum, Messrs. Sinsel and Brown to Col. Horatio B. Hackett, Complaint of Petitioners, December 17, 1934, PHA, RG 196, NA.

7. *Cincinnati Post*, November 22, 1934.

8. *Cincinnati Enquirer*, November 13, 1934; Memorandum, Messrs. Sinsel and Brown to Hackett, December 17, 1934, RG 196, NA.
The charge seemed plausible to many because the beautification of the approach to the Union Terminal had been proposed by a variety of citizens and officials after the terminal's completion in 1933. As early as June 1932, the city had planned a high brick wall along the alley near the Laurel Street approach to shut off the unsightly view of rear tenements facing Botts Street. The Cincinnati Art Commission had even appointed a committee of architects to investigate the possibility of building a housing development near the Laurel Street approach to help beautify it. This plan stalled, however, when the Model Homes Company, approached about building the project, declined because of the high costs. *Cincinnati Enquirer*, March 24, 1934; Minutes, BHL Board of Directors, June 16, 1932, BHL Papers, UC.

9. Adelaide Myer to Eleanor Roosevelt, November 10, 1934, PHA, RG 196, NA; Minutes, BHL Board of Directors, June 16, 1932, BHL Papers, UC.

10. *Cincinnati Enquirer*, November 22, 1934; November 29, 1934; December 7, 1934.

11. CMHA, "Public Housing in Cincinnati: Chronological Developments," p. 3, Rowe Papers, CHS.

12. Memorandum, "Is the Proposed Site a Slum?" CMHA to Col. Horatio B. Hackett, October 3, 1934, Rowe Papers, CHS; "Population in Areas D-E-F-K-J-C. Based on the 1930 Census," in CMHA, "Proposal of Public Housing Project, 1933," Rowe Papers, CHS; Memorandum, CMHA to City Council of Cincinnati, March 12,

1938, p. 3, Rowe Papers, CHS; *Williams' Cincinnati Directory . . . 1933–1934* (Cincinnati: Williams' Cincinnati Directory Company, 1934).

13. Compare this with the city's average of 63 infant deaths per 1,000 live births; 82 tuberculosis deaths per 100,000 residents and 6 arrests per 100 residents. "Population in Areas D-E-F-K-J-C" in CMHA, "Proposal of Public Housing Project," 1933, Rowe Papers, CHS; Ladislas Segoe, "Analysis of Possible Sites for Low-Cost Housing Development, Cincinnati, Ohio," n.d., Segoe Papers, Cornell University.

14. *Cincinnati Enquirer*, January 11, 1935, p. 22.

15. Minutes, CMHA, January 22, 1935, CMHA Files; ibid., February 16, 1935; Straus and Wegg, *Housing Comes of Age*, pp. 82–92.

The Louisville ruling was not the first adverse court ruling against the Housing Division of the PWA. For instance, earlier the court had upheld Comptroller General John Raymond McCarl's decision not to authorize money to the PWA's Emergency Housing Corporation, the vehicle by which the federal government planned to build public housing. McCarl, a Republican appointee, refused to authorize the money because he believed it unconstitutional. The court's ruling forced the Housing Division to dissolve the Emergency Housing Corporation and take over its functions. PWA Housing Division officials reluctantly pursued this course, since the corporate structure would have permitted greater speed in implementing the housing program. For unlike the corporation, the Housing Division was bound by the rules of federal governmental procedure, including audit for all expenses, reference of title problems to the Department of Justice, and competitive bidding on contracts—all time-consuming procedures. Lyle John Woodyatt, "The Origins and Evolution of the New Deal Public Housing Program" (Ph.D. diss., Washington University, 1968), pp. 70–72; Straus and Wegg, *Housing Comes of Age*, pp. 48–51.

16. Minutes, CMHA, June 11, 1935, CMHA Files; ibid., July 16, 1935. The PWA Housing Division dropped its appeal to the Supreme Court over the eminent domain issue on March 5, 1936, a few hours before the court had scheduled the oral arguments, because it decided that the Louisville case was not a good test case. William Eberstein, *The Law of Public Housing* (Madison: University of Wisconsin Press, 1944), p. 45.

17. Press release, August 24, 1935, CMHA Files; *Cincinnati Enquirer*, February 14, 1936; *Report of the CMHA . . . 1937*, p. 1.

18. William Edgemon to A. R. Clas, June 19, 1936, PHA, RG 196, NA. For example, seven pieces of property were owned by lunatics, two of whom were institutionalized in other states. And in three instances, owners were never found. In two of these cases, building and loan associations held mortgages and after foreclosing them, sold the property to the government. In the third case, the county foreclosed its tax lien and the federal government bought the property at a public tax sale.

19. Minutes, CMHA, January 14, 1936, CMHA Files; *Cincinnati Enquirer*, December 8, 1935; January 8, 1935; February 14, 1936.

20. *Report of the CMHA . . . 1937*, p. 6.

21. Minutes, CMHA, February 29, 1934, CMHA Files.

22. *Cincinnati Enquirer*, August 4, 1934.

23. *Cincinnati Times-Star*, August 1, 1935.

24. Harry M. Forwood, "Where the Other Half Lives," *Cincinnati Post*, April 5, 1934.

25. Minutes, CMHA, December 14, 1933, CMHA Files; ibid., January 11, 1934.

26. *Cincinnati Times-Star*, July 19, 1934.

27. Myron Downs to Alfred Bettman, July 23, 1934, in CMHA Minutes, CMHA Files; *Cincinnati Times-Star*, September 28, 1934, CMHA Scrapbook, CHS.

28. *Cincinnati Enquirer*, August 3, 1934; *Cincinnati Post*, August 6, 1934.

29. *Cincinnati Enquirer*, August 3, 1934; *Urban Housing: The Story of the PWA Housing Division*, p. 88.

30. "Laurel Homes. Payment in Lieu of Taxes," March 7, 1938, Rowe Files; Memorandum to Council from the CMHA, March 12, 1938, p. 1, Charles P. Taft Papers, CHS; *Cincinnati Post*, August 2, 1934, CMHA Scrapbook, CHS.

31. Minutes, CMHA, August 28, 1934, CMHA Files; "Laurel Homes. Payment in Lieu of Taxes," Rowe Files.

32. "Laurel Homes. Payment in Lieu of Taxes," Rowe Files; Minutes, CMHA, October 2, 1934; Straus and Wegg, *Housing Comes of Age*, p. 113.

33. "Laurel Homes. Payment in Lieu of Taxes," Rowe Files.

34. Minutes, CMHA, February 18, 1936, CMHA Files.

35. *Cincinnati Enquirer*, April 9, 1936; "Laurel Homes. Payment in Lieu of Taxes," Rowe Files.

36. *Cincinnati Enquirer*, April 9, 1936; *An Act. To waive exclusive jurisdiction over premises of Public Works Administration slum-clearance and low-cost housing projects, to authorize payments to States and political subdivisions in lieu of taxes on such premises, and for other purposes. Statutes at Large*, vol. 49, sec. 2, p. 205 (1936).

37. "Laurel Homes. Payment in Lieu of Taxes," Rowe Files.

38. Ibid.; Memorandum to Council from CMHA, March 12, 1938, Taft Papers, CHS.

39. Memorandum to Council from CMHA, March 12, 1938, Taft Papers, CHS.

40. Ibid. The debt service was the 3-percent interest paid on the $150,000 of additional bonds authorized by council for parks and playgrounds in the Laurel Homes site. Other bonds had already been approved and were simply allotted to the basin site, an area sorely in need of recreation space.

41. *Cincinnati Times-Star*, March 17, 1938; Minutes, BHL Board of Directors, March 17, 1938, BHL Papers, UC. Three different governing units would split the service charge: Cincinnati would receive half while the city school district and the county would divide the other half. Ibid.

42. *Cincinnati Enquirer*, March 23, 1938.

43. Ibid., April 5, 1938; *Cincinnati Times-Star*, April 4, 1938, p. 1; Minutes, CMHA, April 6, 1938, CMHA Files.

44. *Cincinnati Post*, April 4, 1938, CMHA Scrapbook, CHS. Most local realtors were certainly not unbiased observers and had opposed public housing from its beginning. Indeed, the Board of Realtors wired Robert Kohn on August 22, 1933, informing him that it was "unalterably opposed to the financing of any housing projects through federal aid." And when Walter Schmidt, a local realtor, served as president of the National Association of Real Estate Boards in 1935, that organization took a strong

stand against public housing because "it was detrimental to the urge of home owner-ship." Harry J. Mohlman to Robert D. Kohn, August 22, 1933, Rowe Papers, CHS; Straus and Wegg, *Housing Comes of Age*, p. 102.

45. *Cincinnati Post*, April 4, 1938, CMHA Scrapbook, CHS.

46. *Cincinnati Enquirer*, April 6, 1938.

47. Minutes, BHL Board of Directors, March 22, 1938, BHL Papers, UC; *Cincinnati Post*, April 4, 1938, CMHA Scrapbook, CHS; Marquette to CMHA, April 7, 1938, Bettman Papers; *Cincinnati Enquirer*, April 7, 1938.

48. *Cincinnati Enquirer*, April 7, 1938.

49. When the first estimates of building costs were made, they were approximately 36 cents per cubic foot. By the summer of 1936, costs had risen to 44 cents per cubic foot. Minutes, CMHA, February 25, 1936, CMHA Files; ibid., June 30, 1936; October 20, 1936.

50. *Report of the CMHA for the Year 1936* (Cincinnati, 1937), p. 4.

51. Public Housing in Cincinnati: Information for the FDR Visit, October 15, 1935, Rowe Papers, CHS.

52. The BHL used the term "American standard of housing" in its 1936 report. Bleecker Marquette, *Annual Report of the BHL for 1936* (Cincinnati, 1936), p. 5.

53. *Report of the CMHA . . . 1936*, p. 4; *Report of the CMHA . . . 1937*; *Cincinnati Enquirer*, February 17, 1937; September 15, 1939.

Chapter 7

1. On this point, then, I disagree with Peter Marcuse, who has written that "public housing was not, at its outset, low quality housing for the lower-class people, but middle-class housing for working people." Peter Marcuse, "Beginnings of Public Housing," *Journal of Urban History* 12 (August 1986): 354. Remember, many ob-servers were growing uneasy about the type of middle-class housing appearing on the city's fringes. See for example, Douglass, *The Suburban Trend*.

2. In an interesting and provocative article on public tenant unions in New York City—a movement which did not appear in Cincinnati—Joel Schwartz argues that the 1930s "low rent public projects were built on a scale and with a provision for amenities that signaled the interest for them to be [long-term] communities, not way stations." But if public housing is seen primarily as an educational experience in proper com-munity living, then public housing can be viewed as a classroom for good city living, with the expectation that tenants would eventually graduate into new roles of home-ownership and/or civic responsibility. Joel Schwartz, "Tenant Unionism in New York City's Low-Rent Housing, 1933–1949," *Journal of Urban History* 12 (August 1986): 418–19.

3. CMHA, *Tenant Code* (Cincinnati, n.d.), pp. 5–6, Cincinnati Urban League Papers, CHS; CMHA, "Rent, Policies and Standards," in CMHA Minutes, October 3, 1939, CMHA Files.

4. CMHA, *Tenant Code*, pp. 5, 3.

5. *Fifth Annual Report of the CMHA* (Cincinnati, 1938), p. 4.

6. Dorothy I. Cline, Associate Community Relations Counselor, USHA, "Report of Findings Submitted to the Cincinnati Metropolitan Housing Authority: Analysis of

the Administration and Operation of the Community Relations Program, Laurel Homes, Cincinnati, Ohio, May 16–24, 1939," pp. 13–19, PHA, RG 196, NA; *Fifth Annual Report of the CMHA*, p. 4. *Laurel-Ville-Life*, March 1939, Rowe Files.

7. *Laurel-Ville-Life*, March 1939.

8. Cline, "Report of Findings Submitted to the CMHA," p. 6.

9. *Cincinnati Times-Star*, July 29, 1940.

10. Bleecker Marquette, "A Housing Policy—And Planning," *Planners' Journal* (Winter 1936), p. 11. Marquette developed the plan as a guide to Cincinnati's housing program.

11. *Cincinnati Enquirer*, February 22, 1939; D. Delbert Bride, "Unique Low-Rent Housing Plan for Fort Wayne," *American City*, September 1938, p. 103; Loula D. Lasker, "Fort Wayne's Fifty Houses: Analysis of a Pre-Fabricated Experiment," *Survey Graphic*, May 1939, p. 324; Irvan Morgan, "The Fort Wayne Plan: The FHA and Prefabricated Municipal Housing in the 1930s," *Historian* 47 (August 1985): 538–59.

12. Lasker, "Fort Wayne's Fifty Houses," p. 324; *Cincinnati Enquirer*, February 22, 1939; March 22, 1939; April 28, 1939.

13. *Cincinnati Enquirer*, March 3, 1939.

14. Minutes, CMHA, March 20, 1939, CMHA Files.

15. Memorandum, Bleecker Marquette to the CMHA, March 29, 1939, pp. 1–2, Rowe Papers, CHS.

16. Those who supported building prefabricated houses emphasized that these inexpensive dwellings could provide the shelter so desperately needed for the city's relief clients. *Cincinnati Enquirer*, April 28, 1939; February 22, 1939; Minutes, CMHA, March 20, 1939, CMHA Files. Memorandum on Rents, August 20, 1934, Cincinnati Metropolitan Housing Project, p. 1, Rowe Files.

17. Memorandum on Rents, August 20, 1934, Cincinnati Metropolitan Housing Project, p. 1, Rowe Files.

18. CMHA Map, analysis of population by Census Tracts, 1937, in CMHA, Lincoln Court Proposal, 1939, CMHA Papers, CHS; Stanley Rowe, speech delivered to the Cincinnati Business Women's Club, January 8, 1935, Rowe Files.

19. *Cincinnati Enquirer*, November 26, 1935; Notebook of consultants, appointments, certification, April 21, 1936, Justin Hartzog Collection, Department of Manuscripts and University Archives, Cornell University Libraries, Ithaca, New York; Charles Bradley Leach, "Greenhills, Ohio: The Evolution of an American Town" (Ph.D. diss., Case Western Reserve University, 1978), p. 112.

20. *Cincinnati Enquirer*, January 12, 1936.

21. Leach, "Greenhills, Ohio," p. 44; Albert Miller, "Greenhills: The Resettlement Administration's Low Rent Community Near Cincinnati, Ohio," speech given to the Citizens' Committee on Slum Clearance and Low Cost Housing, June 24, 1936, p. 3, Cincinnatus Association Papers, CHS; "Summary of Information: Greenhills, Hamilton County, Ohio," Research Section, Suburban Resettlement Division of the Resettlement Administration, p. 11, John S. Lansill Papers, Special Collections, University of Kentucky (UK); Joseph L. Arnold, *The New Deal in the Suburbs: A History of the Greenbelt Town Program, 1935–1954* (Columbus: Ohio State University Press, 1971), p. 29; "Description of the Town Plan for Greenhills, Ohio," May 1936, RA,

Hartzog Papers, Cornell University. Also see Paul K. Conkin, *Tomorrow a New World: The New Deal Community Program* (Ithaca, N.Y.: Cornell University Press, 1959).

22. Justin R. Hartzog, untitled speech, 1938, Lansill Papers, UK; Warren Jay Vinton, "Report' on Cincinnati, Ohio and the Selection of a Site for Suburban Resettlement," May 24, 1936, Lansill Papers, UK.

23. Robert B. Fairbanks, "Cincinnati and Greenhills: The Response to a Federal Community, 1935–1939," *Cincinnati Historical Society Bulletin* 36 (Winter 1978): 23–41; Vinton, "Report on Cincinnati," p. 64.

24. Letter of Transition for Final Report of the Greenbelt Town Project, John S. Lansill to W. W. Alexander, n.d., p. 6, Lansill Papers, UK.

25. Ibid., p. 7.

26. Milton Lowenthal, Research Section, Suburban Division, RA, "A Study of the Characteristics, Customs and Living Habits of Potential Tenants of the Resettlement Project in Cincinnati, and the Effect of Such Characteristics, Construction and Equipment of the Dwelling Units," February 1936, p. 1. Lansill Papers, UK.

27. Miller became regional coordinator on May 1, 1935. "Summary Chronological History: Greenhills Project," n.d., Lansill Papers, UK; Division of Suburban Resettlement, RA, "Greenhills, Hamilton County, Ohio," May 1936, p. 11, Lansill Papers, UK; Leach, "Greenhills, Ohio," p. 120.

28. Miller, "Greenhills: The Resettlement Administration's Low Rent Community," speech, June 24, 1936, Cincinnatus Papers, CHS.

29. John S. Lansill, untitled speech given at the Annual Meeting of the Regional Planning Commission of Hamilton County, February 3, 1936, Hartzog Papers, Cornell University; Justin Hartzog, "Town Planning of the Greenhills Project," November 1, 1937, p. 14, Hartzog Papers, Cornell University.

30. Justin Hartzog, "Planning of the Suburban Resettlement Towns: Greenhills, Ohio," paper presented at the American City Planning Institute, Princeton, N.J., December 28, 1937, p. 12, Lansill Papers, UK.

31. Hartzog, "Planning of the Suburban Resettlement Towns," p. 13.

32. John S. Lansill, "Suburban Resettlement Division," in Interim Report of the Resettlement Administration (Washington, 1936), Lansill Papers, UK.

33. "Greenhills: Hamilton County, Ohio," Division of Suburban Resettlement, RA, May 1936, pp. 6–9.

34. "Greenbelt Towns," *Architectural Record* (September 1936): 226; Hartzog, untitled speech, p. 6, Lansill Papers, UK.

35. Leach, "Greenhills, Ohio," p. 242. Although the RA was renamed the Farm Security Administration in September of 1937, no fundamental change in the Greenbelt administrative structure occurred. Arnold, *New Deal in the Suburbs*, p. 149.

36. Leach, "Greenhills, Ohio," pp. 220, 228–30; *Cincinnati Post*, September 20, 1938; March 28, 1939.

37. *Cincinnati Enquirer*, April 1, 1940.

38. *Cincinnati Enquirer*, February 21, 1939.

Chapter 8

1. Rosalie Genevro, "Site Selection and the New York City Housing Authority, 1934–1939," *Journal of Urban History* 12 (August 1986): 334–52; Bauman, *Public Housing, Race, and Renewal,* pp. 45–46.

2. Bauman argues that two views of housing—the professional and the communitarian—competed for influence over public housing and ultimately resulted in a "mongrelized housing policy." The professional view, Bauman asserts, characterized the Progressive sanitarians and tenement reformers such as Laurence Veiller, Bernard Newman, and Bleecker Marquette. These men, according to Bauman, were primarily interested in improving the slum through direct action, whether it be tenement regulation or slum clearance. Communitarians, according to Bauman, such as Catherine Bauer and other members of the Regional Planning Association of America, took a broader and more comprehensive neighborhood/regional approach to housing matters. I am not sure how useful these categories were by the 1930s, since in Cincinnati Marquette was clearly showing communitarian sympathies, as was Newman in Philadelphia. Bauman's categories may be more useful in showing change over time: the era of the professional marks the first fifteen years of the twentieth century while the era of the communitarian characterizes the next thirty-five years. Bauman, "Safe and Sanitary without Costly Frills: The Evolution of Public Housing in Philadelphia, 1929–1949," *Pennsylvania Magazine of History and Biography* 101 (January 1977): 114–28; Bauman, *Public Housing, Race, and Renewal,* pp. 1–10, 45–46.

3. For the similarities in Alfred Bettman's and Bleecker Marquette's approaches to slum clearance and public housing see Alfred Bettman, "Housing Projects and City Planning," in *City and Regional Papers,* pp. 92–98; U.S. Congress, Senate, Special Committee on Post-War Economic Policy and Planning, *Post-War Economic Policy and Planning, Hearings before the Subcommittee in Housing and Urban Redevelopment on S.R. 102,* 78th Cong., pt. 2, 1945, p. 1749.

4. *The Housing Act of 1937. Statutes at Large,* vol. 50, sec. 9, p. 891.

5. Ibid., sec. 10(a), p. 891.

6. Minutes, CMHA, December 14, 1937, CMHA Files.

7. Stanley M. Rowe to H. A. Grey, February 5, 1937, in CMHA Minutes; Minutes, CMHA, September 20, 1938, CMHA Files.

8. Minutes, CMHA, February 23, 1940, CMHA Files; ibid., January 6, 1942.

9. Woodyatt, "The Origins and Evolution of the New Deal Housing Program," p. 157; Stanley M. Rowe to members of Cincinnati City Council, October 24, 1938, p. 2, Rowe Papers, CHS.

10. CMHA, *Tenth Annual Report 1943* (Cincinnati, 1944), n.p.; Minutes, CMHA, April 19, 1938, CMHA Files.

11. Stanley M. Rowe to H. A. Grey, September 8, 1937, Rowe Papers, CHS. The Cincinnati public housing strategy, focusing on a combined vacant land/slum clearance site plan, seems to contradict the experience of New York as reported by Rosalie Genevro, who observed that public housing site selection created great antagonism between local officials who wanted slum clearance for the urban core and regional planners controlling the federal program who desired vacant land projects. Genevro, "Site Selection," pp. 334–35.

12. Minutes, CMHA, May 17, 1938, CMHA Files.

13. Ibid.; ibid., June 7, 1938; *Report of the CMHA for the Year 1938*, p. 6.

14. *Cincinnati Enquirer*, September 8, 1938.

15. *Cincinnati Post*, September 8, 1938; *Cincinnati Enquirer*, July 1, 1938; Petition to Council from the Committee on Resolutions [September 21, 1938?], Taft Papers, CHS; *Cincinnati Enquirer*, October 8, 1938.

16. *Cincinnati Enquirer*, July 1, 1938. For a similar response to public housing in New York City, see Genevro, "Site Selection," pp. 336–37. However, unlike New York, where according to Genevro "the most vehement arguments in favor of slum clearance" came from real-estate industry spokesmen, in Cincinnati the strongest support clearly originated from the city's housing reformers, who for years had wrestled with the pathology of the slums.

17. Minutes, BHL Board of Directors, September 21, 1938, UC.

18. Petition to Council from the Committee on Resolutions, Taft Papers, CHS; *Cincinnati Post*, September 22, 1938, CMHA Scrapbook, CHS.

19. Petition to Council from the Hamilton County League of Building and Loan Associations, n.d., Taft Papers, CHS.

20. *Cincinnati Post*, September 22, 1938, CMHA Scrapbook, CHS.

21. *Cincinnati Times-Star*, September 22, 1938, CMHA Scrapbook, CHS.

22. Ibid., September 23, 1938; *Cincinnati Post*, October 6, 1938. Ralph Arthur Straetz, *PR Politics in Cincinnati: Thirty-two Years of City Government through Proportional Representation* (New York: New York University Press, 1958), pp. 226–27.

23. Straetz, *PR Politics*, p. 64.

24. *Cincinnati Enquirer*, October 6, 1938; *Cincinnati Post*, October 6, 1938.

25. *Cincinnati Post*, October 11, 1938; Minutes, CMHA, October 18, 1938, CMHA Files.

26. Minutes, BHL Board of Directors, September 21, 1938; Theodore Berry to R. P. McClain, n.d., Urban League Papers, CHS; *Cincinnati Enquirer*, October 20, 1938.

27. *Cincinnati Times-Star*, October 25, 1938, CMHA Scrapbook, CHS.

28. David L. Krooth, Acting Deputy Administrator, USHA, to the CMHA, October 20, 1938, in CMHA Minutes, October 25, 1938, CMHA Files.

29. *Cincinnati Enquirer*, October 27, 1938; October 31, 1938; November 3, 1938.

30. Ibid., November 3, 1938.

31. Ibid., November 9, 1938; November 11, 1938; *Cincinnati Post*, November 10, 1938; November 26, 1938.

32. *Chronicle* [labor], March 1, 1940.

33. *The State, Ex Rel. Ellis, City Solicitor, v. Sherrill, City Manager, 136 Reports of Cases Argued and Determined in the Supreme Court of Ohio*, 328 (1940). *Cincinnati Enquirer*, November 11, 1938; "State and Local Activity," *Housing Officials' Yearbook*, 1941, p. 150; *Chronicle*, March 1, 1940.

34. CMHA, *Tenth Annual Report 1943*; Citizens' Committee on Slum Clearance and Low Rent Housing, "Housing Facts" for tour, June 15, 1939, p. 7, BHL Papers, UC. And because land costs were lower for Winton Terrace, so were the rents. A three-room apartment at Laurel Homes rented for between $19.35 and $21.35 compared with a Winton Terrace three-room apartment renting for about $18.50 per month (ibid.). *Report of the CMHA for the Year 1939*, p. 4.

35. CMHA, *Tenth Annual Report 1943*.

36. Ibid., pp. 5–6.

37. Total development costs of Laurel Homes, a 20-acre development, were $6,625,607. English Woods, a 107-acre vacant land development, cost the CMHA $3,752,368 to develop. CMHA, *Tenth Annual Report 1943*.

38. Cincinnati Junior League, "Report on Cincinnati Public Housing Projects," December 1941.

Chapter 9

1. CMHA, *Tenth Annual Report 1943*; *Cincinnati Enquirer*, April 22, 1943.

2. CMHA, Proposal of Public Housing Project, 1933, Rowe Papers, CHS. These assumptions were more implicit than explicit in the application. However, see the memorandum from the CMHA to Col. Horatio B. Hackett, September 18, 1934, RG 196, NA. For a general discussion about community in public housing see Albert Mayer, "After the Homes Are Built," *Survey Graphic*, December 1935, pp. 599–601. An interesting discussion about public housing and citizenship can be found in Hilda W. Smith, "Workers Live in USHA Homes," *Public Housing* 3 (December 1943): 4. She concludes her article with an appeal: "To give all these workers a chance . . . to be more responsible citizens of a democratic community, we must build more public housing."

3. Quinn et al., *Population Characteristics by Census Tracts*, pp. 35, 43–45.

4. Culture, according to one college sociology textbook in the 1930s, "is a matter of habits of thoughts and action acquired or 'learned' by interaction with other members of [one's] group." E. B. Reuter and C. W. Hart defined culture as "the mode of life of people. . . . It includes the whole complex of individual activities." Frederick E. Lumley, *Principles of Sociology* (New York: McGraw Hill Book Co., 1935), pp. 253–70.

5. Hirsch, *Making the Second Ghetto*, p. 13; For more on how the government perpetuated racial segregation in its public housing projects see Christopher G. Wye, "The New Deal and the Negro: Toward a Broader Conceptualization," *Journal of American History* 59 (December 1972): 622–29; John F. Bauman, "Black Slums/Black Projects: The New Deal and Negro Housing in Philadelphia," *Pennsylvania History* 41 (July 1975): 311–33; Charles Abrams, *Forbidden Neighbors: A Study of Prejudice in Housing* (New York: Harper and Bros., 1955). Ken Jackson has recently blamed the ghettoization of black public housing on the USHA's emphasis on "local initiative and responsibility." But at least in the Cincinnati case, nothing in the actions of the USHA or the earlier PWA Housing Division suggests that this pattern of segregated public housing would have changed had the federal government held more control. Kenneth T. Jackson, *Crabgrass Frontier: The Suburbanization of the United States* (New York: Oxford University Press, 1985), pp. 224–25.

6. Proposal, Public Housing Project, 1933, Rowe Papers, CHS; Minutes, CMHA, January 23, 1934, CMHA Files; "Chronological Development: Housing Projects in Cincinnati, 1932–1937" (April 13, 1937), Rowe Papers, CHS.

7. "Chronological Development: Housing Projects in Cincinnati, 1932–1937," Rowe Papers, CHS; Minutes, October 8, 1935, CMHA Files.

8. Department of Public Welfare, *A Survey of Housing Conditions in the Basin of the City of Cincinnati* (Cincinnati: n.p., 1933).

9. William S. Edgemon to Horatio B. Hackett, n.d., Rowe Papers, CHS; Report, "Relocation of Tenants, Laurel Homes Housing Project: Historical Narrative of Events Occurring in the Relocation of Tenants in Cincinnati's Basin Housing Project," April 20, 1936, Rowe Papers, CHS; "Placing Dispossessed Tenants: CMHA Project," October 26, 1934, Rowe Files.

10. Report, "Relocation of Tenants, Laurel Homes Housing Project," Rowe Papers, CHS.

11. The Cincinnati Department of Buildings used a four-category classification system for its buildings. Good buildings were those in sound physical condition which had no "important violations of the old building code." Fair buildings required minor repairs and alterations and needed better maintenance. Bad buildings were substandard, requiring extensive repairs and alterations. Very bad buildings were those which had deteriorated beyond rehabilitation. Department of Public Welfare, *A Survey of Housing Conditions in the Basin of the City of Cincinnati*; Rowe Paper, CHS; Report, "Relocation of Tenants, Laurel Homes Housing Project," Rowe Papers, CHS.

12. Minutes, BHL Board of Directors, September 26, 1935, BHL Papers, UC; ibid., October 31, 1935; *BHL Annual Report for 1934–35*, p. 7.

13. Report, "Relocation of Tenants, Laurel Homes Housing Project," Rowe Papers, CHS.

14. "Chronological Development. Housing Projects in Cincinnati, 1932–1937," April 13, 1937, p. 5, Rowe Papers, CHS.

15. Ibid.; Report, "Relocation of Tenants, Laurel Homes Housing Project," Rowe Papers, CHS.

16. Report, "Relocation of Tenants, Laurel Homes Housing Project," Rowe Papers, CHS.

17. Citizens' Committee on Slum Clearance and Low Cost Housing, "Housing Facts," BHL Papers, UC; George W. B. Conrad to Franklin D. Roosevelt, May 21, 1937, PHA, RG 196, NA.

18. J. M. Tadlock to Harold Ickes, December 10, 1935, PHA, RG 196, NA; Minutes, CMHA, January 7, 1936, CMHA Files.

19. Memorandum, A. R. Clas to Dr. Robert G. Weaver, October 25, 1935, PHA, RG 196, NA.

20. Memorandum, Bleecker Marquette to Housing Division of the PWA, August 31, 1935, PHA, RG 196, NA; "Chronological Development: Housing Projects in Cincinnati, 1932–1937. Laurel Homes," Rowe Papers, CHS.

21. Minutes, CMHA, September 15, 1936, CMHA Files.

22. Petition to FDR from Cincinnati Blacks, 1937, PHA, RG 196, NA.

23. Minutes, CMHA, June 1, 1937, CMHA Files; George W. B. Conrad to Franklin D. Roosevelt with clipping of *Cincinnati Post*, March 6, 1937, PHA, RG 196, NA.

24. Minutes, West End Housing Project Committee, December 17, 1937, Cincinnati Urban League (CUL) Papers, CHS.

25. Minutes, CMHA, February 8, 1938, CMHA Files; ibid., August 2, 1938.

26. Minutes, CMHA, July 12, 1938, CMHA Files; Stanley M. Rowe to R. R. Voell, Acting Director of Management Review for the Administration, USHA, November 10, 1938, PHA, RG 196, NA; *Report of the CMHA 1935*, p. 5.

27. Minutes, CMHA, July 12, 1938; August 2, 1938; February 8, 1938; CMHA Files.

28. Memorandum, Housing Committee of the Negro Better Housing Association, [1938], CUL Papers, CHS.

29. Minutes, Citizens' Committee on Slum Clearance and Low Cost Housing, December 6, 1933, BHL Papers, UC.

30. *Report of the CMHA 1938*, p. 4; CMHA, *Ninth Annual Report 1942*, p. 9.

31. Oscar Grear, "Negroes Barred from Living in White Housing Project, says Marquette MHA Head," *Cleveland Call and Post*, November 10, 1938, clipping in CUL Papers, CHS.

32. CMHA, *Tenth Annual Report 1943*.

33. Minutes, CMHA, December 28, 1937, CMHA Files; *Cincinnati Enquirer*, January 29, 1938, CMHA Scrapbook, Rowe Papers, CHS; George H. Wells to Nathan Straus, January 29, 1938, PHA, RG 196, NA; Stanley M. Rowe to Members of Cincinnati City Council, October 24, 1938, Charles P. Taft Papers, CHS; Minutes, BHL Board of Directors, September 21, 1938, BHL Papers, UC; Nathan Straus to Charles P. Taft and Stanley M. Rowe, quoted in *Cincinnati Enquirer*, October 26, 1938.

34. *Cincinnati Enquirer*, December 28, 1939.

35. Ernest Grunwald, "The West End: A Preliminary Ecological Study of an Area in Cincinnati," (M.A. thesis, University of Cincinnati, 1936), p. 59. Theodore Berry, "The Housing Problem in Cincinnati," paper for the Public Welfare Committee of Cincinnati City Council, December 11, 1944, CUL Papers, CHS; *Chronicle*, January 12, 1940.

36. *Chronicle*, January 12, 1940; *Annual Report of the City Manager, 1943* (Cincinnati, 1944), p. 52.

37. *Chronicle*, October 27, 1939.

38. Minutes, CMHA, April 16, 1940, CMHA Files.

39. Cincinnati, *Municipal Activities, 1937. Annual Report of the City Manager* (Cincinnati, 1938), p. 25; *Chronicle*, January 12, 1940; BHL, *What's New in Housing: A Page-a-Month* (BHL newsletter), May 1940.

40. *Cincinnati Enquirer*, March 23, 1940.

41. Minutes, BHL Board of Directors, January 18, 1940, BHL Papers, UC; *Chronicle*, January 12, 1940.

42. In 1940, a survey of 2,838 relief families found that 106 of them lived in houses unfit for habitation while another 618 suffered from overcrowded conditions. *Cincinnati Enquirer*, November 1, 1940; Albert L. France, "Report on the Relocation of Tenants for Lincoln Court Slum Clearance Project," Cincinnati, Ohio, October 28, 1941, Rowe Papers, CHS. That report claimed that 1,346 families were relocated. This figure differs from the CMHA estimate in April 1940, when it predicted that 1,279 families needed relocation. CMHA Minutes, April 16, 1940, CMHA Files.

43. Minutes, CMHA, April 16, 1940, CMHA Files.

44. Ibid.; France, "Report on the Relocation of Tenants"; Minutes, BHL Board of Directors, September 19, 1940, BHL Papers, UC.

45. *Cincinnati Enquirer*, January 22, 1942.

46. Ibid., May 12, 1941; Minutes, CMHA, June 24, 1941, CMHA Files; *CMHA, Eighth Annual Report 1941*, p. 3.

47. France, "Report on the Relocation of Tenants."

48. *Cincinnati Enquirer*, May 12, 1941; Minutes, June 24, 1941, CMHA Files; CMHA, *Eighth Annual Report 1941*, p. 3.

49. *Cincinnati Enquirer*, April 29, 1941; May 12, 1941.

50. Ibid., December 16, 1941.

51. Ibid.; Memorandum, J. Bion Philipson to Philip Klutznick, February 27, 1942, National Housing Agency (NHA), RG 207, NA; CMHA, *Tenth Annual Report 1943*. Even with the A-4 rating, the CMHA did not open the project until December 12, 1942. An inability to acquire copper wire for the project's electrical system proved to be the final delay in Lincoln Court's opening. *Cincinnati Enquirer*, December 12, 1942.

52. Minutes, BHL Executive Committee, November 6, 1942, BHL Papers, UC; J. Harvey Kerns to Henry Emmerich, November 11, 1942, CUL Papers, CHS; Minutes, Division of Negro Welfare, November 9, 1942, CUL Papers, CHS. Housing conditions were so bad in the West End that over 4,200 black families applied for space in Lincoln Court even before it opened. CMHA, *Ninth Annual Report 1942*, p. 9.

President Franklin Roosevelt consolidated all housing-related bureaus on February 24, 1942, into the National Housing Agency. John B. Blandford, Jr., former general manager of the Tennessee Valley Authority, headed the new agency, created to better coordinate the various government housing programs. No stranger to Cincinnati, Blandford had directed the Queen City's Bureau of Governmental Research and served as the city's public safety director during the 1920s. Under the reorganization, the Federal Public Housing Authority replaced the United States Housing Authority as the agency in charge of public housing activities. Blandford appointed Henry Emmerich, a public administrator and garden city advocate, to that post. Philip J. Funigiello, *The Challenge to Urban Liberalism: Federal-City Relations during World War II* (Knoxville: University of Tennessee Press, 1978), pp. 80–119. Keith, *Politics and the Housing Crisis since 1930*, pp. 40–57.

53. Minutes, BHL Board of Directors, December 17, 1942, BHL Papers, UC; CMHA, *Fifteenth Annual Report 1948*.

54. Minutes, BHL Board of Directors, December 17, 1942, BHL Papers, UC; *Cincinnati Enquirer*, May 16, 1943. Minutes, CMHA, January 9, 1941, CMHA Files. The project covered 22.4 acres and replaced 1,346 dwellings, of which 1,129 were substandard. Bleecker Marquette, Memorandum on Lincoln Court, n.d., BHL Papers, UC.

55. Howard B. Myers, "Survey of Vacancies in Dwelling Units of Cincinnati, Ohio," February 1941, CMHA Papers, CHS; Minutes, Housing Committee of the Division of Negro Welfare, October 20, 1943, CUL Papers, CHS.

56. *Cincinnati Enquirer*, August 1, 1940; J. Bion Philipson to Peter Klutznick, February 27, 1942, NHA, RG 207, NA; Memorandum, C. F. Palmer, Coordinator of Defense Housing, to War Department, October 10, 1941, NHA, RG 207, NA. For more on Wright's impact on Cincinnati, see Robert B. Fairbanks and Zane L. Miller, "The Martial Metropolis: Housing, Planning, and Race in Cincinnati, 1940–1955," in *The Martial Metropolis: U.S. Cities in War and Peace*, ed. Roger W. Lotchin (New York: Praeger, 1984), pp. 191–222.

57. *Cincinnati Business*, August 20, 1940.

58. *Cincinnati Enquirer*, August 22, 1940; Minutes, CMHA, November 19, 1940, CMHA Files.

59. Samuel E. Trotter, "A Study of Public Housing in the United States," (Ph.D. diss., University of Alabama, 1956), pp. 170–73; Glenn H. Beyer, *Housing and Society* (New York: Macmillan, 1965), pp. 474–75.

60. Minutes, CMHA, December 10, 1940, CMHA Files. CMHA officials also met with Lockland City Council and asked it to annex the proposed housing site to their city so the government would not have to provide all the essential services. Lockland's council had other plans and formed the Lockland Housing Commission. Members of that group traveled to Washington and requested funds from the Reconstruction Finance Corporation to eliminate all black slum housing in the subdivisions north of Lockland. In their place, local planners would construct between 1,200 and 1,700 units for whites. *Mill Creek Valley News*, December 13, 1940; December 27, 1940; February 28, 1941; Minutes, BHL Board of Directors, Jan. 23, 1941, BHL Papers, UC.

61. Minutes, CMHA, January 28, 1941, CMHA Files. The Federal Works Agency (FWA) succeeded the old PWA. In 1941, the Division of Defense Housing Coordination (created by the National Defense Advisory Commission in 1939) was given the responsibility of defining the needs and standards of defense housing while the FWA controlled actual construction. George Herbert Gray, *Housing and Citizenship: A Study of Low Cost Housing* (New York: Reinhold Publishing, 1946), pp. 240–41.

62. The CMHA was not to spend more than $2,750 per unit. *Cincinnati Enquirer*, February 12, 1941; *Mill Creek Valley News*, February 7, 1941; CMHA, *Eighth Annual Report 1941*, p. 8.

63. *Cincinnati Enquirer*, March 3, 1941; March 27, 1941; *City Constructor*, August 5, 1943.

64. CMHA, *Tenth Annual Report 1943*, Table 1; CMHA, *Eighth Annual Report 1941*, pp. 8–9.

65. CMHA, *Eighth Annual Report 1941*, pp. 8–9; *Cincinnati Enquirer*, March 27, 1941; Minutes, BHL Board of Directors, October 28, 1948, BHL Papers, UC.

66. Minutes, CMHA, June 17, 1941, CMHA Files; Memorandum, C. F. Palmer to War Department, October 10, 1941, NHA, RG 207, NA; Minutes, CMHA, February 10, 1942; Memorandum, Philipson to Klutznick, February 27, 1942, NHA, RG 207, NA; Minutes, CMHA, May 5, 1942, CMHA Files.

67. Top priority was given to applicants to Valley Homes whose homes were beyond reasonable commuting distance from their defense-related jobs. Palmer to War Department, October 10, 1941, NHA, RG 207, NA; Minutes, CMHA, February 10, 1942, CMHA Files.

68. Minutes, Board of Directors, February 2, 1942, BHL Papers, UC; ibid., March 25, 1943; Minutes, CMHA, February 10, 1942, CMHA Files.

69. CMHA, *Tenth Annual Report 1943*.

70. Theodore M. Berry, "The Housing Problem in Cincinnati."

71. Minutes, BHL Board of Directors, September 23, 1943, BHL Papers, UC; ibid., May 18, 1944.

72. CMHA, *Eighth Annual Report 1941*, p. 4; Minutes, BHL Board of Directors, May 27, 1942, BHL Papers, UC.

73. Minutes, CMHA, May 9, 1938, CMHA Files; ibid., May 17, 1938.

74. J.R. Bassiger to Nathan Straus, May 12, 1938, PHA, RG 196, NA; Stanley M. Rowe to Nathan Straus, May 13, 1938, PHA, RG 196, NA; F. W. Willey to Stanley M. Rowe, August 19, 1938, Rowe Papers, CHS; Minutes, CMHA, September 13, 1938, CMHA Files.

75. Minutes, CMHA, March 21, 1939, CMHA Files.

76. Minutes, BHL Board of Directors, February 19, 1942, BHL Papers, UC.

77. Minutes, Conference with William K. Divers, Regional Director, NHA, November 26, 1943, BHL Papers, UC.

78. Even the Model Homes Company raised its rents 9.6 percent because of rising costs. Minutes, BHL Board of Directors, January 8, 1942, BHL Papers, UC.

79. *Cincinnati Enquirer*, November 1, 1942.

80. Division of Negro Welfare, *Bulletin* (Cincinnati), August 1943.

81. Minutes, Meeting to Form Organization Interested in Racial Amity, October 7, 1943, CUL Papers, CHS; Memorandum, Negro Organization Interested in Racial Amity and Good Government to Mayor Stewart's Committee, October 7, 1943, CUL Papers, CHS.

82. Memorandum, William Castellini to Mr. Johnson, January 3, 1944, Cincinnati Human Relations Commission Papers (CHR), UC. The Cincinnati experience fit the national pattern. Following the spectacular Detroit race riot of 1943, more than thirty cities created municipal interracial commissions within a year. Hirsch, *Making the Second Ghetto*, p. 42.

83. Minutes, Conference with Mr. William Divers, November 26, 1943, BHL Papers, UC. Divers pointed out that since July 1, 1941, his agency had given preference to privately financed, converted, and remodeled housing. Minutes, BHL Board of Directors, January 27, 1944, BHL Papers, UC.

84. Bleecker Marquette to Frank Santry, October 31, 1944, CUL Papers, CHS.

85. Minutes, Housing Committee, Division of Negro Welfare, October 20, 1943, CUL Papers, CHS.

86. *Cincinnati Enquirer*, June 4, 1944, in Urban League newspaper scrapbook, 1943–1951, CUL Papers, CHS; Minutes, BHL Board of Directors Meeting, May 24, 1945, BHL Papers, UC; ibid., June 22, 1944. The Norris dwellings sold for an $800 down payment and monthly payments of $31 for a twenty-five-year period.

87. Minutes, BHL Board of Directors, January 27, 1944, BHL Papers, UC; ibid., November 2, 1944.

88. Greene, who had earlier served as a management aid for Laurel Homes, was appointed to her new post in 1942 after much pressure from local blacks. CMHA, *Ninth Annual Report 1942*.

89. Arnold B. Walker to Mayor James Garfield Stewart, December 2, 1943, CUL Papers, CHS.

90. *Cincinnati Call Post*, March 1, 1944, clipping in Urban League Scrapbook, CUL Papers, CHS. August Marx of the BHL exclaimed after hearing of Stewart's choice that putting Skirvin on the CMHA was "like having a Hitler in Congress," *Cincinnati Times-Star*, March 22, 1944, Urban League Scrapbook, CUL Papers, CHS.

91. *Cincinnati Call Post*, March 1, 1944, Urban League Scrapbook, CUL Papers, CHS.

92. Minutes, BHL Board of Directors, January 25, 1945, BHL Papers, UC.

93. Minutes, Joint Committee on Housing and the Cincinnati Negro Citizen, October 26, 1944, CUL Papers, CHS.

94. Memorandum, Negro Housing, January 25, 1945, Rowe Papers, CHS.

95. According to historian John Kirby, Weaver believed that "the integration of Negroes into the American economic system, through expanded federally financed employment and housing opportunities, would not only create a better environment for developing necessary skills and facilitating their entry into a growing industrial society, [but] it would also improve the climate of race relations." John B. Kirby, *Black Americans in the Roosevelt Era: Liberalism and Race* (Knoxville: University of Tennessee Press, 1980), p. 123. For more on the acculturation theory see Stow Persons, *Ethnic Studies at Chicago*, 1905–1945 (Urbana: University of Illinois Press, 1987).

96. Although this study agrees with Hirsch's conclusions about the consequences of slum clearance and public housing in the 1940s, it views the causes quite differently. Hirsch argues that the second ghetto was a result of a conscious decision made by downtown businessmen to sacrifice black homes in areas important to the renewal of downtown Chicago. My study suggests that slum clearance and segregated housing stemmed from planners' and housers' concern with the social as well as economic consequences of slums. Indeed, slum clearance and neighborhood community projects were seen as a way of upgrading the lives of Cincinnati blacks. Hirsch, *Making the Second Ghetto*.

Part IV

1. "The Housing Movement in Retreat," *New Republic*, August 13, 1951, pp. 15–16.

2. Richard O. Davies, *Housing Reform during the Truman Administration* (Columbia: University of Missouri Press, 1966), pp. 116–42.

3. Bauman, *Public Housing, Race, and Renewal*, pp. 125–29.

4. Louis Wirth, "Urbanism as a Way of Life," in *American Urban History: An Interpretive Reader with Commentaries*, ed. Alexander B. Callow, Jr. (New York: Oxford University Press, 1969), p. 492–93; Herbert J. Gans, "Urbanism and Suburbanism as Ways of Life: A Re-evaluation of Definitions," ibid., pp. 512–13.

5. Ibid., p. 512.

6. Ibid., p. 518.

7. Zane L. Miller and Bruce Tucker, "The Revolt against Culture and the Origins of Community Action: A View from Cincinnati" (Cincinnati, 1987), pp. 1–3 (typescript).

Chapter 10

1. *Columbus Metropolitan Housing Authority, Appellant, v. Thatcher, Aud., et al., Appellees*, 140 Ohio 38–50 (1942).

2. Ibid. For a discussion of the ruling see "Tax Exemption of Public Low-Rent Housing and Slum Clearance Projects," *American City* 57 (July 1942), pp. 176–77;

Myres S. McDougal and Addison A. Muellar, "Public Purpose in Public Housing: An Anachronism Reburied," *Yale Law Journal* 52 (December 1942): 42–71.

3. "The Housing Year: A Review," *Housing Yearbook, 1943*, p. 19. Under the 1937 Housing Act, the Federal Public Housing Authority could make loans for projects up to 90 percent of the building costs (including land), therefore leaving local authorities the task of raising the remaining 10 percent for the project through the sale of bonds.

4. *Cincinnati Enquirer*, November 15, 1942; April 7, 1943; Minutes, BHL Board of Directors, June 11, 1942, BHL Papers, UC; ibid., January 28, 1943.

5. BHL, *What's New in Housing: A Page-a-Month*, July 1951; *Cincinnati Enquirer*, June 30, 1951.

6. For more on the federal defense housing efforts see the following highly critical works: Abrams, *Future of Housing*, pp. 296–311; and Funigiello, *The Challenge to Urban Liberalism*, pp. 80–119.

World War I defense housing was experimental, community-oriented and publicly built. World War II defense housing tended to be more traditional, temporary, and privately built. During World War II defense housing was treated more as a commodity than as an instrument for community. Abrams, *Future of Housing*, pp. 296–302.

7. Summary of talk by Joseph P. Tufts to the Citizens' Committee on Slum Clearance and Low Cost Housing, June 21, 1940, BHL Papers, UC.

8. Memorandum, the BHL and the Citizens' Committee on Slum Clearance and Low Rent Housing to City Council, November 20, 1945, p. 1, BHL Papers, UC.

9. Ibid., pp. 3–4.

10. *Cincinnati Enquirer*, December 1, 1945.

11. Ibid., December 11, 1945; "Report of the Mayor's Committee on Housing," January 2, 1946, Rowe Files.

12. "Report of the Mayor's Committee on Housing," January 2, 1946, Rowe Files.

13. *Cincinnati Enquirer*, December 13, 1945; December 20, 1945.

14. CMHA, *Thirteenth Annual Report 1946*; *Cincinnati Enquirer*, January 15, 1946.

15. CMHA, *Thirteenth Annual Report 1946*; CMHA Minutes, March 5, 1946, CMHA Files, *Cincinnati Enquirer*, April 24, 1946. The Ohio General Assembly passed the State Veterans Housing Act in August 1946, which provided $540,262 to the Hamilton County Commissioners to build housing for veterans. They constructed one prefabricated project for seventy-five white families at a site near Longview Hospital and another project for blacks in the Steel Street Subdivision in North College Hill. *Cincinnati Enquirer*, August 29, 1946; October 1, 1946; October 5, 1946; April 9, 1947.

16. *Cincinnati Enquirer*, March 8, 1946; Minutes, CMHA, March 5, 1946, CMHA Files.

17. A three-room apartment rented at $28 per month, four rooms at $31, five rooms at $33. All rents included gas, electricity, and water. The CMHA not only managed the units but also handled the details of their construction. Minutes, BHL Board of Directors, June 27, 1946, BHL Papers, UC; *Cincinnati Enquirer*, January 15, 1946; April 24, 1946.

18. *Cincinnati Enquirer*, August 6, 1946; Minutes, BHL Board of Directors, January 22, 1947, BHL Papers, UC.

19. *Cincinnati Enquirer*, October 15, 1946; February 21, 1947.

20. Memorandum on Proposed Emergency Housing Committee, April 14, 1946, BHL Papers, UC; Minutes, CMHA, January 23, 1945, CMHA Files; *Cincinnati Enquirer*, May 9, 1942.

21. The necessary legislation for this program, the Veterans' Emergency Housing Act, became law on May 22, 1946. Keith, *Politics and the Housing Crisis since 1930*, pp. 59–63; Mary Frost Jessup, "Trends in Housing during the War and Postwar Periods," *Monthly Labor Review* 61 (January 1946): 92–93.

22. Memorandum on Proposed Emergency Housing Committee, April 19, 1946, BHL Papers, UC.

23. Minutes, BHL Board of Directors, June 27, 1946, BHL Papers, UC; Memorandum on Proposed Emergency Housing Committee, April 19, 1946, BHL Papers, UC; *Cincinnati Enquirer*, January 1, 1947.

24. *Report of the Cincinnati Committee to Expedite Housing* (Cincinnati, 1947), pp. 48–49. The report discussed the movement of new housing outside the city limits and noted how that made the city's Building Department statistics of little value.

25. Ibid., p. 11.

26. Minutes, CMHA, September 12, 1944, CMHA Files.

27. *Cincinnati Enquirer*, August 23, 1947; Minutes, BHL Board of Directors, May 22, 1947, BHL Papers, UC; ibid., October 28, 1948; *Cincinnati Enquirer*, September 28, 1948; Minutes, CMHA, June 25, 1946, CMHA Files.

28. *Cincinnati Enquirer*, May 9, 1942.

29. U.S., Work Projects Administration (WPA), "Real Property Survey, Cincinnati, Ohio, 1939–1941," p. 2 (mimeograph); *Cincinnati Constructor*, October 2, 1939; *Cincinnati Enquirer*, September 19, 1941.

30. Minutes, BHL Board of Directors, April 29, 1943, BHL Papers, UC; WPA, *Real Property Survey*, p. 29.

31. Minutes, CMHA, February 17, 1942, CMHA Files; ibid., May 4, 1943; *Cincinnati Enquirer*, May 9, 1942.

32. WPA, *Real Property Survey*, p. 31.

33. Minutes, BHL Board of Directors, January 8, 1942, BHL Papers, UC.

34. Richard High, "The Planning Process in a 20th Century American City: The Case of Cincinnati, 1935–1948" (Senior thesis, University of Cincinnati, May 1974), p. 9; Sherwood L. Reeder, "Revamping the Master Plan," *Journal of the American Institute of Planners* 12 (1946): 4.

35. Ibid.; George P. Stimson, "They Cared: A Citizens' Planning Association, 1944–1948; The Citizens' Development Committee, 1948–1968," unpublished paper, n.d., pp. 11, 13, CDC Papers, CHS.

36. Interview, Stanley M. Rowe, December 6, 1979; Stimson, "They Cared," pp. 11–13.

37. Interview, Rowe, December 6, 1979; Interview, Ladislas Segoe, December 4, 1979; George P. Stimson, "It Happened Here," *Queen City Heritage* 41 (Summer 1983): 21; Industrialist John J. Emery also played an important role in the the initial

stages of the planning movement. High, "The Planning Process in a 20th Century American City," pp. 10–15.

Many of those in the planning movement, then, were leading businessmen, some with specific downtown interests. It does not appear, however, that they, or their predecessors on earlier boards or committees associated with low-cost housing or planning, were motivated solely by a preoccupation with preserving their economic interests in the urban core. Rather, they seemed to buy into the social arguments that a well-planned and well-housed city produced good citizens and good workers, something which might benefit them as employers, and would certainly benefit the city in which they worked and lived. No doubt the deterioration of the core was perceived as a problem by the 1940s—but not as the only problem, or even the most important problem. See for example, how the Urban Land Institute approached Cincinnati's downtown problem in 1940 from a metropolitan perspective. *Proposals for Downtown Cincinnati* (Chicago: Urban Land Institute, 1941).

38. Neil H. McElroy was a vice president at Procter and Gamble; John J. Hurst presided over the Central Labor Council; Charles F. Cellarius was an architect; W. Howard Cox was president of the Union Central Life Insurance Company; Milton H. Schmidt practiced law; and Charles W. Dupuis served as president of the Central Trust Company. Stimson, "They Cared," p. 16. On February 21, they incorporated as the Cincinnati Planning Association, a not-for-profit corporation.

To compare the Cincinnati postwar development experience with other cities see Silver, *Twentieth-Century Richmond*; Carl Abbott, *Portland: Planning, Politics and Growth in a Twentieth Century City* (Lincoln: University of Nebraska Press, 1983). John F. Bauman, "Visions of a Post-War City: Perspective on Urban Planning in Philadelphia and the Nation: 1942–1945," *Urbanism Past and Present* 6 (Winter/Spring, 1981): 1–11; Blake McKelvey, "Housing and Urban Renewal: The Rochester Experience," *Rochester History* 27 (October 1965): 1–28; William R. Barnes, "A National Controversy in Miniature: The District of Columbia Struggle over Public Housing and Redevelopment, 1943–1946," *Prologue* 9 (Summer 1977): 91–104.

39. Statement of Stanley M. Rowe on his election to the presidency of the Citizens' Planning Association, December 21, 1943, Rowe Files.

40. Hirsch, *Making of the Second Ghetto*, p. 101; Bettman, "Statement to the Sub-Committee on Housing and Urban Redevelopment, Committee on Postwar Planning, U.S. Senate," in *City and Regional Planning Papers*, p. 101. Marc A. Weiss's provocative study on the national origins of urban renewal also argues how urban renewal owes its origins to downtown merchants, banks, large corporations, newspaper publishers, and others with "substantial business and property interests in the central business district." Although he provides a convincing argument that the National Real Estate Board's Urban Land Institute played a critical role in the wording of both the 1949 and 1954 Housing Acts, his study neglects to explore the larger context of social concern which also influenced the development of those bills. Moreover, he argues as does Hirsch that the planning profession was merely a tool of big business, and at odds with the social concern of public housing supporters. Such a claim does not seem valid for Cincinnati. Weiss, "The Origins and Legacy of Urban Renewal," p. 54.

41. For a more detailed look at the search process see High, "The Planning Process

in a 20th Century American City," pp. 41–61. See also Cincinnati City Planning Commission (CCPC), *The Master Plan. Report on Program and Progress* (March 1946), pp. 1–2; Reeder, "Revamping the Master Plan," p. 14.

42. CCPC, *Cincinnati Metropolitan Master Plan and the Official City Plan of the City of Cincinnati, 1948* (Cincinnati: City Planning Commission, 1948), pp. 31–32, 69–70, 79–104. Although Arnold Hirsch has argued that in Chicago downtown business interests used the war and postwar housing emergency and planning as an opportunity to secure subsidies for the redesign and reconstruction of the central business district, the Cincinnati plan shows no such intent. That plan discussed the central business district only in connection with other focal points and issues and did not call for redevelopment of any sort within the business district itself. The plan did address the central riverfront as a problem, however, treating it as a separate and discrete locale and suggesting that it should be redeveloped. Hirsch, *The Making of the Second Ghetto*, pp. 102–6; CCPC, *Cincinnati Metropolitan Master Plan 1948*, pp. 141–49. In Cincinnati, downtown redevelopment planning began in the mid-1950s. See Zane L. Miller and Geoffrey Giglierano, "Downtown Housing: Changing Plans and Perspectives, 1948–1980," *Cincinnati Historical Society Bulletin* 40 (Fall 1982): 177–88. The plan, then, was exactly what the title indicated, a metropolitan master plan. Its key conceptual element, the residential community, occupied the central place and was explicated first in the plan.

43. The following material on the master plan of 1948 first appeared in Fairbanks and Miller, "The Martial Metropolis," pp. 204–9. Miller drafted that part of the article. CCPC, *The Economy of the Cincinnati Metropolitan Area* (Cincinnati: City Planning Commission, 1946); CCPC, *Cincinnati Metropolitan Master Plan 1948*, p. 10.

44. CCPC, *Cincinnati Metropolitan Master Plan 1948*, pp. 11, 27–34, figure 17; CCPC, *Residential Areas: An Analysis of Land Requirements for Residential Development, 1945–1970* (Cincinnati: City Planning Commission, 1946), figure 2.

45. CCPC, *Communities* (Cincinnati: City Planning Commission, 1947), pp. 2–6.

46. Ibid., pp. 6, 21–22. The self-contained community idea was not unique to Cincinnati planners, see "To Make Our Big Cities Friendly Groups of Well Planned Neighborhoods," *American City* 61 (February 1, 1946): 79–80; Harland L. Bartholomew and Associates, "A Master Plan for Dallas, Texas," Report No. 10, "Housing" (December 1944), pp. 27–35.

47. CCPC, *Communities*, pp. 21–22.

48. Ibid., p. 9.

49. CCPC, *Residential Areas*, pp. 17–18.

50. Ibid., p. 18.

51. Ibid., pp. 42–50.

52. Ibid., pp. 76–78.

53. Ibid., pp. 34–35, 54–55, 81. For a map of the residential and nonresidential redevelopment sites, see figure 7.

54. Alfred Bettman to Herbert U. Nelson, April 4, 1942, CDC Papers, CHS.

55. William L. C. Wheaton, "The Housing Act of 1949," *Journal of the American Institute of Planners* (February 1949): 26–27. Title I authorized the federal government to loan up to $1 billion and grant up to $500,000 for clearance over a five-year period (p. 29); Public Law 171, July 15, 1949, sec. 1070, 81st Congress; Walter S.

Schmidt, "The Ohio Redevelopment Law," *Urban Land: News and Trend . . . in City Development* 8 (July-August, 1949): n.p.; *Citizens' Development Committee Bulletin* 8 (June 1951), n.p. Rowe helped secure federal subsidies for public housing by educating his friend, Robert A. Taft, on the need for slum clearance and public housing. As a result, the Cincinnati-born U.S. senator supported the cause through the passage of the federal legislation of 1949. James T. Patterson, *Mr. Republican: A Biography of Robert A. Taft* (Boston: Houghton Mifflin, 1972), pp. 187, 315–30.

56. Zane L. Miller first called this added appeal of rehabilitation and conservation to my attention.

57. See, for instance, the 1948 master plan's discussion of the need for relocation housing for the poor, pp. 70–71.

58. *Cincinnati Enquirer*, May 15, 1948.

59. Ibid., April 8, 1949. Cincinnati voters passed a $41-million bond issue for such public works as the viaduct and the River Road improvement. Statement of Randolph Sellars before the Ohio Urban Redevelopment Commission, Columbus, November 20, 1945, CDC Papers, CHS.

60. Minutes, BHL Board of Directors, September 23, 1948, BHL Papers, UC; *Cincinnati Enquirer*, September 1, 1948.

61. Minutes, CMHA, September 17, 1948, CMHA Files.

62. *Cincinnati Enquirer*, October 26, 1948.

63. Ibid., May 24, 1950; May 6, 1950; Minutes, CMHA, May 23, 1950, CMHA Files; ibid., June 27, 1950; Office of the City Manager, Cincinnati, Ohio, Redevelopment, "Preliminary Report on Relocation and Rehousing," August 8, 1951, Charles P. Taft Papers, CHS; *Cincinnati Enquirer*, April 21, 1951. Funding for the relocation project came from the Weaver Fund, set aside for a proposed Woodward playground. *Cincinnati Enquirer*, May 11, 1950.

64. Urban Redevelopment Data, "Relocation Housing," presented to Council, Committee of the Whole, June 25, 1951, p. 10, Taft Papers, CHS; *Cincinnati Enquirer*, February 3, 1949.

65. *Cincinnati Enquirer*, April 22, 1948; Statement Regarding the Formation of the Cincinnati Community Development Company, April 22, 1948, CDC Papers, CHS.

66. *Cincinnati Enquirer*, February 7, 1948; August 26, 1948, p. 1. Statement Regarding the Formation of the CCDC, April 22, 1948, CDC Papers; Preliminary Proposal for Purchase and Development of Greenhills Tract submitted to the Public Housing Administration, Rowe Files.

67. "Report to the Stockholders of the CCDC," February 1, 1950; p. 8, CDC Papers; ibid., September 2, 1952.

68. *Cincinnati Enquirer*, May 6, 1949; "Report to the Stockholders of the CCDC," February 1, 1950, p. 1, CDC Papers, CHS. It hoped eventually to build 400 units on the site.

69. CCDC, "Review of Activities, 1950, 3rd Report," p. 1, CDC Papers, CHS; *Report of the Cincinnati Mayor's Housing Committee* (Cincinnati: July 1950), p. 39.

70. Urban Redevelopment Data, "Relocation Housing," Presented to Council, Committee on the Whole, June 25, 1951, p. 6, Taft Papers, CHS.

71. Ibid.

72. Ibid., p. 7.

73. The Laurel-Richmond plan proposed to develop two community projects made up of low-density housing, community facilities including a school and hospital, and commercial areas for local shoppers. The main controversy over this project revolved around its target clientele. Some wanted the area to be developed "as a beauty spot for the city," i.e., attractive high-rent apartments, while others wanted the area reserved for those displaced by public works projects "and others of modest means." *Journal of Housing* 17 (March 1960): 99.

74. Office of the City Manager, Cincinnati, Ohio, Urban Redevelopment, "Preliminary Report on Relocation and Rehousing," August 8, 1951, Taft Papers, CHS; City Planning Commission, "Facts about Cincinnati's Slum Clearance and Urban Redevelopment," October 1951, p. 18, CDC Papers, CHS.

75. Office of the City Manager, "Preliminary Report on Relocation and Rehousing," August 8, 1951, Taft Papers, CHS.

76. The report argued that building for more prosperous blacks outside the targeted slum area would help the needy blacks through a filter-down process. It also claimed that 18 percent of those black families in the Laurel-3, Richmond-1 area could pay rent of at least $50 per month and thus qualify for the new housing (pp. 3–6).

77. *Cincinnati Enquirer*, September 6, 1951; *City Bulletin*, September 18, 1951, Ordinance No. 346-1951, p. 6; "Declaration of Urban Redevelopment Policy," adopted September 5, 1951, Taft Papers, CHS; BHL, *What's New in Housing: A Page-a-Month*, December 1951; Minutes, BHL Board of Directors, November 29, 1951, BHL Papers, UC. Although the city eventually used other money for the project, delays continued. Awards of the land weren't made until 1958 when council accepted the proposals of the Midland Redevelopment Corporation and the Cincinnati Redevelopment Corporation. However a price war with federal agencies along with soaring interest rates and construction costs ultimately led both developers to withdraw. Not until February of 1960 were two new developers found: Reynolds Metals Company of Louisville and the Hamilton Company of Cincinnati. *Journal of Housing*, 15 (July 1958): 236; (March 1960): 99.

78. CCDC, "Interim Report on Site Selection Studies," June 30, 1950, pp. 1–3, CDC Papers, CHS.

79. The CCDC had originally planned to build five conventional houses at the Lindale site but cancelled this when the Chester Road homes sold slowly. Lawrence H. Tucker to Earle J. Wheeler, January 17, 1952, CDC Papers, CHS; "Report to the Stockholders of the CCDC . . . September, 1952," p. 3, CDC Papers, CHS.

80. "Report to the Stockholders of the CCDC . . . September 1, 1952," p. 3, CDC Papers, CHS.

81. Cincinnati voters had already approved bonds for the city's part in the expressway program in 1950. *Citizens' Development Community Bulletin*, February 1953, p. 2.

82. Office of the City Manager, Division of Slum Clearance and Urban Redevelopment, "Relocation Plans: A Manual for Family Relocation Services," typescript, 1953, CDC Papers, CHS.

83. *Cincinnati Enquirer*, June 30, 1951; October 13, 1951; Minutes, CMHA, October 23, 1951, CMHA Files. The Public Housing Administration succeeded the Federal Public Housing Administration in 1947.

84. *Cincinnati Enquirer*, June 16, 1952.

85. The local attack on the neighborhood unit approach to public housing was symptomatic of a ·national debate. See the National Public Housing Conference, *A Housing Program . . . for Now and Later* (n.p., February 1948), pp. 43–46; and Reginald R. Isaacs, "Attack on the Neighborhood Unit Formula," *Land Economics* 25 (February 1949): 73–78.

86. Resolution 461, Approving the Use of the Kirby Road Site and Authorizing the Acceptance of an Option to Purchase the Real Property, Minutes, CMHA, April 22, 1952, CMHA Files. As of 1946, there were 2,063 vacant land parcels comprising "a marginal supply of odds and ends" suitable for housing (ibid.).

87. Minutes, BHL Board of Directors, October 25, 1951, BHL Papers, UC.

88. Ibid., March 27, 1952.

89. Minutes, CMHA, February 26, 1952, CMHA Files; Resolution No. 461, ibid., April 22, 1952.

90. Minutes, BHL Board of Directors, June 19, 1952, BHL Papers, UC; Minutes, CMHA, April 22, 1952, CMHA Files.

91. Minutes, BHL Board of Directors, June 19, 1952, BHL Papers, UC; *Cincinnati Enquirer*, November 23, 1952. According to the *Enquirer*, Ruebel would build 150 prefabricated homes on the site and sell them for between $9,000 and $13,000.

92. *Cincinnati Enquirer*, July 24, 1952; BHL, *What's New in Housing: A Page-a-Month*, September 1952; October 16, 1952.

93. *Cincinnati Enquirer*, July 25, 1952. The local referendum campaign against public housing appeared to be part of a nationwide effort orchestrated by the National Association of Real Estate Boards after they failed to defeat the 1949 Housing Act. Public housing advocates pointed out that the NAREB published *Public Housing on the Community Level*, a document that outlined a program for local groups to use to defeat public housing. The pamphlet specifically cited the referendum tactic. Davies, *Housing Reform*, p. 127.

94. *Cincinnati Enquirer*, July 24, 1952; October 13, 1952.

95. Ibid., July 29, 1952; October 10, 1952; November 4, 1952; BHL, *What's New in Housing: A Page-a-Month*, December 1952.

96. BHL, *What's New in Housing: A Page-a-Month*, February 1953. The East Westwood Property Owners' Association also filed an injunction suit against the project but it was dismissed. Minutes, CMHA, March 24, 1953, CMHA Files.

97. Minutes, CMHA, June 2, 1953, CMHA Files; ibid., November 12, 1953; October 26, 1954; Minutes, BHL Board of Directors, May 28, 1953, BHL Papers, UC; BHL, *What's New in Housing; A Page-a-Month*, December 1955.

98. Minutes, CMHA, March 2, 1954, CMHA Files; ibid., August 17, 1954; May 11, 1954; Minutes, BHL Board of Directors, July 8, 1954, BHL Papers, UC; CMHA, *Twenty-Seventh Annual Report*, 1960, p. 4. There were several exceptions: the CMHA was able to find two sites for public housing for the elderly, and it built a small project for blacks in Lincoln Heights during the late 1950s (ibid.).

99. William H. Hessler, "The Refugees from Civic Progress," *Reporter*, July 9, 1959, pp. 27–29; Thomas F. Johnson et al., *Renewing America's Cities* (Washington D.C.: Institute for Social Science Research, 1962), p. 41.

100. *A New Town: Report of the Sponsors by a Combined Panel from Three Coun-*

cils of the Urban Land Institute (Washington, D.C.: December 1952), pp. viii, 21–22; Interview, Ladislas Segoe, November 30, 1979; Zane L. Miller, *Suburb: Neighborhood and Community in Forest Park, Ohio, 1935–1976* (Knoxville: University of Tennessee Press, 1981), pp. 8–27.

101. Interview, Segoe, November 30, 1979; Miller, *Suburb: Neighborhood and Community*, pp. 28–45; *Community Development Committee Bulletin*, February 1956.

102. For instance, see *Architectural Record*'s discussion of St. Louis's massive high-rise public housing project, Pruitt-Igoe, built in 1954. The article discusses how the project's designers arranged space in such a way to create neighborhoods within each building. "Four Vast Housing Projects for St. Louis," *Architectural Record* 120 (August 1956): 182–89.

103. Professor Miller first called my attention to the shift from community services to individual desires. See his *Suburb: Neighborhood and Community*, pp. 28–29.

104. John Bauman neatly details the new approach to low-cost housing in his examination of Philadelphia's public housing. See Bauman, *Public Housing, Race, and Renewal*, pp. 160–86.

105. *Housing Act of 1954, Statutes at Large*, vol. 68, sec. 220 (1954).

106. Cincinnati, Department of Urban Development, *Cincinnati: No Pause in Development* (Cincinnati: n.p., 1970), p. 14. The refocusing of planning concurred with a national pattern that according to Howard Gillette, Jr., shifted the emphasis of neighborhood planning in the 1950s and 1960s "from the kind of social and civic concerns associated with its origins in the Progressive Era to the protection of business investment and the growth of city revenues." Gillette, "Evolution of Neighborhood Planning," p. 431.

107. CCPC, "Central Business Report," 2 vols., 1958.

108. "Cincinnati: CDC is a Real Spearhead of Progress," *Journal of Housing* 17 (1960): 19; *Cincinnati Enquirer*, March 15, 1958.

109. CCPC, "Central Business District and Riverfront Report," November 1961, p. 3.

110. D. Reid Ross, "A Guide to Officials in Organizing Citizen Support for Urban Renewal," *Journal of Housing* 13 (July 1956): 235; Cincinnati, Office of City Manager, "A Workable Program for Urban Renewal," 1955, p. 30 (mimeographed).

111. John Clayton Thomas, *Between Citizen and City: Neighborhood Organizations and Urban Politics in Cincinnati* (Lawrence: University Press of Kansas, 1986), p. 28. For more on this approach to neighborhood planning see Christopher Silver, "Neighborhood Planning in Historical Perspective," *Journal of the American Planning Association* 51 (Spring 1985): 171. For more on the shift in Cincinnati see Miller and Giglierano, "Downtown Housing," pp. 167–90; Zane L. Miller, "History and the Politics of Community Change in Cincinnati," *Public Historian* 5 (Fall 1983): 17–35.

112. Cincinnati, Department of Urban Development, *Cincinnati: No Pause in Development*, p. 14.

Bibliographic Note

   This book benefited from a number of excellent, well-preserved manuscript collections, many of them housed in Cincinnati. The Urban Studies Collection, part of the Archival Collection of the University of Cincinnati Libraries, contained the extremely valuable Better Housing League (BHL) Papers, which offered a number of published and unpublished reports about Cincinnati's housing problems, and even more important, included the valuable minutes book of the BHL's board of directors. While the BHL Papers provided a detailed look at Cincinnati's low-cost housing reform, the Alfred Bettman Papers, also of the Urban Studies Collection, closely documented local planning developments. The Bettman papers not only helped link Cincinnati's planning activities with the broader national movement, but also suggested that a revaluation of the relationship between planners and housers was necessary.

   Several other holdings of the Urban Studies Collection helped illuminate the history of the planning and housing movements in Cincinnati and the nation. They include the Jacob G. Schmidlapp Papers, the Census Tract Center Data Files, the Cincinnati Human Relations Commission Records, and the Charles H. Stamm Papers. The University Archival Collection also contained the Cincinnati City Planning Commission Records and the Hamilton County Regional Planning Commission Records as part of its Ohio Network Collection.

   The Cincinnati Historical Society's Manuscript Department provided the other major holdings of source material. Clearly the most important of these collections were the Stanley M. Rowe Papers. They not only contained materials documenting the formation and early programs of the Cincinnati Metropolitan Housing Authority, but included records from Rowe's involvement in the Citizens' Planning Association and from the Citizens' Development Committee. Although they were uncataloged when I used them, the Rowe Papers have since been neatly organized and cataloged.

   The Cincinnati Historical Society also holds the papers of Charles P. Taft, long-time political reformer, councilman, and mayor of Cincinnati. The Taft Papers are a storehouse of useful information on a variety of Cincinnati topics between 1920 and 1960, including the controversy between city council and the CMHA over the placement of public housing. The CHS's Cincinnati Urban League (CUL) Papers provide insight to how black leaders responded to the public housing program. Another collection, the Citizens' Development Committee (CDC) Papers, included valuable records of not only the CDC and the Citizens' Planning Association, but also of the Cincinnati Community Development Company. Both proved indispensable in portraying the complex interrelationships between planning, low-cost housing, and urban redevelopment after World War II.

Several CHS collections proved more helpful in understanding earlier developments in Cincinnati's low-cost housing movement. Particularly important in this regard were the Associated Charities/Family Services Records, the Cincinnati Chamber of Commerce Records, the Woman's City Club Papers, the BHL Papers, and the Model Homes Company Records. Besides the material found in the Manuscript Department, the CHS's main library contained a number of valuable published reports by both private organizations and public agencies. The reports of the Anti-Tuberculosis League closely covered one of the city's earliest better housing movements.

The Max Senior Papers and the records of the United Jewish Charities of Cincinnati are both located at American Jewish Archives on the campus of Hebrew Union College–Jewish Institute of Religion in Cincinnati. Both of these collections provided a helpful perspective of the role played by the city's Jewish leadership in combatting Cincinnati's tenement problem at the turn of the century.

The city's political reform tradition may help explain its impressive number of detailed local government reports. Many of these, including reports of city departments, can be found at the University of Cincinnati's library or at the downtown branch of the Public Library of Cincinnati and Hamilton County. These records were supplemented by the minutes of city council, kept at city hall, and an assortment of material, including the minutes of the Cincinnati City Planning Commission, located in the City Planning Commission Office. The very valuable Cincinnati Metropolitan Housing Authority minutes were found at the offices of the CMHA in downtown Cincinnati.

The local search for information also led me to interview two of the city's major actors in the low-cost housing story—Stanley M. Rowe and Ladislas Segoe. Although elderly, both exhibited clear minds and provided valuable supplementary information which helped me gain a better feel for the era under investigation. Rowe also allowed me to reproduce a number of valuable papers from his office files in Mariemont, Ohio.

In addition to relying on local sources, I found materials from outside Cincinnati quite valuable. The book's chapters on public housing benefited greatly from the Public Housing Administration Records (RG 196) and the Housing and Home Finance Agency files (RG 207) at the National Archives. The detailed applications for limited dividend housing found in the PHA Records proved particularly helpful in better understanding the community development strategy to housing betterment.

The Ladislas Segoe Papers, part of the Department of Manuscripts and University Archives, Cornell University Libraries, provided more helpful documentation about the city's first effort at large-scale slum clearance and community-based low-income housing.

The Justin Hartzog Papers, also located at Cornell, gave valuable insight to the development of Greenhills. Even more useful in this regard were the John S. Lansill Papers, part of the Special Collections and Archives of the University of Kentucky

Libraries. These papers clearly demonstrated that Greenhills was part of a community development strategy for metropolitan Cincinnati.

This book also relied heavily on local newspapers. Guided by the massive index of local newspapers at the downtown branch of the Public Library of Cincinnati and Hamilton County, I looked at thousands of entries for the city's three daily newspapers—the *Cincinnati Enquirer*, the *Cincinnati Post*, and the *Cincinnati Times-Star*. Other special-interest newspapers were also consulted, including the suburban *Mill Creek News*, labor's *Chronicle*, and the local black newspaper, the *Cincinnati Union*. Unfortunately, no complete run of this last paper any longer exists.

For a more extensive list of unpublished as well as published works consulted, see the bibliography of my dissertation, "Better Housing Movements and the City: Definitions of and Responses to Cincinnati's Low-Cost Housing Problems, 1910–1954," at the University of Cincinnati Library.

Index

Abrams, Charles, 89
Addams, Jane, 51
Alfred, Helen, 197n11
Allen, Martha Francis, 112
Alms, William H., 35
American City, 4
American Institute of Architects, 23
Americanization Committee, 63
American Journal of Sociology, 39
American Reform Judaism, 183n24
American social thought: changing assumptions in, 147–48
American Society of Planning, 6
Anderson, Melvin, 134
Anderson Park: as site for temporary housing, 154
Anomie, 1, 104
Anti-Tuberculosis League, 26–28
Architectural firms: Samuel Hannaford and Son(s), 77, 92; Tietig and Lee, 77; Potter, Tyler and Martin, 77, 92; Rapp and Meacham, 78
Armstrong, Albert, 193n65
Associated Charities: support of tenement reform, 18, 19, 20; promotion of model tenements, 20–21; promotion of tenement regulation, 23; mentioned, 25
Augur, Tracy, 159
Avondale, 35, 125, 163, 176
Avondale-Corryville neighborhoods: as a neighborhood renewal project, 175–76

Baltimore, Md., 14, 18
Bartholomew, Harland, 199n24

Bassiger, J. R., 141
Bauer, Catherine, 114, 210n2
Bauman, John F., 114, 210n2
Bauman, Oscar E., 172
Beaman, R. E., 132
Beekman Street, 88
Berry, Theodore M.: support of public housing, 102, 120; promotion of housing opportunities for blacks, 130, 169
Better Housing League of Cincinnati: and housing reform, 4, 5, 29–33; identification of citywide housing problem, 24; establishment, 29–30; promotion of housing education, 30–31; and visiting housekeepers, 30, 62, 65, 67, 195n12; association with the Community Chest, 31, 62; and its model housing company, 31, 33–34; support of city planning, 32, 41, 69, 190n30; community development strategy, 32–34, 37; support of zoning, 44–45, 69; on Mariemont, 54; metropolitan vision of, 55; promotion of tenant education, 59; reevaluation of its approach to the housing problem, 59; response to the black housing crisis, 65; promotion of basin housing survey, 80; on Fort Wayne housing experiment, 107; and relocation problem, 128–29; opposition to temporary dwelling units, 142; on postwar housing shortage, 153; board of directors, 186n24; expanding vision, 194n68; mentioned, 37
Better Housing League of Cincinnati and Hamilton County. *See* Better Housing League of Cincinnati

Bettman, Alfred: background, 5, 41–42; involvement in Cincinnati housing reform, 5, 29–30; significance to national planning movement, 5, 6; planning philosophy of, 6; as founder of the United City Planning Committee, 41–42; on patchwork planning, 43; as author of planning legislation, 49; support of the Charter cause, 61; association with the Ferro limited dividend slum clearance project, 75, 78; on basin housing studies, 79–80; promotion of the Citizens' Committee on Slum Clearance and Low Cost Housing, 84; and state enabling legislation permitting public housing, 85; at CMHA meetings, 86; support of public housing, 114; establishment of Citizens' Planning Association, 158–59; observation of core deterioration, 158; promotion of comprehensive planning, 164; as member of the BHL board of directors, 186n24; in the Ohio State Conference on City Planning, 191n36
Bettman, Henry, 156
Biddle, Jeanne, 134
Bifocal: defined, 192n42
Bigelow, Herbert, 119
Big Missouri tenement house, 14–15
Blacks: housing conditions, 14, 60, 62–63, 66–69 passim, 83, 112, 125, 139, 141–42; in Washington Terrace, 36; development of suburban subdivisions, 55, 67, 193n65; during the Great Depression, 73; effects of community development strategy on, 124–25; role in PWA public housing controversy, 126–31; demand for more say in housing policy, 131–32, 143; effects of Cincinnati housing policy on, 131–32; and Lincoln Court, 135–37; failure to fill Valley Homes, 138–39; housing shortages and social tensions, 141–42
Blandford, John B. Jr., 215n52
Blighted areas: defined, 201n48; mentioned, 43
Blockbusting, 67
Blum, Harry, 93
Bohn, Ernest J., 5, 85
Bond Hill, 166
Borchert, James, 193n66
Boyer, M. Christine, 181n3
Boyer, Paul: on social groups, 9

Bradstreet, E. P., 30, 186n23
Breakdown of order and community, 9
Breed, W. D., 23
Bricker, John W., 99
Broadway House Wrecking and Material Company of Cleveland, Ohio, 96
Brookings Institution, 152
Bundy, Ellsworth, 102
Bureau of Census, 144, 199n33
Burgess, Ernest, 10
Burleson, Frank E., 31, 186n23
Business Men's Benevolent Advisory Committee, 184n38

Camargo Road housing site, 173
Camp Washington, 125
Campbell, Wendell B., 95, 101
Carl Mackley Homes, 199n27
Carnegie Institute of Technology, 7
Casell, Omar H., 107
Cash, Albert D., 118, 166
Cellarius, Charles.F., 84, 92, 158, 221n38
Census tract 5, 108, 117
Census tracts, 80, 200n37
Central business district, 148
"Central Business District and Riverfront Report," 176
Central Labor Council, 20
Changing conception of the metropolis, 175
Chapman, Henry G., 128
Charities Bulletin: discussion of model tenements, 21
Charities' Review: critique of the building code, 22
Charterites. *See* See City Charter Committee
Charter reform movement, 61–62
Chester Road Development, 169
Cheviot, Ohio, 56
Chicago, 14, 18
Chicago school of sociology, 148
Chronicle (labor), 20, 185n15
Cincinnati: growth and development, 3–4, 17; as setting for low-cost housing study, 3–7; as "Progressive" city, 7; tenement types, 14–15; decline of German community, 58–59; financial crisis, 60–61; during the Great Depression, 73; establishment of census tracts, 80; official housing policy of, 106
Cincinnatian, 56

Cincinnati Art Commission, 204*n*8
Cincinnati basin: housing problems in, 45, 47; as a slum, 106
Cincinnati Board of Education, 157
Cincinnati Board of Health, 15, 17, 20, 63
Cincinnati Building Code: tenement regulations, 24
Cincinnati Building Department, 26, 185*n*6
Cincinnati Bureau of Municipal Research, 26, 167, 184*n*3
Cincinnati Business Men's Club, 41
Cincinnati Chamber of Commerce: promotion of tenement reform, 28; support of city and metropolitan planning, 41, 56, 188*n*1; sponsorship of the "Cincinnati Industrial Survey, 1925," 46, 48; boost of wartime industry, 137; establishment of census tracts, 200*n*37
Cincinnati Chapter of the NAACP, 130
Cincinnati City Council: tenement code, 23–24; and Laurel Homes, 98–108 passim; approval of 5-percent charge in lieu of taxes, 100; finance committee of, 101; impact of 1937 election on, 119; and blacks' protest of CMHA discrimination, 131; and the Lincoln Court Community Building, 136; financing of temporary housing, 153–54, 165–66; funding of the *Cincinnati Metropolitan Master Plan,* 159; mentioned, 32, 157
Cincinnati City Housing Bureau, 62, 65, 68
Cincinnati City Planning Commission; described, 42; promotion of planning, 42–43; promotion of zoning, 44, 72; approval of black subdivisions, 55; evaluation of limited dividend low-cost West End housing projects, 77–78; basin housing studies, 79; development of North and West Central Basin District Plan, 79–82 passim; cooperation with the CMHA, 86; involvement in postwar planning, 158; and postwar redevelopment, 167, 169; and plans for the central business district, 175; mentioned, 6, 157
Cincinnati City Welfare Department: relief housing policy, 133–34
Cincinnati Committee to Expedite Housing, 156
Cincinnati Community Chest, 31, 62, 65
Cincinnati Community Development Com-

pany (CCDC): formed, 166; accomplishments, 166–68, 174; and housing for blacks, 169; and Forest Park development, 174
Cincinnati Department of Buildings, 213*n*11
Cincinnati Enquirer: announcement of Mariemont, 49; on Laurel Homes, 97–98; on Fort Wayne housing experiment, 107; on the vacant land public housing controversy, 129; on delays in temporary housing, 155
Cincinnati Housing Bureau, 60, 139, 195*n*21
Cincinnati Housing Corporation, 77, 78, 198*n*22
Cincinnati Housing Department, 15, 17
"Cincinnati Industrial Survey, 1925": discussed, 46; on metropolitan growth, 48
Cincinnati Mayor's Friendly Relations Committee, 142
Cincinnati Metropolitan Housing Authority (CMHA): established, 85–86; and basin redevelopment plan, 87–88; relationship with the Housing Division of the PWA, 89, 90, 92–102 passim; relationship with the United States Housing Authority, 90, 121; relationship with city council, 90, 115, 117, 118–21; as defender and advocate of public housing, 92–102 passim; promotion of local contributions to public housing, 97–98; involvement in tax controversy, 98–103 passim; defense of Laurel Homes Community Building, 102–3; promotion of a community development strategy, 103, 121; on Fort Wayne housing experiment, 107; on Laurel Homes rent, 108; promotion of a balanced public housing program, 114; and protest from the Cincinnati Real Estate Board, 117; called a "Super Government," 118; and north-of-Lockland project, 124, 130; and public housing for blacks, 124–25; and relocation report, 129; agreement to build Valley Homes, 138; opposition to temporary housing, 142; request for wartime housing, 142; reinforcement of established racial patterns, 145; breach of contract with the FPHA, 152; and overincome families in public housing, 156–57; and postwar public housing, 157; and Irving Street Project, 165–66; on postwar public housing, 170–71, 173; involvement in public housing controversy, 171–72; prob-

lems in finding housing sites, 171; and
Millvale projects, 172–73; agreement with
goals of the Housing Division of the PWA,
202n2; mentioned, 1, 5, 115
Cincinnati Metropolitan Master Plan (1948):
promotion of community development
strategy, 147; discussed, 159–64; compared with *Cincinnati City Plan* (1925),
164; limited focus on the central business
district, 222n42; mentioned, 4, 6
Cincinnati Model Homes Company: established, 34, 35; and Washington Terrace,
36; and post-World War I housing crisis,
65, 66; proposal of a limited divided slum
clearance project, 74; and high building
costs, 196n30; and West End beautification, 204n8; mentioned, 5, 95
Cincinnati Post: on federally sponsored slum
clearance, 97
Cincinnati postwar planning: compared with
Chicago's, 159
Cincinnati Public Health Federation, 61, 65,
187n32
Cincinnati Railroad Transit System, 61
Cincinnati Real Estate Board: on Cincinnati's
tenement house law, 24; on need for tenant
education, 30; opposition to Laurel Homes,
101; housing policy toward blacks, 143–44
Cincinnati Redevelopment Corporation,
224n77
Cincinnati relief: compared to Cleveland's re-
lief program, 133–34
Cincinnati Relief Union, 13–14, 20
Cincinnati Social Unit Organization, 51–52
Cincinnati Tenement House Department, 26,
27, 185n6
Cincinnati Times-Star: on Laurel Homes, 97
Cincinnati zoning law (1924): discussed,
45–46
Citizens' Committee on Slum Clearance and
Low Cost Housing: established, 84; promo-
tion of public housing, 85; on post-World
War II housing shorage, 153, 154, 172; op-
position to large-scale public housing
projects, 170–71
Citizens' party, 22
Citizens' Planning Association (CPA): estab-
lished, 158; mentioned, 4
Citizenship: threatened by bad housing, 25
City: as a whole, 11; as a social entity, 148

City Charter Committee: promotion of politi-
cal reform, 7; support of housing reform
and comprehensive planning, 7; discussion
of public housing, 118–19; loss of major-
ity status, 119
City Housing Corporation, 192n43
City planning: in Cincinnati, 32–45 passim
City planning enabling bill: described, 42
City planning movement: and the metropo-
lis, 59
Civic activists: and segregation, 2
Civic leaders, 20
Clarke, R. E., 132, 143
Clas, A. R., 99, 130
Cleveland, Ohio, 73
Cleveland Wrecking and Material Company
of Cincinnati, Ohio, 96, 134, 135
Clifton, 163
Commission form of government, 182n16
Committee to Amend the City Charter for
Public Housing, 172
Community: as a problem, 1
Community council movement, 176
Community development projects: defined, 1;
purpose, 2; Washington Terrace as ex-
ample, 36
Community development strategy: promoted
by the CMHA, 114–15; as a controversy,
122–23; decline of, 147–48; promoted in
the *Cincinnati Metropolitan Master Plan*,
160–62, 164; challenged, 171; shortcom-
ings of, 174, 177–78; mentioned, 3, 8
Comprehensive planning for the central busi-
ness district, 175–76
Comprehensive regional planning, 40
Conference of Charities and Benevolent Or-
ganizations, 20
Conference on Home Building and Home
Ownership. *See* President's Conference on
Home Building and Home Ownership
Conrad, George W. B., 129, 131, 132
Consumer Services Corporation, 112
Cooper, Myers Y., 186n24
Council of Social Agencies, 31
County Welfare Department, 129
Courte, C. V., 142
Covington, Ky., 48
Cox, George B., 5, 7, 22, 26, 61
Cox, Howard S., 77
Cox, W. Howard, 158

Crabbs, George Dent, 77
Craig, Wiley, 119
Croly, Herbert, 51
Crosley Radio, 58
Cumminsville, 163
Cummunsville-Northside, 125

Dabney, W. P., 62
Davis, Clark W., 21
Deer Creek Valley, 14
Defense housing, 152
Delhi Hills, 173
Department of Charities and Correction, 27
Deupree, R. R., 158
Devou, William, 62–63
Dillard, C. E., 128
Dinwiddie, Courtenay, 29, 186n24
Divers, William K., 142
Division of City and Metropolitan Planning, 159
Division of Defense Housing Coordination, 216n61
Douglass, Harlan Paul, 192n42
Downs, Myron: development of North and West Central Basin District Plan, 56, 79; criticism of the Ferro limited dividend slum clearance project, 77–78; at CMHA meetings, 86, 90; on Cincinnati's excessive land costs, 98; on Greenhills, 110; background, 199n24
Draper, Walter A., 158, 186n24
Dunbar, W. M., 188n1
Dunham, H. Kennan, 185n11
Dupuis, Charles W., 158, 221n38
Dykstra, Clarence A.: support of the Ferro limited dividend slum clearance project, 75; at CMHA meetings, 86; on Laurel Homes, 97; mentioned, 7, 99

East End, 62
Edgemon, William S.: management of Laurel Homes land acquisition, 88, 92, 96, 204n6
Edwards, Morris, 165
Elizabeth Gamble Deaconess Home, 23
Ellis, John D., 121
Elmwood Place, 169
Elzner, A. O., 30, 31, 186n24
Emergency Housing Bureau, 153, 154
Emergency Housing Corporation, 205n15

Emergency Relief Appropriations Act, 91, 204n3
Emergency Relief and Construction Act, 73
Emerson, Dr. Haven, 65
Emery, John J., 158, 220n37
Emery, Mary: establishes Mariemont, 49
Emery, Thomas, Jr., 20, 35
Eminent domain: defined, 210n53
Emmerich, Henry, 136, 215n52
English Woods: land coverage, 121; discussed, 121–22; under FHPA's control, 152; mentioned, 1, 2
Espy, Arthur, 77
Este Avenue site, 116
Estes, J. I., 193n65
Eubank, Earle, 200n37
Euclid v. Amber, 6
Everett, Rollin, 155, 165

Fairchild, Rev. F. S., 20
Federal Emergency Relief Act of 1935, 109
Federal Emergency Relief Administration, 91
Federal Housing Administration (FHA), 106–7, 143, 192n55
Federal Housing Agency: promotion of defense housing, 152
Federal Housing Authority, 153
Federal Land Acquisition Division, 96
Federal Public Housing Administration, 136, 157, 213n52
Federal Works Agency, 137–38
Federated Improvement Association, 41
Ferro Concrete Construction Company: proposal of limited dividend slum clearance project for West End, 74–77 passim
Ferro limited dividend slum clearance project: adoption of the community development stretegy, 77
Field, Tylor: involvement in BHL housing company, 33; initiation of Ferro limited dividend slum clearance project, 74; mentioned, 186n24
Filter-down theory of housing: discussed, 46; failure of, 65, 68, 69; mentioned, 59
Findlater, Ramsey, 155, 170
Five-percent service charge, 102
Fleischman, Julius, 183n24
Flood of 1937, 91, 96
Ford, George, 42
Ford, Henry, 59

Foreman, Clark, 137–38
Forest Park, Ohio, 174
Fort Wayne, Ind.: scattered-site low-cost housing, 106
Fort Wayne Housing Authority, 106
Fort Wayne housing experiment: discussed, 106–7; criticized, 107–8
France, Albert, 134
Frankenstein, Eli G., 121
Freiberg, Maurice, J., 77

Galvin, John, 61
Gamble, James N., 188n1
Gans, Herbert J., 148
Garber, Frederick W., 84, 87, 92
Garties, George, 140, 155
Geier, Frederick A., 35, 158, 186n24
Genevro, Rosalie, 211n16
George-Healy-Russell bill, 100
Gerholz, Robert, 174
Gillette, Jr., Howard, 226n106
Glen Industrial Home, 23
Glen Meadows, 167, 169
Good community: discouragement of integration, 177
Good low-cost housing: neglect of the city's neediest, 109
Goodrich, E. C., 42
Gould, E. R. L., 21
Gradison, Willis: on taxing Laurel Homes, 99–101 passim; criticism of public housing, 119, 120; support of temporary housing, 154; mentioned, 157
Grear, Oscar, 132
Great Depression: effect on black housing, 125
Greater Cincinnati Metropolitan Area, 156
Greater Cincinnati Savings and Loan Exchange, 172
Greenbelt, Md., 110
Greendale, Wisc., 110
Greene, Verna, 105, 132, 143
Greenhills, Ohio: as mirror of community development strategy, 109–13 passim; as model for suburban development, 110; adapted to Greater Cincinnati, 110–11; built by federal initiative, 110; tenant selection process, 112; town plan described, 112; opponents of, 117; mentioned, 5, 166, 170, 174

Haley-Livingston Company, 193n65
Hall, Joseph B., 165
Hamilton Company of Cincinnati, 224n77
Hamilton County, 137
Hamilton County Commissioners, 56, 157
Hamilton County Department of Public Welfare: promotion of basin housing survey, 80, 128; mentioned, 198n16
Hamilton County Home: as site for temporary housing, 154
Hamilton County League of Building and Loan Associations, 117, 118
Handlin, David, 189n2
Hannaford, Samuel, 23
Hartzog, Justin, 109, 111
Harvard University, 7, 42
Hess, William, 93
High, Douglas G., 143–44
Hill, William E., 116
Hill people, 142
Hirsch, Arnold: on residential segregation, 125; on acculturation, 144; on Chicago's postwar development, 159
Hirsch, Max, 186n24, 188n1
Historical discontinuity, 3
Historical landmarks, 189n7
Hock, Fred, 143
Holmes, John R., 185n6
Home Builders Association, 172
Home, Health and Happiness, 31
Home Owners Loan Corporation, 153, 192n55
Home Savings and Loan Companies, 172
Hooper, Henry N., 35
Hoover, Herbert, 1, 5, 6, 73
Housing: changing focus of, 32–33; relationship to planning, 114; as a cause, 151
Housing Act of 1937: discussed, 115–16; effect on Cincinnati's public housing program, 115–23 passim; effect on the CMHA, 133; amended, 137; requirement of local governmental contributions, 151; mentioned, 5, 89, 103
Housing Act of 1949: goal, 1; as a community development strategy, 147; discussed, 165, 222n55
Housing Act of 1954: Section 221 program, 173; reflection of metropolitan mode of thought, 175

Housing Division of the Public Works Administration (PWA): established, 74–75; encouragement of limited dividend housing in Cincinnati, 74–79 passim; promotion of public housing, 84, 85; demand for collateral, 92; role in the Cincinnati tax controversy, 99–101; approval of Laurel Homes project, 124; cutting of allocations to the CMHA, 125; rejection of the north-of-Lockland housing site, 130; promotion of a community development strategy, 202n2; requirement of local sponsorship, 203n1; mentioned, 7

Housing: Forward or Backward? 68

Housing and Home Finance Administration, 167

Housing movement: and the metropolis, 59

Housing problem: redefined, 32–33, 36–37, 69

Housing reform: compared to tenement reform, 39, 47; relation to zoning, 44–47 passim; decline of leadership, 174

Howard, Ebenezer, 50

Hubbard, C. M., 23, 25

Hubbard, DeHart, 143

Hunt, Henry T., 26, 28, 61

Hurst, John J., 158, 221n38

Hutchinson, Woods, 28

Hyde Park, 35

Hynicka, Rudolph K., 7, 61

Ickes, Harold L., 88, 91, 92, 130, 155

Ideson, Ethel, 155

Iglaver, Samuel, 185n11

Individual desires: as replacement to community needs in public housing, 248–49

Intemperate behavior: as cause of poverty, 13

International City Managers Association, 7

Irving Street Project, 166

Jackson, Kenneth T., 212n5

Jackson, Lois, 134

Johnson, Clyde P., 198n14

Johnson, Ernest B., 92

Johnson, Morse, 155

Johnson Park: as site for temporary housing, 154

Joint Industrial Homes Committee, 20

Julian, W. A., 33, 186n24

Junior League, 122

Kellogg, William R., 155

Kerns, J. Harvey: protest of proposed billeting of white soldiers at Lincoln Court, 134

Kessler Park Plan of 1907, 43, 188n2

Keyserling, Leon, 5

Kirby, John, 218n95

Kirby Road public housing site, 171

Kohn, Robert D., 85, 88

Korean War, 147

Kroger, B. H., 200n37

Kuhn, Setty S.: establishment of Better Housing League, 29, 30; as member of the CMHA, 86; mentioned, 201n58

Lane Gardens: as limited dividend housing project, 78–79

Lane Seminary site: rejected, 117

Lang Brothers, 143

Lanham Act, 137, 154

Lansill, John: on Greenhills, 111

Large-scale community development, 85

Laurel Homes: land acquisition for, 86–87, 135; development of, 89, 91–103 passim; construction of, 91–98 passim; rents in, 99, 108; expenses criticized, 101; as a community development strategy, 104–6; neglect of the city's neediest, 104; promotion of cultural transformations, 104; associational life, 105; relationship to surrounding slums, 105–6; tenant handbook of, 105; example of neighborhood unit plan, 106; security guards from, 106; as a response to the housing problem of the 1930s, 113; land costs, 116, 121; demolition for, 128; as whites-only project, 130; racial quota system in, 131; addition of black units, 139; competition with Valley Homes, 139; as a biracial project, 140–41; addition to, 141

Laurel-3 and Richmond-1: population characteristics of site, 167

Laurel-Ville-Life, 105

Laurence, Daniel, 193n65

Lee, Walter H., 92

Lehman, Mrs. Alvin, 84

Letchworth, England, 50

Lincoln Court: relocation of building-site oc-
cupants, 133–34; delayed by World War
II, 134–35; demolition of housing site,
134; land acquisition, 134–35; to billet sol-
diers, 135–36; as a community develop-
ment strategy, 136; community building
of, 136; compared to Laurel Homes, 136;
competition with Valley Homes, 139; under
FPHA's control, 152; priority admission to
war workers, 156
Lincoln Heights, 164, 169. *See also* north-of-
Lockland
Lindale Subdivision, 169
Livingood, Charles J., 35, 49, 51
Local Planning Administration, 7
Locker, Jesse, 143, 155
Lockland City Council, 216*n*60
Lockland Housing Commission, 216*n*60
Louisville, Ky., 104
Low-cost housing and planning experience:
conventional wisdom, 3
Lower West End: inappropriateness for hous-
ing reform, 82
Lukenheimer Company, 58

McCarl, John Raymond, 99, 205*n*15
McCarthyism, 147
McClain, R. P., 120
McDonnell, Timothy L., 203*n*6
McElroy, Neil H., 158, 221*n*38
McKenzie, Roderick D., 2
Madisonville: as housing site, 173; men-
tioned, 125
Mann, Annette, 186*n*22
Marcuse, Peter, 187*n*35, 203*n*7, 207*n*1
Mariemont, Ohio: founding of, 49; as a community development strategy, 49–51; arrangement of living space, 49–50;
compared to Letchworth, 50; relationship
to the Cincinnati metropolitan region, 50;
compared to tenement reform, 51; and
city's wage earners, 54; housing costs of,
54; as a failure, 69; compared with Greenhills, 109; mentioned, 5, 37, 40, 57
Mariemont Company, 193*n*64
Marquette, Bleecker: significance of, 5; background, 5, 31–32; promotion of model
housing, 33; on the tenement house problem, 45, 67; on black suburban subdivisions, 55; on post-World War I housing

crisis, 60; support of Charter cause, 61; exchange with W. P. Dabney, 62; opposition
to direct federal aid to low-cost housing
needs, 72; on basin housing studies, 79–
80; on failure of natural slum clearance,
82; encouragement of the formation of the
Citizens' Committee on Slum Clearance
and Low Cost housing, 84; and the metropolitan housing authority law, 85; involvement with the CMHA, 86, 90; on Fort
Wayne housing experiment, 107–8; justi-
fication of West End redevelopment plan,
114; support of public housing, 114; on
black housing, 130; opposition to billeting
of white soldiers in Lincoln Court, 135–
36; promotion of black defense housing,
137; on black housing shortages, 140; on
core deterioration, 158; executive secretary
of the Cincinnati Public Health Federation,
187*n*32; mentioned, 40, 53, 65, 210*n*2.
See also Better Housing League of
Cincinnati
Massive slum clearance: as a housing im-
provement strategy, 71
*Master Plan of 1948. See Cincinnati Metro-
politan Master Plan* (1948)
Mathes, H. C., 188*n*1
Matthews, Stanley, 84
Matthews, William Procter: as selected mem-
ber of the CMHA, 86
Mayer, Albert H., 101
Mayor's Committee on Housing, 154
Meacham, Standish, 92, 155
Mead Amendment, 154
Meade, S. D. J., 21
Medosch farm site, 137–38
Mennonite Mission, 23
Men's City Club, 188*n*1
Metropolitan community: expansion, 59
Metropolitan Community, The, 2
Metropolitan districts, 191*n*33
Metropolitan housing authority law, 5
Metropolitan mode of thought, 2, 177
Metropolitan planning: decline, 147–48
Metropolitan region: defined, 111
Midland Redevelopment Corporation, 224*n*77
Millcreek Expressway, 172
Mill Creek Valley, 14, 28
Miller, Albert L., 111
Miller, Wallace E., 20–21, 22

Miller, Zane L.: on the "revolt against culture," 148; on the *Cincinnati Metropolitan Master Plan,* 159–65; on Jews in Cincinnati, 183 *n*24
Millvale North, 172–73
Millvale South, 172
M. J. Boyajohn Company of Columbus, Ohio, 135
Model Homes Company. *See* Cincinnati Model Homes Company
Model tenements: as housing reform strategy, 18, 20–22
Mohawk Brighton, 52, 62, 67
Monday Evening Club, 22, 184 *n*38
Mullen, Michael, 23
Mumford, Lewis, 6
Municipal Housing Bureau, 30
Murphy, Richard, 23
Myer, Adelaide, 93

National Association of Housing Officials, 5, 147
National Association of Real Estate Boards, 172, 206 *n*44, 225 *n*93
National Conference on City Planning, 6
National Housing Agency, 135, 142, 153–54, 155, 215 *n*52
National Housing Association, 28, 29, 51
National Housing Conference, 147
National Industrial Recovery Act, 74, 204 *n*3
National Public Housing Conference, 197 *n*11
National Resources Board, 7
Natural slum clearance: as a strategy, 46, 68, 72; failure of, 79, 83
Negative cultural traits, 144
Negro Citizens' Advisory Committee, 132
Negro Civic Welfare Association, 63
Negro Housing Association, 131–32
Negro Welfare Division of the Council of Social Agencies, 130
Negro Working Peoples Conference, 130
Neighborhood community: as promoter of metropolitan consciousness, 53, 54
Neighborhood conservation, 163, 165
Neighborhood rehabilitation, 163
Neighborhood slums: discovered, 9
Neighborhood unit: described, 51; mentioned, 81
"New City" as a threat, 17
New Deal, 7

New Republic: on public housing, 147
New York City, 14, 18
New York City and Suburban Homes Association, 21
New York state housing law (1926): described, 73
New York State Tenement House Committee, 5
New York State Tenement Law of 1867, 17
New York Tenement House Law of 1901: goals, 10, 11
New York Times: on Mariemont, 5, 51
Newman, Bernard, 114, 210 *n*2
Newport, Ky., 48
Noertker, Joseph A., 156
Nolen, John: on town planning, 41; plans for Mariemont, 49; connection with Greenhills, 109; mentioned, 33
Norris Homes, Inc., 143
North and West Central Basin District Plan: as a community development strategy, 81
North Fairmount site: approved, 117
North-of-Lockland site: rejected, 116; mentioned, 86
Northside–South Cumminsville–College Hill–Mt. Airy Home Owners Association, 171
Northwestern University, 7
Norwood, Ohio, 35, 50, 56, 163

O'Grady, Father John, 198 *n*18
Oakley, Ohio, 35, 50, 125
Official City Plan of Cincinnati, Ohio (1925): described, 43–48 passim; on decentralization, 43, 46; as example of comprehensive planning, 43–44; promotion of homogeneity, 44; on community development, 47; on metropolitan planning, 47–48; reflection of earlier mode of thought, 71; discussion of natural slum clearance, 71; mentioned, 4
Ohio Bureau of Labor: tenement house survey, 18–19
Ohio General Assembly: revision of housing authority law, 170; mentioned, 17
Ohio Real Estate Board, 86
Ohio State Board of Housing, 73, 77, 85
Ohio State Conference on City Planning, 191 *n*36
Ohio State Housing Authority Law: discussed, 85; amended, 152; mentioned, 151

Ohio State Housing Law: described, 73, 93, 121
Ohio Supreme Court: on public housing, 121, 151–52, 170
Omwake, John, 77
Oppenheimer, Benton, 185n11
Our Cities: Their Role in the National Economy, 7
Over-the-Rhine neighborhood, 58
Overton, Boyd W., 132

Palmer, C. F., 137
Park, Robert, 39
Parker, William H., 185n11
Pastner, Robert, 93
Penker Construction Company: promotion of limited dividend housing, 78–79, 138
Perry, Clarence: development of the neighborhood unit, 51, 52
Peters, William H., on redevelopment, 72
Philadelphia, Penn., 14, 18
Philanthropy and 5 percent, 187n40
Phillips, Wilbur C., 51–52
Philpott, Thomas: on the "business creed," 21; on private enterprise, 69
Planning: citizens' input into, 176
Political reform: and financial crisis, 61; and the city as a whole, 62
Pollak, Julian A.: on Mariemont, 51
Pollak, Louise, 29, 186n24
Post-World War I housing shortage, 60
Post-World War II: housing shortage, 157; planning, 159
Pounsford, Nicholas G., 188n1
President's Conference on Home Building and Home Ownership: described, 52–53; on homogenous communities, 53; mentioned, 5
President's Research Committee on Social Trends, 2
Pritz, Sidney E., 35
Problem of poverty, 2
Process of problem solving, 3
Procter, William Cooper, 77
Procter and Gamble Company, 58
Professional norms, 90
Progressive Era, 10, 18
Property Owners Association: protest of public housing, 117
Pruit-Igoe housing projects, 226n102
Public housing: goals, 2, 144; projects built by the PWA, 89, 91–103 passim; social purpose of, 89; tax controversy, 98–103; vacant-land projects, 117–23; targeting of ambitious blacks, 124; connection to assimilation, 144; as a reform movement, 147; decline of, 147–48; as relocation housing, 170; public referendum on, 172; on the community level, 225n93
Public Housing Administration: sale of excess Greenhills land, 174; mentioned, 170
Purdue University, 107

Racism: defined, 3; mentioned, 3
Radburn, 192n43
Raffety, J. Stanley: hired to manage Laurel Homes, 105; on Laurel Homes, 106; development of Valley Homes, 138
Real-estate lobby, 177
Real Property Survey of Cincinnati and Urbanized Hamilton County, 157–58
Realtors: on Laurel Homes rent, 108
Realty Owners Association: promotion of West End public housing, 117
Reconstruction Finance Corporation (RFC), 73, 137, 216n60
Red Bank–Corsia Road housing site, 173
Reed, Lawson, 210n59
Reeder, Sherwood L., 159
Regional metropolitan planning: discussed, 55–56
Regional Plan Association of New York Association, 52
Regional Plan of New York and Its Environs, 52
Regional Planning Association of America, 6, 40, 188n3, 210n2
Regional Planning Commission: formed, 56; cooperation with the CMHA, 86; on Greenhills, 111; and low-cost housing, 173
Reiner, Rev. Joseph, 186n24
Relief program: and housing, 133
Relocation: of Laurel Homes site occupants, 128; of relief families from Laurel Homes housing site, 129; need for, 151; as a problem, 165
Rempe, Dora, 193n65
Rempe, Edward, 193n65
Republican party: attitudes toward public housing, 118
Resettlement Administration: adoption of

community development strategy, 109–10; selection of Cincinnati for greenbelt town, 110; survey of the Cincinnati metropolitan region, 111; mentioned, 5

Reynolds Metals Company of Louisville, 224*n*77

Rhodes, Rev. Dudley Ward: on curse of tenements, 14–15

Richards, John R., 185*n*6

Rockhill, Mrs. Charles, 186*n*24

Roosevelt, Eleanor, 93

Roosevelt, Franklin D.: emphasis on jobs, 91; petitioned, 93, 129, 130; authorization of Valley Homes, 138

Rose, Charles O., 98

Roselawn, 166

Ross, D. Reid, 176

Rothass, Ernestine N., 105

Rowe, John J., 77, 154

Rowe, Stanley M.: on census tract 5, 109; as selected member of the CMHA, 86; on Laurel Homes, 97, 99, 102–3, 128, 131; on the Fort Wayne housing experiment, 107; support for a balanced public housing program, 118; promotion of black defense housing, 137; resignation from the CMHA, 143; as head of Citizens' Planning Association, 158; involvement in post-World War II planning, 158; on Myron Downs, 199*n*24. *See also* Cincinnati Metropolitan Housing Authority

St. Bernard, Ohio, 163, 169

St. Louis, Mo., 14

Santry, Frank, 142

Savings and Loan Association: protest of public housing, 117

Saylor Park, 125

Scherer, Gordon, 171

Schmidlapp, Jacob G.: promotion of model housing, 34–36 passim; building difficulties in Norwood, 35; death of, 66; mentioned, 5

Schmidt, Milton H., 158, 221*n*38

Schmidt, Walter S., 53, 206*n*44

Schultz, William J., 121

Schwan, George H., 33

Schwartz, Joel, 207*n*2

Schwartz Realty Company: proposal of limited dividend slum clearance project, 74

Seasongood, Murray, 7, 53, 61, 183*n*24

Section 221 of the National Housing Act, 173

Segoe, Ladislas: significance of, 5; background, 6; on zoning, 46; support of Charter cause, 61; plans for the Ferro limited dividend slum clearance project, 75; development of *Cincinnati Metropolitan Master Plan*, 159; development of Forest Park plan; mentioned, 39

Segoe and Associates, 7

Segregation: impact on blacks, 63; promotion by BHL, 67; promotion by CMHA, 105, 124–25, 130–31, 134; as source of problems for CMHA, 117–18; reinforcement by *Metropolitan Master Plan*, 163

Self-contained public housing projects: criticized, 170–71

Sellars, Randolph: opposition to vacant land public housing, 117

Senior, Max: criticism of tenement code enforcement, 25; support of the creation of the BHL, 30; role in Model Homes Company, 35; mentioned, 186*n*22, 186*n*24

Separate but equal facilities: discussed, 144

Shapiro, Henry D.: on place, 9

Sharonville, Ohio, 173

Sharpe, Carleton F., 112, 113

Sherrill, Clarence O., 119, 121, 157

Shoemaker Health and Welfare Center: established, 67

Sibbald, Walter K., 121

Silver, Christopher, 199*n*34

Silverton, 56

Simkhovitch, Mary Kingsbury, 197*n*11, 198*n*18

Simpson, Frank, 156

Skirvin, W. Ray: opposition to vacant land public housing, 117; appointment to CMHA, 143

Slums: impact of, 1, 2, 10, 45, 124; culture of, 39, 113; changing definitions, 72; defined, 210*n*48

Smith, Scott, 26

Smith Act of 1911: impact on Cincinnati, 61

Social problems: and tenement districts, 10

Southwestern Kansas University, 20

Special committee on black housing, 65–66

Spiegel, Frederick, 183*n*24

Spilker, John L., 86, 156, 201*n*59

Stamm, Charles H.: as head of the CCEH,

156; as head of the Urban Redevelopment Division, 167; on relocation problem, 167, 169; as lobbyist with federal government, 174

State ex rel. Ellis v. Sherrill, 121

Steele, C. W., 193*n*65

Stein, Clarence, 6, 192*n*43

Sternberg, George M., 34, 35, 187*n*40

Stevens, Herbert, 176

Stewart, James G.: on Laurel Homes, 104; elected mayor, 119; opposition to vacant land public housing, 120; appointment of Ray Skirvin to CMHA, 132; response to racial tension, 142; response to housing shortage, 154, 155

Stonorov, Oskar, 199*n*27

Stratford Manor, 169

Straus, Nathan, 118, 122, 133, 141

Suburban Division of the Resettlement Administration. *See* Resettlement Administration

Sunnyside, 192*n*43

Survey Graphic, 7

Survey of Housing Conditions in the Basin of the City of Cincinnati, 80–81

Tadlock, Joshua M., 130

Taft, Charles P., 61, 118, 120

Taft, Robert A., 223*n*55

Taft, William Howard, 120

Tarr, Gordon, 143

Tax exemption: and public housing, 151

Tax problem, 152

Technical Advisory Corporation of New York (TAC): survey of Cincinnati, 42–43; on metropolitan community, 44; on zoning, 44; mentioned, 6, 61

Technical University of Budapest, 6

Tenant House Association, 20

Tenant relocation, 134

Tenement code of 1909: enforcement problems, 25–26

Tenement district: as object of reform, 9–10, 17–18; evils of environment discussed, 10

Tenement house codes: as legacy of Progressive Era, 10–11

Tenement problem, 26–27

Tenement reform: goals and concerns, 3, 9–10; leadership, 20; and the "business creed," 21; as tenement regulation, 17–20, 22, 24; as model tenement building, 20–22 passim; ties with political reform, 22, 26; reorganization of enforcement mechanism, 26; aims of, 28

Tenements: as a problem, 13; defined, 181*n*5, 184*n*42

Tenhundfeld, A. R., 172

Thomson, Alexander: refusal to accept nomination to the CMHA, 86

Title VI program, 155

Tocker, Charles A., 23

Todd, Robert E., 26, 185*n*11

Travelers' Aid Society, 63

Truman, Harry S., 155

Tucker, Lawrence H., 166

Tugwell, Rexford: selection of Cincinnati for greenbelt town, 110

Undeserving poor, 109

Union Bethel, 23

Union Terminal, 204*n*8

United City Planning Committee (UCPC): founded, 41–42; employment of TAC, 42–43; promotion of regional metropolitan planning, 55–56; mentioned, 4

United Jewish Charities of Cincinnati (UJC): support for tenement reform, 19, 23; mentioned, 25, 29

United States Housing Authority (USHA): compared to the Housing Division of the PWA, 115; relationship with CMHA, 116; and black public housing, 132; mentioned, 106, 215*n*52

University of Cincinnati, 1, 7, 175

Upson, Lent D., 191*n*32

Urban, Charles H.: as member of the CMHA, 86; on Laurel Homes taxes, 99; on slumless Cincinnati, 119; mentioned, 201*n*58

Urbanism Committee, 7

Urban Land Institute, 221*n*37, 221*n*40

Urner, Henry, 101

Vacant land projects: as promoters of community development strategy, 117; controversy surrounding, 117–21; CMHA policy on, 123; mentioned, 114

Valley Homes: development of, 136–39; slow

occupancy, 138–39; as site for temporary housing, 154

Veiller, Lawrence: on Cincinnati's housing problems, 4, 28; on Cincinnati housing reform, 25; as representative of the Progressive Era approach to housing reform, 40; on Cincinnati slum clearance, 73; mentioned, 5, 10, 11, 31, 32, 210n2

Veterans' Emergency Housing Act, 220n21

Veterans' Emergency Housing Program, 155

Vinton, Warren Jay, 111

Visiting housekeepers. *See* Better Housing League of Cincinnati

Vogel, Jacob, 188n1

Wagner, Robert F., 5, 197n11

Waldvogel, Edward N., 118

Walker, Arnold B., 143

Walnut Hills, 35, 62, 125, 163–64

Walnut Hills Congregational Church, 18

War Manpower Commission, 140, 156

Warner-Kanter Company, 169, 174

War Production Board, 142, 156

Washburn elementary school, 141

Washington Sanitary Improvement Company, 34–35

Washington Terrace, 36. *See also* Cincinnati Model Homes Company

Weaver, Robert: on role of housing for blacks, 144–45; 218n95

Weiss, Marc A., 203n5, 221n40

Wells, George H., 130

West End: population turnover, 30, 63, 74; congestion, 63–64, 67, 133, 144, 156; as a slum, 74; as an economic and social liability, 87–88; redevelopment of, 167–68, 172, 224n77; mentioned, 65, 73, 164

West End expressway project, 166

West End Plan of 1933. *See* North and West Central Basin Redevelopment Plan of 1933

West End Property Owners Association, 92

Western and Southern Life Insurance Company, 167

Western Hills Business Men's Association, 120

West Side Real Estate Owners Association: promotion of census tract 5 redevelopment, 118

Westwood Civic Association, 120

Westwood Improvement Association, 120

Wheeler, Earle J., 166

Whitney, N. R., 156

Wilson, James, 186n24

Wilson, Mrs. M. E., 62

Wilson, Russell, 101, 118

Winkler, Willis, 155, 156

Winton Terrace: land coverage, 121; discussed, 122; attraction of whites from Laurel Homes, 140; under FPHA's control, 152; as site for temporary housing, 153, 154; admission of war workers, 156; as a "little city," 170

Wirth, Louis, 148

Withrow, Samuel P.: production of "Darkest Cincinnati," 27

Woman's City Club: established, 29; establishment of BHL, 29, 30; on unregulated metropolitan planning, 55; promotion of city planning, 41; membership, 186n19; mentioned, 84

Wood, Edith Elmer, 197n11

Woodlawn, 169

Workable program, 176

Working-class poor, 9

Works Progress Administration, 107

World War I: as end of reform, 58, 59; postwar housing shortage, 63–67 passim; mentioned, 5–6, 32

World War II: impact on Lincoln Court, 134–35; housing shortage during and after, 152–59 passim, 157

Wrenn, Robert, 134

Wright Aeronautical Corporation, 137, 138

Wurlitzer, Rudolph, 188n1

Wyatt, Wilson W., 155

Wyman, John W., 53

Zoning: ordinance introduced, 44; relationship to better housing, 44–46

Zunz, Olivier, 59

A Note on the Author

Robert B. Fairbanks received his Ph.D. degree from the University of Cincinnati in 1981 and is now assistant professor of history at the University of Texas at Arlington. An urban historian, he has published in the *Journal of Urban History*, *Planning Perspectives*, *Ohio History*, and *Queen City Heritage: The Journal of the Cincinnati Historical Society*. He is currently working on a history of Dallas, Texas, between 1930 and 1960, with special reference to the changing nature of federal-urban relations in that sunbelt city.